CANADA'S NATIONAL PARKS

A VISITOR'S GUIDE

Marylee Stephenson

Prentice Hall Canada Inc.
Scarborough, Ontario

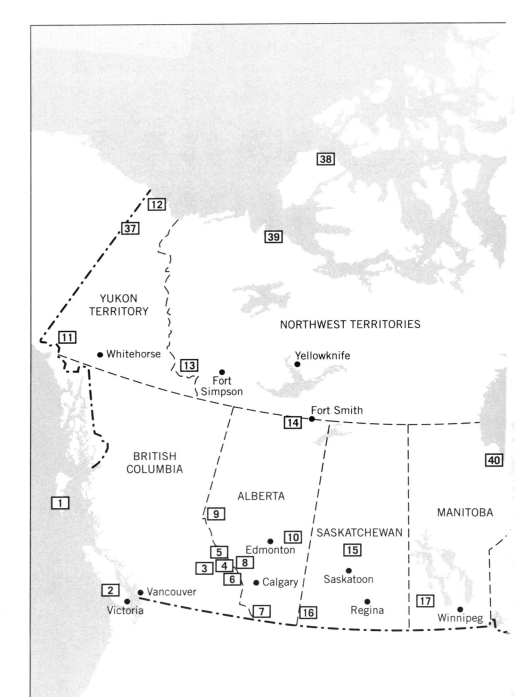

CANADA'S NATIONAL PARKS

1	Gwaii Haanas	21	Georgian Bay Islands
2	Pacific Rim	22	Point Pelee
3	Mount Revelstoke	23	St. Lawrence Islands
4	Glacier	24	La Mauricie
5	Yoho	25	Saguenay/St. Lawrence
6	Kootenay	26	Mingan Archipelago
7	Waterton Lakes	27	Auyuittuq
8	Banff	28	Forillon
9	Jasper	29	Kouchibouguac
10	Elk Island	30	Fundy
11	Kluane	31	Prince Edward Island
12	Ivvavik	32	Kejimkujik
13	Nahanni	33	Cape Breton Highlands
14	Wood Buffalo	34	Gros Morne
15	Prince Albert	35	Terra Nova
16	Grasslands	36	Ellesmere Island
17	Riding Mountain	37	Vuntut
18	Pukaskwa	38	Aulavik
19	Bruce Peninsula	39	Tuktut Nogait
20	Fathom Five	40	Wapusk

N

BAFFIN ISLAND

27
Pangnirtung •

NEWFOUNDLAND

QUEBEC

34
Corner Brook

35
St. John's

Sept Iles •   26

28 Gaspé

PRINCE EDWARD ISLAND

NTARIO

25

33
Sydney

Moncton 31
Charlottetown

NOVA SCOTIA

Quebec
24

29
30 • Halifax
Saint 32
John

der

18

Sault
Ste. Marie
— Ottawa — • Montreal

19
North Bay 23

NEW BRUNSWICK

20 21
Toronto Kingston

Windsor • 22

For my mother,

Carey Margaret Stephenson
1914–1995

Curiosity is, in great and generous minds,
the first passion and the last:
(Samuel Johnson, *Rambler* 150)

Canadian Cataloguing in
Publication Data

Stephenson, Marylee, 1943–
Canada's national parks :
a visitor's guide

ISBN 0-13-575028-8

1. National parks and reserves –
Canada – Guidebooks.
2. Canada – Guidebooks. I. Title.

FC215.S83 1997   917.104'648
C97-930360-5
F1011.S83 1997

 © 1997
Prentice-Hall Canada Inc.
A Division of
Simon & Schuster/
A Viacom Company

Prentice-Hall, Inc., Upper Saddle
River, New Jersey
Prentice-Hall International (UK)
Limited, London
Prentice-Hall of Australia, Pty.
Limited, Sydney

Prentice-Hall Hispanoamericana, S.A.,
Mexico City
Prentice-Hall of India Private Limited,
New Delhi
Prentice-Hall of Japan, Inc., Tokyo
Simon & Schuster Southeast Asia
Private Limited, Singapore
Editora Prentice-Hall do Brasil, Ltda.,
Rio de Janeiro

ISBN 0-13-575028-8

Managing Editor: Robert Harris
Acquisitions Editor: Sara Borins
Production Editor:
Mary Ann McCutcheon
Copy Editor: Dianne Broad
Editorial Assistants: Susanne Frame,
Paula Thiessen
Production Coordinator: Julie Preston
Cover and Interior Design:
Kyle Gell, art & design
Maps: Allan Moon, Valentino Sanna
Art Direction: Mary Opper
Page Layout: Kyle Gell, art & design

1 2 3 4 5   WC   01 00 99 98 97

Printed and bound in Canada

Visit the Prentice Hall Canada Web site!
Send us your comments, browse our
catalogues, and more.

www.phcanada.com.

Contents

Acknowledgements

A s with the previous two editions of this book, I have drawn on the assistance of many people, at the parks, in the administration of Parks Canada, at the publishers, and among friends and associates. At Parks Canada headquarters, Jean-Robert Gauthier's aid was unstinting and enjoyable throughout this process. Andre Guindon was very helpful with photo supplements. Those listed below, park by park, made corrections and suggestions for the materials on their parks, and I am particularly grateful for their promptness and thoroughness. Also, for this third edition I visited Isles des Mingan and Saguenay-St. Lawrence Marine Parks and received a great deal of on-location help from those cited here. They are very busy people, but they found the time to show me around and answer my questions—and see some birds and whales along the way.

I went on these visits with Pamela Sachs, and her help and patience were great assets, especially because the visits began just days after the death of my much-beloved mother.

Sara Borins, Paula Thiessen, and Mary Ann McCutcheon of Prentice Hall Canada have been very patient throughout this process, which always takes longer than one anticipates. Dianne Broad has been very helpful as a copy editor.

Because of pressure of my "day job" as the head of my own company, I simply could not have completed this third edition without the constant help of Jeannie McIntosh. Her background in biology and her organizational and computer skills were invaluable in preparing the materials for final submission to the publisher.

I would like to thank again Scott Meis, the person who first introduced me to the outdoors of Canada. He was instrumental in the completion of the first two editions of this book, and his continued encouragement of all my work continues to be of great importance to me.

Even though the people listed below were very careful in their reviews of the chapters, I assume the responsibility for any errors.

Fundy National Park   Ellen Bertrand, Patrick McKinley

Grasslands National Park   Jim Masyk

Prince Edward Island National Park   Barbara MacDonald

Gros Morne National Park   Anne Marceau, Michael Burzynski

Kouchibouguac National Park Barry Spencer

Kejimkujik National Park Peter Hope

Saquenay/St. Lawrence Marine Park Claude Filion, Eric LeBel, Jacque Hebert, Marc Pagé, Marcel Ward, Louise Jomphe, Hélène Lauzière, Lorraine Côté, Catherine Morisset, Marie Lachance, Paul Cyr, Josée Normandin

Mingan National Park Reserve Eric LeBel, Hélène Lauzière, Marie Lachance, Marcel Ward, Lorraine Côté, Guylaine Côté, Catherine Morissette

Cape Breton Highlands National Park David Lawley, Geraldine LeVert

Georgian Bay Islands National Park Greg Gemmell, Mike Walton

Bruce Peninsula and Fathom Five National Parks Andrea Kettle, Ellen Hill

Gwaii Haanas National Park Reserve Roger Hamilton, Margaret Stronge

Riding Mountain National Park Helen Ewasiuk

Prince Albert National Park Adam Pidwerbeski, Cathy Corrigal

Wood Buffalo National Park Natalie Humenuk-Bourke, Jeff Dixon

Nahanni National Park Reserve Christian Bucher, Carl Lafferty

Waterton Lakes National Park Merv Syroteuk, Duane W. Barrus

Auyuittuq and Ellesmere Island National Park Reserves Yves Bosse, Jonah Kilabuk

Kootenay National Park John Pitcher

Kluane National Park Reserve Brent Liddle, Eric Carmichael

Banff National Park Ann Morrow

Pacific Rim National Park Reserve Bill McIntyre

Yoho National Park Sacha Veelbehr, Kathryn Cameron

Jasper National Park Kim Forster

Elk Island National Park Ken Green

Pukaskwa National Park Sharon Otiquam, Bob Reside

Point Pelee National Park Lily Meleg, Laurel McIvor

St. Lawrence Islands National Park Ken Robinson

La Mauricie National Park Jacques Pleau

Forillon National Park Marc Trudel

Terra Nova National Park Greg Stroud

Mount Revelstoke and Glacier National Parks Pat Dunn

Aulavik and Ivvavik National Parks Vicki Sahanatien

Vuntut National Park Duane West

MAP LEGEND

Highway ⬌

🔲 Park Gate/Entrance

Secondary Road ⟋

🏠 Accommodation

Marsh

🔺 Mountain

Information Centre 🔲?

🏠 Shelter

Administration Ⓐ

┼┼┼ Railway

Trails ⋯

Icefield/Glacier

Camping 🔺

Lake/River/Creek

Group Camping ⩗

Ⓔ Interpretive Centre/Exhibit

Primitive Camping* 🔲

🔥 Base Camp

Viewpoint 🔲

⛵ Shipwreck

Warden Station Ⓦ

🔲 Flowerpot

---

*This designation means there are no flush toilets, kitchen shelters, hook-ups or waste disposal units for trailers. These campgrounds usually have pit toilets and well or fresh stream water. Be sure to purify all the water you use.

Readers should note that conversions from metric to imperial measure in the text are not exact. They are intended to provide a rough guide.

Introduction

Canada's national parks are simply splendid. One is as far south as the border of northern California, and several are located above the Arctic Circle. You can take a long detour around buffalo in the baking prairie sun, or listen to beavers chewing their evening meal beside a Rocky Mountain stream. Kayaking, walking, swimming, exploring a trail in a wheelchair, driving in your car, or bumping along on horseback—there's no end to the ways you can get close to the natural wonders encompassed by our national parks. And, it has to be said, in some parks the shopping and restaurants, ski lifts and tour boats, can also add much to your enjoyment. Given this vast natural richness and the multitude of possibilities for fun, learning, and spiritual renewal that our parks provide, this book is designed to help you match your interests with what Canada's national parks have to offer. In planning a trip, or arriving at your destination, this book should be treated as a friend who has been there before you, and who continues to walk along with you, chatting about what you're seeing now, and mulling over what to do next.

Canada's 39 national parks and three national marine conservation areas protect some of the most precious natural resources of our country and, in many cases, of our world. The goal of the park system is:

> To protect for all time representative natural areas of Canadian significance in a system of National Parks, and to encourage public understanding, appreciation, and enjoyment of this natural heritage so as to leave it unimpaired for future generations.
>
> It would be naive to think that this protection is complete, or that this system could not be improved upon, but what we have is truly marvellous.

The national system began in 1885, with the creation of what is now Banff National Park. The establishment of Banff and its sister parks, such as Yoho, Glacier, and Waterton Lakes, came about largely because the federal government acted in conjunction with the railway companies, or other commercial interests, to set aside for tourism the spectacular scenic areas through which the railways passed. In some cases, there were a few local people who were aware that the environment was being threatened by the rapid encroachment of settlement, hunting, mining, or logging, but this was not the primary impetus for early park establishment. In fact, hunting, mining, and logging continued in a number of parks for decades, and town-based commercial development remains a major feature of a number of the parks today, as any visit to Banff, Riding Mountain, Prince Edward Island or Bruce Peninsula national parks readily reveals.

Gradually, however, there has been a shift in the balance between protecting resources for commercial exploitation and protecting natural resources for their own inherent values. Now the primary rationale for establishing parks is to set aside forever at least one significant segment of each of Canada's types of natural regions. Thirty-nine of these regions are terrestrial—like the Northern Yukon Region or the Northwestern Boreal Uplands, and 29 are marine—like the Labrador Sea or Queen Charlotte Sound. In terms of the establishment of parks in terrestrial regions, 23 of the 39 regions are represented by national parks. Of the 29 marine natural regions, five are represented in parks. (One of these marine conservation areas, Gwaii Haanas, formerly South Moresby, represents two distinct marine natural regions.) Much has been done to preserve at least some part of a number of natural regions, but there is still a long way to go before the national park system has met its goals for representation and protection.

Since the second edition of this book was published, there have been major changes to the internal operations of the national parks systems, changes that I view with some concern. That is, as part of the federal government's budgetary cutbacks and emphasis on a "business" approach to government services, the parks system is dealing with a funding reduction of nearly $100 million from 1994 to 1999. One way in which the system must adjust to this reduction is to divest itself of many functions it traditionally exercised and to have many of these provided on a privatized basis. There are staff cuts that go with this, and in many cases staff are invited to organize as a private or non-profit organization to provide the services they once offered as federal employees. These changes can range from park maintenance, to campground operations, or interpretation. A much greater role is played by other profit or non-profit groups as well, whether or not they include former staff.

In addition, Parks Canada is expected to compensate for funding cuts by engaging in revenue-generating activities. This translates directly into more services having fees for the first time, and existing fees being increased. You may pay for firewood now, and for guided walks in some parks and historic sites. I think you will find that these fees are modest, and the services offered are good value for the money. And in some cases there is no doubt that the new way of operating has brought about an improvement in services, with a fresh approach and an increased emphasis on efficiency and quality.

But there are losses, too. Sometimes there are losses in quality of service, because it is not economical for a company to provide a water taxi service in a park that receives relatively few visitors and those for just a few months of the year. Where once the park could have included this service in its budget and ensured that it was available throughout the season, now there may be no service. Or what service there is may be irregular and over-priced. The parks do what they can to assure that private concessionaires meet reasonable standards of service, but there are gaps. But, as I say, there are definite successes in these new approaches to service as well.

I'm not happy about what I see as a significant negative change on the part of government (no matter what the party in power, because this is simply an accelerating trend of more than a decade) about its own role in supporting our natural and historical heritage. However, you should know that Parks Canada staff have responded to these changes with the dedication and imagination that has, to my mind, always characterized their work. They work with the private sector to ensure that services and programs meet high standards. They make every effort to ensure that their own staff services are organized in the most efficient and effective manner. Taking the parks system as a whole, you have every chance of having the most wonderful experience of your lifetime, and it will be entirely worth whatever you may now pay.

As you plan your trip, you can determine in advance exactly what services are available and any associated costs. This is because part of the response of the parks to all these changes has been to assume a much stronger role in communicating about their own services and in serving as a kind of centralized information centre for all of the other organizations in the area that may become a part of your visit. So be sure to contact the park first and ask for a list of services and associated fees for anything that you will be interested in — camping in the park or outside it, other accommodations, interpretive programs, guided tours, recreational opportunities such as golf, tennis, kayaking, skiing. The parks have excellent information to share, and it will be the most up-to-date on available services and any associated fees.

Also, the provincial tourism offices, whose names and numbers are provided in the chapters of this book, are also invaluable sources of information. I've found them to be very prompt in supplying an array of attractive information on their regions.

I've given a lot of advice in this introduction, and there will be much more in each chapter. Perhaps readers would like to know the basis of the information and opinions I am presenting.

I am a sociologist by training, but I've been a natural history enthusiast for nearly 30 years. For the first edition of this book, I worked sporadically for close to four years, visiting 25 of the then 29 parks, excluding only Wood Buffalo, Nahanni, Auyuittuq, and the newly established Grasslands. For these last four, I interviewed people who were very familiar with them, and I read widely. For the 25 I visited, I spent an average of five days and four nights in each. I interviewed staff, went to most of the interpretive events, hiked most major trails, camped in at least one or two of the campgrounds, and visited virtually all the rest to assess their location and facilities. I checked commercial facilities near the parks, where possible. Though I was usually alone in my visits, I based my evaluations on my idea of what visitors, such as retired couples, or families with children, or keen hikers, might look for in a park.

In preparing the second edition, I revisited Banff, Fundy, and Georgian Bay Islands National Parks, because so much had changed in them. I also visited Gwaii Haanas, Bruce Peninsula, and Fathom Five. These visits were from two to five days, and I was able to interview staff and explore what areas could be covered in this more limited time. Of course, there is a lot of written material to draw on for describing the parks, and I have used it, as well. For the third edition I visited Mingan Archipelago National Park and Saguenay-St.Lawrence Marine Park, also spending several days in each, interviewing, reading, walking, and boating.

The interpretive and visitor-services staff, at the parks and at several regional offices, reviewed the revised chapters and, therefore, the materials are as up-to-date and accurate as possible. But circumstances can change so contacting the parks in the area you plan to visit is important. Addresses and phone numbers are listed at the end of each chapter.

Goals for This Book

My goals for this book have evolved over the years. The first goal has not changed. I want the book to make your visit to the national parks of Canada easy and enjoyable. Even though I have reservations about the changes to some of parks' operations, the fact is that staff at all levels are amazingly dedicated to their work and extremely skilled in making the very best of the situation. I hope that this book is an entry point into the national parks for you, even if you are unable to actually visit. If you are able to visit, then I hope you will make use of the information here, for planning your visit days or even years ahead. Once you are in the park, this book should help you plan your day so that you can use your undoubtedly limited time to the fullest.

My second goal also is the same, though it is expressed more implicitly than the first. I hope that your visit to the national parks will encourage you to participate in national and local debate on the direction Canada takes in protecting and preserving our amazingly rich national heritage. If this book makes it easier for you to learn about our parks and increases your desire to cherish them and to act upon that desire in whatever way you see fit, then my second goal will have been met.

Finally, there is a third goal for this third edition. You will find that there is a new section for most parks, about related places of natural and historic interest that I suggest you visit. In the earlier editions of this book I concentrated on the national parks alone, in an almost "territorial" manner. But this is too narrow and impractical an approach. It is too narrow, because the preservation of our natural or human history, our natural environment or our historical heritage, does not start or stop at some park boundary. We have to take the wider view, and I want this edition of the book to help you do that. So I have selected sites of natural or historical interest that are either a part of the larger Parks Canada system — specifically national historic parks and sites — or are provincial parks or sites that can extend your experience of the natural and historic region that a given national park encompasses.

There are also very practical economic reasons for including suggestions for visiting related sites. On the one hand, Canada is a large country. People often travel quite far to visit the parks and they usually have limited time to do so. You may want to come to one place and spend all of your precious days and nights there, but I think that adding some of these other sites to your itinerary can enrich your experience even further. Also, consider visiting parks in the "shoulder seasons," which usually means spring and fall. The parks have significantly extended their services and activities beyond the traditional vacation periods. This is a quieter time, with fewer visitors, but most services are still open. Also, there is a major increase in winter activities in the national parks. You can do overnight cross-country ski tours or join winter camping expeditions, or watch regional cross-country championships in a national park. Again, the park has the information to help you plan.

On the other hand, let's face it, tourism is a major economic resource for communities. If you stay another few days in an area, visiting other places of interest, eating in different places, staying in other campsites or hotels or RV parks, then the local economy is further strengthened. I'm all for that, as long as our natural and historic heritage is protected.

Canada's national parks are surely one of the greatest treasures of our world. It may seem a contradiction to write a book that encourages more people to visit these parks, when great numbers of people could destroy that heritage. But I believe that support for our natural and historic heritage is created and strengthened by direct experience of that heritage. Perhaps this book will play a role in bringing that experience to you.

Using the Third Edition of this Book

In each the chapters that follow, you will see that I begin with a description of the main natural and human history themes of the park. Then there is a section on how to see the park. I have related the main themes to examples of activities you might engage in to experience those themes — trails, special sites to visit, particular interpretive opportunities. Then there are details on park services and facilities, like campgrounds, and recreational features of the parks, such as golf or swimming or winter sports. This is followed by information on other accommodation, food, gas, supplies, whether inside or outside of the park boundaries. There is a new section in this edition and that is a brief listing of related historic or natural history sites that are readily visitable as a part of your trip to the park being described. I haven't visited most of these related places, but in my review of the informational materials I collected on them, they seemed very attractive and interesting. If you read the previous editions of this book, you will remember that I listed other books you might want to read. Now that most parks have "cooperating associations" (usually called the "Friends of...Park") the giftshops and bookstores they often operate are excellent places to purchase the latest, best publications on a specific park. Be sure to visit them when you go, and you might even contact them beforehand, in that they are increasingly the source of trail maps and local field guides. Plus, they need and deserve your support. Finally, at the end of each chapter there is the information on whom to contact at the national park to gather more information for planning your trip. I hope it is a wonderful one — mine always have been.

You can reach the Parks Canada web site at

http:\\parkscanada.pch.gc.ca

GWAII HAANAS

National Park Reserve/

Haida Heritage Site

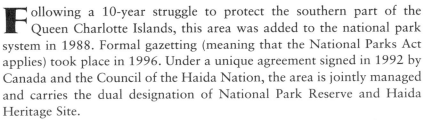

Following a 10-year struggle to protect the southern part of the Queen Charlotte Islands, this area was added to the national park system in 1988. Formal gazetting (meaning that the National Parks Act applies) took place in 1996. Under a unique agreement signed in 1992 by Canada and the Council of the Haida Nation, the area is jointly managed and carries the dual designation of National Park Reserve and Haida Heritage Site.

The Queen Charlotte Islands are located 80 kilometres (50 miles) west of the mainland. Gwaii Haanas (Haida for "Islands of Wonder") encompasses the lower third of the Queen Charlottes, with South Moresby Island itself comprising the main land mass. The reserve contains 138 islands, and uncounted islets. The larger or better-known islands include Moresby, Lyell (famous for attempts by Haida people and environmentalists to halt logging, in the final days before the park's reserve status was declared), Hotspring, and Anthony (or Sgan Gwaii). Anthony Island, home of the village of Ninstints, is the location of a hauntingly beautiful group of totem poles and has been selected as a UNESCO World Heritage Site.

Gwaii Haanas is both a terrestrial and a marine park. The land mass represents the Pacific Coast Mountains natural region. It is dominated by the San Christoval Range, its slopes and watershed clad in magnificent rain forests, its upland bogs dotted with stunted "bonsai" pine. Highlights for wildlife watchers include bears and eagles feeding on salmon in the many rivers and streams, rich and colourful intertidal areas, and, on the water, whales, dolphins, sea lions, and puffins. At a number of old village sites visitors can learn first-hand about Haida culture from the Haida Gwaii Watchmen, who remain there to ensure protection of the sites.

Because Gwaii Haanas is a wilderness area, visitor numbers are restricted and a reservation for visiting is required. Access is by chartered plane, boat, or kayak. There are no roads and only minimal development, mainly at the Watchmen basecamps. This, in fact, is part of the Gwaii

Parks Canada

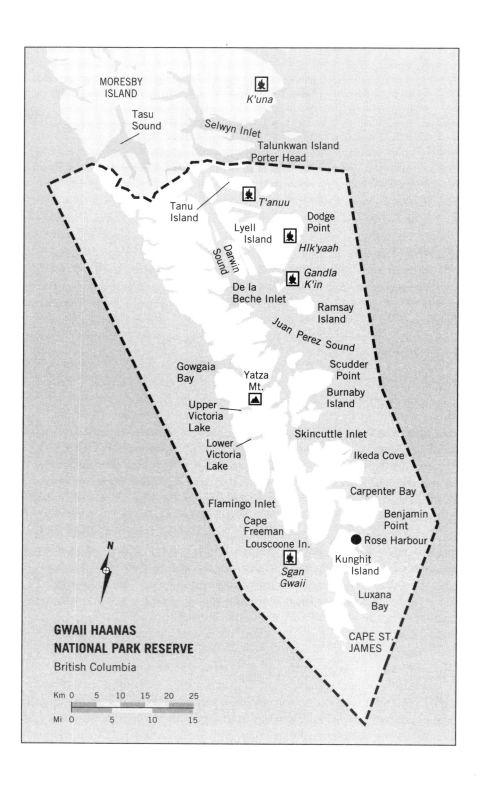

MORESBY
ISLAND

Tasu
Sound

Selwyn Inlet

K'una

Talunkwan Island
Porter Head

Tanu
Island

T'anuu

Dodge
Point

Lyell
Island

Hlk'yaah

Darwin
Sound

Gandla
K'in

De la
Beche Inlet

Ramsay
Island

Juan Perez Sound

Gowgaia
Bay

Yatza
Mt.

Scudder
Point

Burnaby
Island

Upper
Victoria
Lake

Skincuttle Inlet

Lower
Victoria
Lake

Ikeda Cove

Carpenter Bay

Flamingo Inlet

Benjamin
Point

Cape
Freeman
Louscoone In.

Rose Harbour

Sgan
Gwaii

Kunghit
Island

Luxana
Bay

CAPE ST.
JAMES

**GWAII HAANAS
NATIONAL PARK RESERVE**

British Columbia

Km 0   5   10   15   20   25

Mi 0   5   10   15

Haanas experience—people have been an integral part of this landscape for thousands of years, yet throughout most of the area, it is still possible to feel as though you're the first person to set foot there. To ensure that it remains that way, and that visitors "travel without trace," the Management Board provides an orientation program that all visitors must attend before travelling into Gwaii Haanas.

Sea-kayaking is a favourite way to see the area, but you must be very experienced or travel with a licensed tour operator. The area is exposed to Pacific swells and storms, and the rugged coastal landforms combine with wind and tide to create hazardous conditions. "Small-craft warning" conditions are in effect at all times here, and canoeing generally is not considered to be safe in these waters. Hiking opportunities exist, if you are willing to manoeuvre through heavy bush in terrain that is often difficult, wet, and slippery. Some basic trails may be developed in the future but for now, good route-finding skills are essential. Although you may camp wherever you find a suitable place, it is important that you leave no traces of your visit whatsoever.

Plan your trip to Gwaii Haanas well in advance. Contact the Parks Canada office for the most up-to-date information on reservations, orientation, lists of licensed operators, and services and facilities available in the

Marylee Stephenson

Ninstints is the location of a beautiful group of totem poles

Marylee Stephenson

Rugged coastline of Gwaii Haanas

surrounding area. In the towns and villages of the Queen Charlottes as a whole, there are a number of fascinating visitor sites, many of which reflect the Haida heritage and the rich natural history of the whole archipelago.

Related Activities or Places of Natural or Historic Interest

Discover British Columbia is an excellent information service for all kinds of visitation in the province. Call 1-800-663-6000 (or 663-6000 within Greater Vancouver). The Queen Charlotte Travel Infocentre can be reached at (604) 559-4742.

Activities and Places to Consider Visiting:

- The Queen Charlotte Island Museum, near Skidegate, houses excellent displays of the art and culture of the Haida.

- Naikoon Provincial Park, located at the northeast tip of Graham Island. Known for its long sandy beaches and Tow Hill, a volcanic plug is located midway along the northern beach.

FURTHER READING

Ecological Classification of Gwaii Haanas (Archipelago Management Board, 1994).

Paradise Won: The Struggle for South Moresby by Elizabeth May (McClelland and Stewart, 1990).

For More Information

Gwaii Haanas National Park Reserve/
Haida Heritage Site
P.O. Box 37
Queen Charlotte, British Columbia
V0T 1S0
Phone: (604) 559-6317
Fax: (604) 559-8366

PACIFIC RIM

National Park Reserve

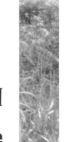

The Pacific Ocean has shaped much of the natural and human history of the West Coast, and Pacific Rim National Park is the place to go to experience the ocean's powerful, ever-changing nature.

Pacific Rim is a thin strip of land along the southwestern coast of Vancouver Island. The park is composed of three segments. The most accessible is the northern, or Long Beach, area, which has an interpretive theatre, marked trails, and kilometres of uninterrupted beach.

Southeast of the Long Beach section are the Broken Group Islands. This second segment is located in Barkley Sound, and is composed of about 100 islands, covering an area of about 58 square kilometres (22 square miles). Some of the islands are tiny exposed rocks with a bit of vegetation clinging to them, and some are several hundred hectares in area—big enough for people to land their boats, to hike, or to camp on.

The third segment of the park is managed as a wilderness area. It lies at the southern tip, a narrow, 72-kilometre (45-mile) strip from Bamfield to Port Renfrew, along which runs the West Coast Trail. The trail was originally laid out in 1891 as a telegraph line route, and later, between 1908 and 1915, as a "lifesaving trail." This trail was needed because so many lives were lost in shipping disasters off the coast. The park has restored sections of the trail to make it safer and easier to hike.

To understand the natural and human history of Pacific Rim, it is best to picture it as a series of long, thin strips of water and land, running from north to south, parallel to each other. These strips include the sub-tidal zone of deep water; the intertidal zone, which lies between the highest and lowest reach of the tides; the foreshore zone of gravel bars, drift logs, and patchy plant life; and, finally, the forest zone, with its own successive bands of plant life.

The location of Pacific Rim, its relatively mild climate, and its rich marine life and forest growth have made it a place with a long human history. The Nuu-Chah-Nulth (West Coast) people lived, fished, hunted, and

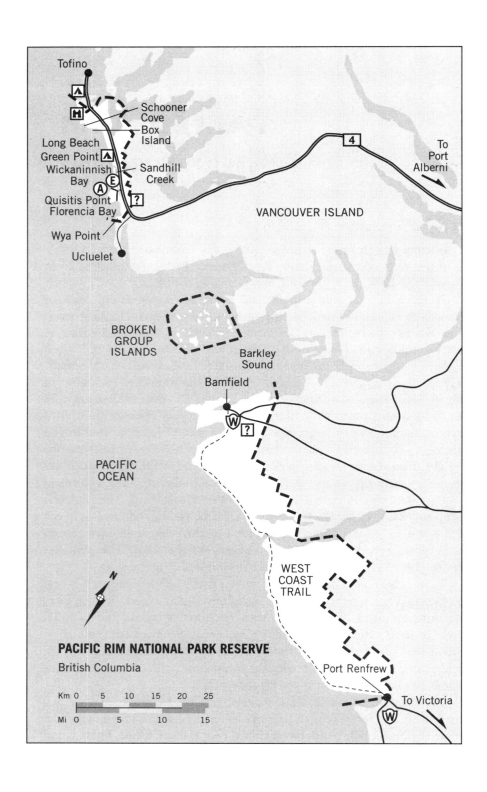

Tofino

Schooner
Cove

Box
Island

Long Beach
Green Point
Wickaninnish
Bay

Sandhill
Creek

Quisitis Point
Florencia Bay

Wya Point

Ucluelet

VANCOUVER ISLAND

4

To
Port
Alberni

BROKEN
GROUP
ISLANDS

Barkley
Sound

Bamfield

PACIFIC
OCEAN

N

WEST
COAST
TRAIL

PACIFIC RIM NATIONAL PARK RESERVE

British Columbia

Port Renfrew

To Victoria

Km 0   5   10   15   20   25

Mi 0   5   10   15

gathered here for thousands of years. People came as fur traders, then for logging, gold mining and fishing, and finally as settlers.

In the late 1960s, before Pacific Rim was established as a national park, the Long Beach area became a celebrated refuge for young people who wanted to live unfettered by the demands of modern city life. Today, this environment is somewhat more developed for visitor use, and park operations are in place to manage and protect it.

HOW TO SEE THE PARK
The Long Beach Area

You can experience much of the Long Beach segment on your own. Good maps and informative brochures show the hiking trails, or describe the plant and animal life found in the forests or in the ocean, and I would suggest participating in the interpretive program. It is well-coordinated, pleasing and certainly will enrich your own ramblings and observations.

The **sub-tidal zone** covers an underwater area, including the Continental Shelf. Conditions are ideal for kelp, which grows here in rafts, some as deep as 30 metres (100 feet). These rafts are frequented by grey whales, which feed off the bottom life in and near kelp beds. People come to Pacific Rim from afar, in the hope of glimpsing the grey whales puffing out clouds of vapour as they surface from their dives to the bottom. It's not unusual to see sea lions basking on islands, or swimming in the surf.

For a closer view of the life of the sub-tidal zone, you can scuba dive or snorkel in the park and reach relatively deep waters. The underwater life is very rich, but the water is extremely cold, often rough, and the currents are hazardous. Unfortunately, most good dive sites are in exposed locations.

To explore the **intertidal zone,** you must get a copy of the Tofino tide tables for the Long Beach area. They are available at the Park Information Centre, and are posted on bulletin boards throughout Long Beach. Wherever there are sandy beaches, you can walk at high or low tide. The park offers visitors an 11-kilometre (six-mile) stretch of sandy beaches to explore, from Wickaninnish Beach in the south, along Combers Beach in the middle, to Long Beach at the north.

Where it is rocky, you can scramble out on little headlands. You should know the tide schedule for the day, however, in order to avoid having to beat a hurried and damp retreat. Rocky areas harbour the beautiful tide pools. At low tide, they are a marvel of brightly coloured anemones, starfish, barnacles, and nearly invisible little fish darting to avoid your shadow.

Naturalists explain the survival strategies of animal and
plant life of the sub-tidal zone

My favourite place for observing the intertidal zone was **Wya Point**, located at the south end of **Florencia Bay**. Four trails lead to Florencia Bay, and then there's a pleasant walk to Wya Point itself. The southern-most location, the **Willowbrae Trail**, actually starts outside the park but emerges nearest the point.

The **South Beach Trail**, starting behind the Wickaninnish Centre, is a 1.5-kilometre (one-mile) return hike leading to a wonderful pebbled beach surrounded by rocky bluffs. The first 300 metres (900 feet) of the trail, as far as Lismer Beach, is paved and is wheelchair accessible. Lismer Beach was named after one of Canada's famous Group of Seven painters, Arthur Lismer, who was a regular visitor here.

An excellent place for sandy beach, tide pools, and islets is Schooner Cove. There you'll see Box Island, with its striking layers of rock, which give the effect of rows and rows of circular saw blades packed together and resting in an upright position.

Parks Canada

Trail through the rain forest at Florencia Bay

The interpretive programs concentrate on the intertidal zone. A number of guided walks are offered each week during July and August, as well as several related evening slide shows that you won't want to miss. (The Green Point camping fees include theatre admission.)

For the wilderness visitor, the **Broken Group Islands** and the **West Coast Trail** provide marvellous opportunities to experience first-hand the intertidal zone. Although no formal interpretation is provided, a number of books or pamphlets on intertidal life are available, which are published by the park, and by the British Columbia Provincial Museum.

The Foreshore: A Transition Zone

Any walk on the beaches bordering the forest reveals the log-strewn upper beach, with its fine, wind-blown sand and its sparse plant life struggling to take hold.

The foreshore area at **Florencia** is very different, in that it is bounded by gravel cliffs, pitted with the small holes made by nesting rough-winged swallows.

At the northern end of Florencia Bay, a little lagoon has been formed by the entry of **Lost Shoe Creek** into the ocean. The gulls love it, and I saw several black oystercatchers washing themselves in the stream water where it met the ocean. It's particularly easy to access from a parking lot at Florencia Bay. The road goes off to the left, from the Wickaninnish Road, and allows you to join the **Wickaninnish Trail**.

The Forests

Most of the land area of Pacific Rim is forest, with the exception of the occasional break where logged sections are now recovering, and the area of marine estuary at **Grice Bay**.

A variety of trails highlight several different forest communities, from shorepine bog, to Sitka spruce fringe, to coastal rain forest.

The **Shorepine Bog Trail** is an excellent self-guiding trail through a typical sphagnum bog habitat. This one-kilometre (0.6-mile) boardwalk loop-trail is wheelchair accessible. The dominant tree species is the shorepine, dwarfed and misshapen because of nutrient deficiency. Although some of these trees are hundreds of years old, they stand only a few metres tall.

A striking contrast to the trail through the bog is the **Rain Forest Trail**. There are two short loop trails, one on either side of Highway 4, about 16 kilometres (10 miles) north of the Park Information Centre. In this area the amabilis fir grows, along with the cedar and hemlock, as the dominant trees in a fully mature, climax rain forest. Boardwalks and staircases are often provided to ease the way for hikers.

Off Highway 4, toward the Tofino end, there is the **Schooner Trail** down to Schooner Cove. The trail is only one kilometre (0.6 mile) long, but it descends by a winding, stairstepped trail from the cedar/hemlock forest through the Sitka spruce fringe to the open beach.

Another short trek is the trail leading from **Green Point**. Near the top of the cliffs, you can see what has happened to some of the tallest cedar trees from their constant exposure to the salty winds from the sea.

As the trail flattens out at the bottom of the cliffs it runs behind the gnarled wall of Sitka spruce *krummholz* that borders the foreshore. This very short trail branch goes to another opening on to the beach where two of the park's environmentally friendly, solar-powered composting toilets are located. These are the latest in environmental management technology! Being so close to the ocean, but completely screened from it, clearly demonstrates the effectiveness of the gnarling and overlapping of the trees, as an adaptation to the constant wind.

The **Gold Mine Trail**, one of the trails that leads down to the beach at Florencia Bay, provides visitors with an opportunity to observe a forest that is undergoing the process of regeneration. The forest here was logged of its native amabilis fir, red cedar, and hemlock, and replaced with seedlings of Douglas fir and Sitka spruce in the mid-1900s. The original species re-established themselves in the plantation, and the creation of the park in 1970 has ensured that this process will continue.

A good place to get a bird's-eye view of the forests of Pacific Rim and the grey whales is from the viewpoint on top of **Radar Hill** at the northern terminus of the park. A wheelchair-accessible viewing platform and outhouse are provided here.

PARK SERVICES AND FACILITIES

The Park Information Centre is located just inside the park boundary, on the main highway. The Centre is open daily from mid-March to Thanksgiving. Check at the Centre for information on park-use fees that are in effect all season when full services are provided. Annual, daily, and hourly permits can be purchased on site.

Interpretive Program

The most outstanding service that the park provides is its interpretive program. Modest fees are charged to cover the cost of this service, which includes special family rates. To be comfortable on the walks, take a raincoat or windbreaker, and wear rubber boots or shoes with good traction. A variety of programs cover the human history of the area. The interpretive theatre at Green Point offers interpretive programs each night, from late June through Labour Day. The theatre is wheelchair accessible, as is Wickaninnish Centre, a beautiful interpretation facility, which is open from March to Thanksgiving each year. All-terrain manual wheelchairs can be borrowed from the Centre.

Camping

Two camping options are available in the Long Beach area of the park, both of which are located at **Green Point**. There are 94 drive-in sites in a wooded area at the top of the bluffs. The beach is a five-minute walk down a well-kept trail. The washrooms have hot and cold water, faucets every few sites for cooking water, picnic tables and fire grates at each site; firewood is provided. Although kitchen shelters, showers, electricity, and trailer hook-ups are not provided, there is a trailer-waste disposal system and bear-proof garbage containers. A seven-day stay limit is imposed. Note that this campground is extremely popular and fills every day. A reservation service is available (1-800-689-9025).

Walk-in camping is also available at Green Point, in wooded sites and on the beach. There are solar-powered composting toilets and fresh water from faucets. The walk to the campsite from the parking lot is about 200 metres. It is lovely, a bit winding and steep.

Primitive Camping

There are eight designated sites with either pit or solar-powered composting toilets on Broken Group Islands—on **Clark, Dodd, Gilbert, Hand, Willis, Benson, Turret,** and **Gibraltar** islands. Water is usually available, but may run dry in late summer, so consider bringing your own. Sites are very busy during the summer, and the park has a quota system. Modest camping fees are charged.

Wilderness hiking can be found on the **West Coast Trail**. A quota and reservation system is in effect. Call 1-800-663-6000 for details. All backpackers must have a park-use permit to hike the West Coast Trail. The permit fee in 1996 is $70, exclusive of reservation service fees ($25) and ferry crossing charges. Backpackers must be fully provisioned and capable of self-reliant hiking for as long as a week. Campers usually choose locations near streams. Drinking water is obtained from these streams, so dispose of personal waste carefully and far from fresh water. Driftwood is used for small fires, which should be built only on sand or rock, below the high-tide line. Once you've registered for your park use permit, you will receive a complete list of trail conditions and what you need to do to be prepared to hike the rugged West Coast Trail.

Other Camping

Several small commercial campgrounds are offered in the area that are approved by Tourism B.C. Advance reservations are strongly recommended as sites fill early and the campgrounds are extremely busy from late June to late September. Contact the Ucluelet or Tofino Chamber of Commerce for listings.

Other Accommodation, Gas, Food, and Supplies

Tofino, Ucluelet, and surrounding areas have a number of oceanfront bed and breakfasts, resorts and motels. Because they fill quickly, it is important to phone or write ahead for reservations.

Victoria, Port Alberni, Ucluelet, and Tofino all have a full range of restaurants, gas stations, grocery and supply stores. They also have shops with local arts and crafts. Quality gift galleries including original works by well known West Coast artists are located in Ucluelet and Tofino.

Recreational Services

Swimming   Supervised swimming is available at North Long Beach in summer, but the water is cold and often rough. Extreme care should be taken, even when wading, because of currents, which usually occur near any rocky headlands.

Scuba Diving, Kayaking, Surfing   All of these activities can be done in park waters, but cold water, high winds, and strong currents require skill and experience. Keep away from rocks and carefully watch the weather.

Fishing   Fishing is allowed from the shore. A federal salt-water fishing licence is required. Information and licences are available from the Department of Fisheries and Oceans, 1090 Pender Street West, Vancouver, B.C. Licences are available in most stores and marinas in Ucluelet and Tofino. Fresh-water fishing requires a B.C. licence.

A wide range of charter-boat fishing opportunities are offered in both Tofino and Ucluelet. Check with the local Chambers of Commerce for listings.

Shellfish Gathering   Scuba divers may catch a few crab or abalone, but the gathering of clams, mussels, or oysters for food is often prohibited, because of the presence of highly toxic "red tide." Ask at the park or confirm with Federal Fisheries offices before attempting to collect any of these molluscs. A federal tidal waters fishing licence is required. Shellfish collecting is not recommended in national parks, in support of conservation and protection of park resources.

Boating   Rentals and charters operate out of Tofino and Ucluelet for whale and wildlife viewing, bird-watching, or fishing. Check with the local Chambers of Commerce and Tourism B.C. Information Centres for a list of operators. Complete marine facilities are available at Ucluelet and Tofino.

Canoeing   You can canoe at Grice Bay, Kennedy Lake, Clayoquot Sound, Clayoquot Arm, and in sheltered areas of the Broken Group Islands.

Hiking   The park's *Official Guidebook to Pacific Rim National Park Reserve* contains a complete description of all trails within Long Beach, including maps. You can order it from the park before you leave or you can buy it there. The West Coast Trail is *only* for experienced hikers. When you register you will receive the appropriate information from the park. There are also guidebooks published about the Trail.

HOW TO GET THERE

For the Long Beach section of the park, most vistors drive up the east side of Vancouver Island to Parksville and Nanaimo and then turn west toward Port Alberni. Stop at Port Alberni if you have time (they've made the waterfront into a very pleasant place to visit), and then drive on to the west coast and park itself. Give yourself a leisurely day to do the trip, stopping at interesting or beautiful sites along the way. If you drive straight through, it will take about four hours from Nanaimo. Access to the West Coast Trail is from the northern trailhead and Information Centre, at Camp Ross, Pachena Bay, five kilometres (three miles) from Bamfield. Bamfield is 90 kilometres (56 miles) by car from Port Alberni, along a gravel logging road. The West Coast Trail can also be accessed via Port Renfrew at the southern end. There is no public transportation to either trailhead. In the summer the motor vessel *Lady Rose* also carries passengers to and from Port Alberni and Bamfield, several times weekly.

Related Activities or Places of Natural or Historic Interest

Discover British Columbia is an excellent information service for all kinds of visitation in the province. Call 1-800-663-6000 (or 663-6000 within Greater Vancouver). The Pacific Rim Tourism Association (604-720-2808), the Ucluelet Chamber of Commerce (604-726-4641), and the Tofino Chamber of Commerce (604-725-3922) can also provide information on local opportunities.

Activities and Places to Consider Visiting:

- Nearby provincial parks include Taylor Arm, Stamp Falls and Sproat Lake, all located between Port Alberni and Pacific Rim; Maquinna, north of Tofino; and Carmanah Pacific, off the West Coast Trail.

- Amphitrite Point Lighthouse, at the entrance to Ucluelet harbour, provides some excellent viewpoints. The grounds are open to the public.

- The annual Pacific Rim Whale festival takes place during a three-week period from mid-March to mid-April. It is a series of family-oriented events celebrating the spring migration of 20 000 grey whales, which pass close to the shore through park waters. The celebrations are organized by the commu-

Related Activities Cont'd

nities of Ucluelet and Tofino, and there are special programs and guest lectures by whale researchers and other scientists in the park.

- Hot-springs aficionados might be interested in a visit to Hot Springs Cove, located 65 kilometres (40 miles) north of Tofino. The hot springs are part of Maquinna Provincial Park. Access is by float plane or boat.

National Historic Sites:

- Port Alberni: McLean Mill National Historic Site.

FURTHER READING

Official Guidebook to Pacific Rim National Park (1996).

For More Information

The Superintendent
Pacific Rim National Park Reserve
Box 280
Ucluelet, British Columbia
V0R 3A0
Phone: (604) 726-7721/726-4212
Fax: (604) 726-4720

MOUNT REVELSTOKE AND GLACIER
National Parks

With respect to their human history and genesis, Mount Revelstoke and Glacier National Parks are quite different. Revelstoke National Park was established in 1914 as a result of lobbying by the people of Revelstoke to protect a nearby mountain environment with its spectacular wildflower displays. Glacier National Park was set aside in 1886, along with Yoho National Park, and its history is intertwined with the early years of the Canadian Pacific Railway.

In terms of their natural history, however, Glacier and Revelstoke are best considered as two segments of the same park, with Mount Revelstoke as the "little sister" of Glacier. These two parks preserve essentially the same habitat—sections of the Columbia Mountains in eastern British Columbia.

The Columbia Mountains lie to the west of the Rockies, and can be subdivided into four mountain groups: the Purcells, Selkirks, and Monashees extending in narrow north-south strips from east to west, and the Cariboos forming a steep triangle at the northern end of the system. The Columbia River forms a low valley border that runs directly north-south between the Monashees and Selkirks. Mount Revelstoke National Park lies within sight of the Columbia River, and Glacier National Park, less than 50 kilometres (30 miles) east, includes parts of both the Selkirks and the Purcells.

The Columbias differ from the Rockies, in that they are an older mountain system and are composed of much harder rock. Most mountains start out jagged and rough-edged, but wind, rain, freezing, and thawing pare them down. However, the Columbias resist erosion. This is an area of sharp, angular mountains, with narrow, steep-walled valleys.

The combination of steep mountain walls, huge collections of snow, and near-freezing or even warmer-than-freezing temperatures creates ideal conditions for avalanches. In Glacier National Park, avalanche slopes are so numerous and extensive that they cover a considerable portion of what would otherwise be forest areas.

Marylee Stephenson

27

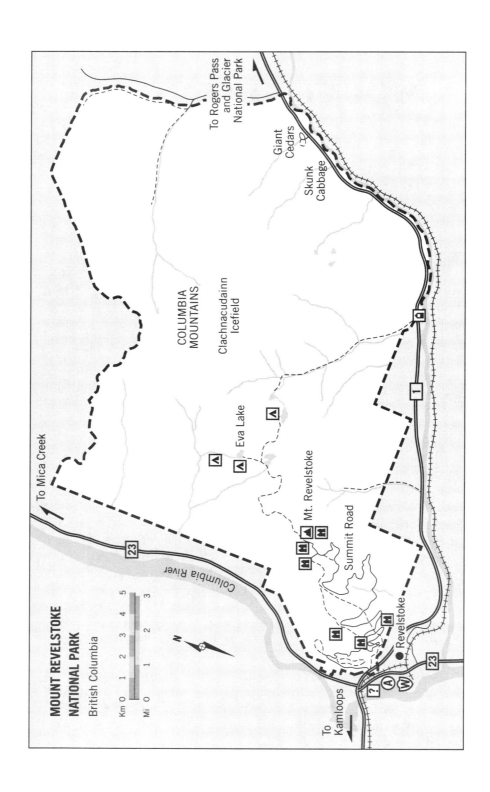

MOUNT REVELSTOKE
NATIONAL PARK

British Columbia

Km 0   1   2   3   4   5

Mi 0   1   2   3

N

To Mica Creek

To Rogers Pass
and Glacier
National Park

Giant
Cedars

Skunk
Cabbage

COLUMBIA
MOUNTAINS

Clachnacudainn
Icefield

Eva Lake

Mt. Revelstoke

Summit Road

Columbia River

Revelstoke

To
Kamloops

23

1

23

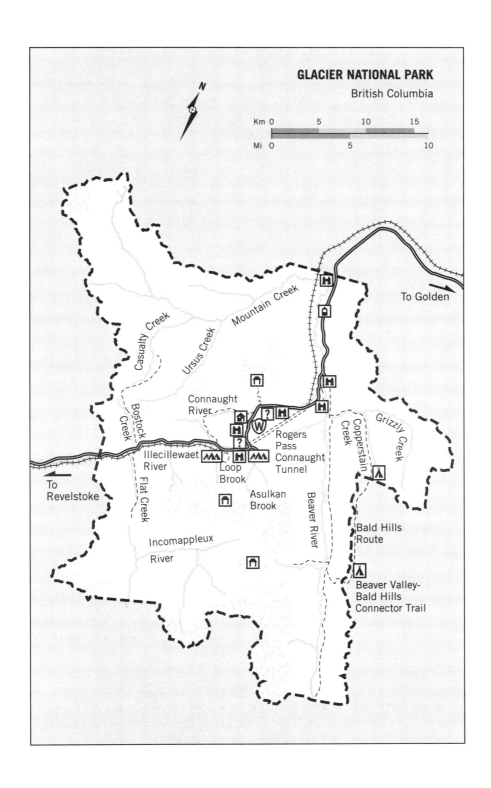

GLACIER NATIONAL PARK

British Columbia

Km 0   5   10   15

Mi 0   5   10

To Golden

To Revelstoke

Casualty Creek

Ursus Creek

Mountain Creek

Bostock Creek

Connaught River

Rogers Pass Connaught Tunnel

Illecillewaet River

Loop Brook

Asulkan Brook

Beaver River

Copperstain Creek

Grizzly Creek

Flat Creek

Incomappleux River

Bald Hills Route

Beaver Valley-Bald Hills Connector Trail

Huge amounts of snow have also created a multitude of glaciers. Glacier National Park has over 400 glaciers, comprising 10 percent of its area.

The ruggedness of the Columbias posed enormous problems in the late nineteenth century, when there was great interest in finding a southern transport route through the western mountains to the sea. The first problem was to find a pass and the second was to make the passage safe for train travel. Rogers Pass was discovered in 1881, but steep grades, avalanches, and climate would all work together to tear apart in seconds what had taken weeks, or even years, to build. Finally, construction began on the eight-kilometre (five-mile) Connaught Tunnel under Mount Macdonald.

New techniques have now resulted in a fairly good method of predicting when and where avalanches are likely to occur. Then the park acts before nature does. Seventeen circular emplacements have been built along Rogers Pass, where 105-millimetre howitzer cannons can be rolled up, aimed, and fired on the danger spots. The potential avalanche is released before too much snow builds up, or the slides move safely across one of the numerous snow sheds that bridge the road and carry the snow harmlessly farther down slope.

HOW TO SEE THE PARKS

Even though Mount Revelstoke and Glacier National Parks are located close to each other and have the same type of habitat, the facilities and services of each park are designed for different uses. Glacier is a multi-use park, offering campgrounds, many trails, and interpreter-led hikes. Mount Revelstoke is primarily for day use, with a road to its summit, and a series of shorter trails leading from there to the alpine meadows.

Glacier National Park

Glacier National Park offers an assortment of trails that allows visitors to explore the varied terrain, from the narrow river valley to alpine meadows. All trails begin from the Trans-Canada Highway or from the campgrounds just off the highway.

Eastbound from Rogers Pass, a small "hiker" sign marks the access road leading to the short **Bear Falls** trail. Bear Falls itself, located on Connaught Creek, is a rewarding destination, but hikers can also continue across Connaught Creek on a wooden bridge for a short hike through spectacular old-growth forest to the Beaver River.

The **Hemlock Grove** interpretive trail is a recently constructed short boardwalk through old-growth hemlock forest. This short trail is wheelchair accessible.

Several trails start at the Illecillewaet Campground, which seems the most popular place to stay. Trails here range in length from one to 11 kilometres.

Parks Canada

Glacier lily

Most of the trails reach as far as the timberline, if the snow has retreated that far (which means July at the earliest). Scan the avalanche slopes for grizzly bears, but probably you'll just see the glacier lilies, whose blossoms and roots the bears feed on. Many trails overlook glaciers.

More adventurous hikers might be interested in visiting the **Nakimu Caves**. The park allows a set number of visits offered by commercial and private caving groups.

Human History at Glacier

You can see the evidence of the building of the railway at **Rogers Pass** from the road or near the campgrounds. The **Loop Trail** follows the route of the old railway line, starting at the Loop Brook Campground. It's an easy 30-minute walk through the thickest of rain forests—full of ferns and fungi, cedar, and hemlock. In places, you pass the huge stone pillars that once supported the train trestles.

Another trail that touches on the railway history of the park is called **Meeting of the Waters**. The trail is mostly very level, and it stays in the forest. It leads past a footbridge, to a point where the creek from the Asulkan Glacier meets the Illecillewaet River. The Asulkan Brook is usually much milkier from glacial debris than the Illecillewaet and, for a little while, at the "meeting of the waters," they flow side by side, each retaining its distinctive colour.

Parks Canada

Glaciers like this one can be seen from many of the hiking trails
at Glacier National Park

The final railway history trail is called **Abandoned Rails**. A very level trail, it will take about a half-hour, one way. It follows the route that the railway took, before the Connaught Tunnel was built.

Mount Revelstoke National Park

Mount Revelstoke is mostly a place of dense forest, rushing streams, and sub-alpine meadows, which lead to tundra and its major glacier and ice-field. However, it also has one small place that is reminiscent of the quiet river valleys meandering across the inland trench, to the east of the Columbias. Where the Illecillewaet River is slow and wide enough for a marshy area to have formed, there is a beautiful self-guiding trail, inelegantly named **Skunk Cabbage**. It runs behind the Skunk Cabbage Picnic Area, about eight kilometres (five miles) east of the park entry kiosk. This short trail is almost entirely boardwalk. The richness and variety of plant life make it the best area for bird-watching in the park. The best time of year for bird-watching is late May until about mid-July. The most noticeable marsh plant near the boardwalk is the skunk cabbage, which, in the west, is different from the plant of the same name in the east. They are both early-spring plants, but the western one grows to mammoth proportions. **Giant Cedars Trail** provides an intimate experience of the interior rain forest of the Columbias. A parking lot and picnic area have been cleared next to the trail. The trail is a gently sloping and winding boardwalk, marvellously designed, and carefully banked for walking ease.

To experience the full transition of life zones in Mount Revelstoke, take the Meadows in the Sky Parkway that starts at the edge of the City of Revelstoke, by the information kiosk and fee station, and then winds its way up to the peak of the mountain. The parkway is closed to double-axle vehicles such as tour buses, however, and is not recommended for vehicles pulling trailers. A trailer drop-off parking lot is located at the base of the parkway. The road is free of snow only from mid-July through September, and is paved as far as Balsam Lake. As it progresses, the road has a number of picnic areas and viewpoints from which you can see the great sweep of the **Columbia River Valley** and of the Monashees, the westernmost mountains in the Columbias. Several hiking trails cross the road, some of which start at pull-off areas partway up the road. At Balsam Lake, a shuttle-bus service takes visitors to Heather Lake, near the actual summit.

The road is one of the few places in the park system where it is possible to drive to the summit of a mountain high enough to reach alpine meadows. You can picnic at **Balsam Lake,** below the summit. At the summit, you can stroll in the immediate area, choose from a number of short trails that lead to vista points, or start off on longer hikes to several of the alpine lakes that are scattered five or six kilometres (3.5 miles) farther along the crest of this mountain range. The **Meadows in the Sky** (formerly **Mountain Meadows**) trail is self-guiding.

Wildflowers are abundant here in late summer; they grow as thick as grass. An annual pilgrimage is held by the park, for residents and visitors, on the Monday of the long weekend in August, when everyone is invited to walk with the naturalists to the **Eva Lake Meadows** and enjoy the day together.

PARK SERVICES AND FACILITIES

Interpretive Program

The park's interpretive program is currently being revamped. Guided hiking opportunities (or shorter "guided strolls") will likely be offered but fees will vary. Check the bulletin boards or Information Centre for schedules and fees.

Another aspect of interpretation is the Rogers Pass Centre. Built at the summit of Rogers Pass, the Centre resembles the snow sheds that characterize the battle against the avalanches. You can receive all of the park's brochures there, and see pictures and artifacts illustrating the Columbias and their natural and human history.

Camping

Camping facilities are only available in Glacier National Park. Two small campgrounds are located just off the Trans-Canada Highway, and they tend to fill by the early afternoon. An overflow campground is currently being developed. Until 1989, a third, larger campground, Mountain Creek, was also available, but it had to be closed due to widespread root-rot and the danger of falling trees. It was also discovered that the area was important territory for moose and grizzly and black bears, so the campground is being rehabilitated and all structures removed. Commercial camping can be found both east and west of the Glacier Park.

With only 59 sites, **Illecillewaet Campground** is not a large campground, but it is centrally located and is the starting point for most hiking. Five sites are wheelchair accessible. The campground is moderately wooded and beautifully situated along the narrow Illecillewaet River. There are kitchen shelters, washrooms with flush toilets and cold running water, depots for water and wood, and picnic tables and fire grates at each site.

With only 20 sites, **Loop Brook Campground** is also a small campground. It is very similar to Illecillewaet, being situated by a river, and has identical facilities. The Loop Brook Trail starts here, and should not be missed.

Since both campgrounds are small and popular, campers are advised to arrive early in the day to get a site.

Primitive Camping

Back-country campsites are being established in some of the more popular areas, including Eva Lake and the Jade Lakes in Mount Revelstoke National Park, and along the Bald Hills in Glacier National Park. An old connector trail between the Bald Hills and the Beaver Valley has been reopened by the Friends of Mount Revelstoke and Glacier, which makes possible a spectacular, but strenuous, three- to four-day loop trip. Some route-finding is necessary for this loop, however, and interested campers should speak with a park staff person who has completed the trip. All backpackers must register first and have a back-country wilderness pass. Also, inquire about fire regulations, bears, feasible routes, and so forth, before setting out.

Other Accommodation, Gas, Food, and Supplies

Aside from a large hotel that is located at Rogers Pass, the nearest accommodation is located in the City of Revelstoke, 68 kilometres (42 miles) from Rogers Pass and right at Mount Revelstoke. The city is not large, but has a reasonable number of motels and small hotels. Golden, British Columbia, is 82 kilometres (51 miles) from Rogers Pass, and also has motels and hotels.

The only place in the parks to purchase gas is at Rogers Pass, at the hotel. If possible, fill up elsewhere, since gas can be particularly expensive here. The Rogers Pass hotel has a large restaurant and a small general store. Revelstoke and Golden have a full range of gas stations, and grocery and supply stores.

Recreational Services

Hiking This is the most popular use of the parks. There are 140 kilometres (93 miles) of established trails in Glacier, and 65 kilometres (40 miles) at Mount Revelstoke. Often the elevation gain is considerable, but the trails are well maintained and the scenery is magnificent. An excellent hiker's guide, *Footloose in the Columbias*, is available at the bookstore in the Rogers Pass Centre.

Fishing   Fishing is poor in the rivers, because they are glacially fed. However, in some of the lakes on the summit area of Mount Revelstoke, you can fish for trout. A national park licence is required, and can be obtained from the Rogers Pass Centre or the park administration office in Revelstoke, at 313-3rd Street West.

Winter Use   In Glacier Park, the conditions are usually too rigorous for light cross-country skiing, but the park has much to offer the experienced touring skier. If you are interested in alpine ski touring, however, be advised of the avalanche hazards. You must register at the administration office and purchase a back-country wilderness pass for any off-highway travel in either Glacier or Mount Revelstoke. The Illecillewaet Campground is open for winter camping. The washrooms and kitchen shelters are maintained. Snowmobiles are not allowed in either park.

In Mount Revelstoke, there are several cross-country skiing trails. At the base of the mountain, near Revelstoke, there is a two-kilometre (1.2-mile) trail and another that is five kilometres (three miles) long. The two-kilometre trail is lit at night. Trails are also available at Maunder Creek and Summit Road. You do not need a wilderness pass to ski on the trails at the base of the mountain or the Summit Road, or to toboggan on the toboggan hill at the base of the mountain—a very popular Revelstoke activity!

At the 12-mile mark on the Meadows in the Sky Parkway is a cabin that is available in winter and is accessible by the Summit Trail. Cabin passes are available for $10 per person and reservations can be made through the administration office for the park in Revelstoke.

Related Activities or Places of Natural or Historic Interest

Discover British Columbia is an excellent information service for all kinds of visitation in the province. Call 1-800-663-6000 (or 663-6000 within Greater Vancouver). The Revelstoke Chamber of Commerce can also provide information on local opportunities, phone (604) 837-5345.

Related Activities Cont'd

Activities and Places to Consider Visiting:

- Nearby provincial parks include Martha Creek, on the east side of Lake Revelstoke; Blanket Creek, on the west side of Upper Arrow Lake; and Arrow Lakes, near Shelter Bay.
- Boating opportunities include whitewater rafting on the Illecillewaet River and boat tours on the Columbia.
- For historic interest, the Revelstoke Museum has a large collection of artifacts dating back to the 1880s. A self-guided heritage walking and driving tour brochure, identifying 60 historic buildings, is also available here.
- The Revelstoke Railway Museum houses a restored engine and railcars, as well as artifacts and archives pertaining to the steam era.

National Historic Sites (all pertaining to the story of the railway):

- Glacier National Park: Rogers Pass
- West of Revelstoke: Craigellachie National Historic Site
- Kaslo: S.S. Moyie National Historic Site

FURTHER READING

Glacier Country: A Guide to Mt. Revelstoke and Glacier National Parks by John G. Woods (Douglas & McIntyre, 1987).

For More Information

The Superintendent
Mount Revelstoke and Glacier National Parks
Box 350
Revelstoke, British Columbia
V0E 2S0
Phone: (604) 837-7500
Fax: (604) 837-7536

YOHO
National Park

Y oho is the more northern of the two Rocky Mountain parks situated in British Columbia. Bordered on the east by Banff and Kootenay National Parks, it is bisected from east to west by the Trans-Canada Highway. Yoho is the second-smallest of the Rocky Mountain parks at 1313 square kilometres (506 square miles).

Yoho's most impressive peaks are those located near its eastern boundary, adjacent to the Continental Divide. These mountains are part of the Eastern Main Ranges of the Rockies. Their dramatic cliffs and lofty heights result from the nature of their rocks—limestones and erosion-resistant quartzose sandstone. During the mountain-building process, these sturdy rocks were heaved up in great chunks, producing the massive blocks of mountains we see today.

Farther west, approximately even with the village of Field, the character of the mountains changes. The limestones are interspersed with softer rocks, such as shales. Over time, these mountains have weathered more than the peaks along the Continental Divide, as you can see by their less jagged shapes.

Yoho's famous Burgess Shale fossils outcrop in the rocks between the Eastern and Western Main Ranges. At one time this area was covered by a subtropical sea. About 515 million years ago, living sea creatures were buried in mudslides that carried them into deep stagnant water. In this low-oxygen environment, normal decay did not occur and thus both the animal's soft and hard tissues were preserved. The incredible detail of their fossilized remains now gives scientists an excellent record of life at that time. The Burgess Shale is an important part of Yoho's contribution to the selection of the four mountain parks as a World Heritage Site. These parks join an international list of locations, including the Egyptian pyramids and other famous sites, that evidence humanity's natural and cultural heritage. Yoho's fossils are now heavily protected. The fossil beds are now closed to the public, except for guided hikes offered by concessionaires.

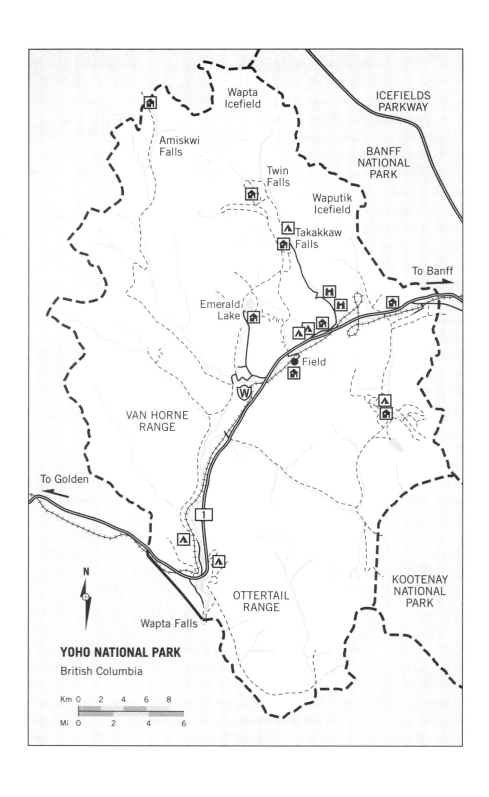

Wapta
Icefield

ICEFIELDS
PARKWAY

Amiskwi
Falls

Twin
Falls

Waputik
Icefield

BANFF
NATIONAL
PARK

Takakkaw
Falls

To Banff

Emerald
Lake

Field

VAN HORNE
RANGE

To Golden

1

KOOTENAY
NATIONAL
PARK

N

OTTERTAIL
RANGE

Wapta Falls

YOHO NATIONAL PARK

British Columbia

Km 0   2   4   6   8

Mi 0   2   4   6

The location of the park and the shape of the mountains had considerable consequences for its human history. One of the two train routes through the Rockies runs through Yoho National Park. The Canadian Pacific Railway was stymied for years by the height of the Rocky Mountain passes and by the steepness of the western slopes. Eventually, the Kicking Horse Pass was chosen as the route across the Great Divide.

The steepness limited the number of train cars that could be pulled up the grade or that could safely be run down the slope toward the west coast. This problem was solved with the construction of the Spiral Tunnels. In 1909, nine kilometres (5.5 miles) of tracks were looped out from the main direction of the line, to pass through two mountains that sit astride the route. The Spiral Tunnels Viewpoint is one of the most visited interpretive sites in the park.

The railway played a considerable role in the mining of lead and zinc in Yoho. These metals were discovered in two areas at the head of the Kicking Horse Valley, just before the railway was completed. One mine entrance that can be seen from the road is on the side of Mount Field, next to Kicking Horse Campground.

It was not until 1927 that a car road was built through the Kicking Horse Pass. It has been upgraded with time, and now is part of the Trans-Canada Highway.

HOW TO SEE THE PARK

There are four main sections of the park with easy visitor access. Starting from the north they are the Lake O'Hara area; the Yoho Valley road, which starts at the Kicking Horse Campground and leads along a beautiful and very winding drive to Takakkaw Falls and the back-country trail system beyond; the Emerald Lake and Natural Bridge area to the south of Field; and the Trans-Canada Highway, in particular the Spiral Tunnels Viewpoint, and the quiet trails and campgrounds at the west end of the park.

Lake O'Hara

The **Lake O'Hara** section of Yoho is almost a separate park in itself. The core is Lake O'Hara, a small lake backed by magnificent castellated mountains. There are 25 other lakes or ponds within a five-kilometre (three-mile) radius of Lake O'Hara. Within an eight-kilometre (five-mile) radius are 80 kilometres (50 miles) of trails.

This zone of interconnecting trails, running through alpine meadows and past icy-blue lakes is, to my mind, one of the most beautiful and exciting areas in the entire park system. The extreme fragility of the alpine meadows, and the great popularity of the place, have made it necessary to control access to it. This not only protects the area from damage, but also allows hikers to enjoy the scenery without crowds. A few people hike along the 13-kilometre (eight-mile) trail to the lake, but most people reserve a place on the bus that runs between mid-June until the end of September. You can visit for the day only, or you can stay at the Parks Canada campground or at the luxurious, privately run Lake O'Hara Lodge. Certain parts of the Lake O'Hara area are subject to seasonal area closures in order to protect grizzly-bear habitat and reduce human/bear encounters. These areas are the Odaray Plateau and Prospect region and the McArthur Creek Valley. Closures are in effect from May 1 to November 20 annually.

Yoho Valley and Takakkaw Falls

This combination drive and walk takes you from the broad valley of the **Kicking Horse River** steadily upward, as it follows the more sharply descending and turbulent **Yoho River**. On Canada Day 1989, Kicking Horse was dedicated as a Canadian Heritage River—the first ever within the boundaries of British Columbia. This designation recognizes its unique place in Canada's history, its beauty, and its significance as a classic example of a glacially fed mountain river. The drive to **Takakkaw Falls** is narrow and winding. Because trailers cannot negotiate some of the turns, a drop-off area for trailers is situated near the beginning of the road. The road takes you through sub-alpine forest areas, which are periodically stripped of tree growth by avalanches. The vegetation that survives or first recurs is low, supple, and bushy, and full of flowers and berries. Along the side of the road, you can frequently see mountain goats and marmots; please note that it is illegal to feed or entice wildlife. The 13-kilometre (eight-mile) road ends in a parking area at Takakkaw Falls. This is one of the highest waterfalls in Canada.

From the viewing area, you can begin your walk up the Yoho Valley. The usual destination is **Twin Falls**, or a good view of the falls from the **Twin Falls Chalet** below. This hike is ideal for seeing the interplay of the faulting patterns of these mountains and the power of water. From Takakkaw Falls, the trail passes four more falls of varying shapes and sizes: **Laughing Falls**, **Point Lace Falls**, **Angel's Staircase Falls**, and, **Twin Falls**.

The trail is about nine kilometres (six miles) long, but it is easy and rolling with only two steep parts—one just beyond Point Lace Falls and

Parks Canada

Twin Falls from near the Chalet teahouse

one just before the Twin Falls teahouse. A back-country campground is located on the river, just before that final ascent. The trail continues beyond the chalet, although many people turn back after a rest. You can go up to the **Yoho Glacier** or join a very large network of rigorous back-country trails, before returning to Takakkaw Falls. On a personal note, the highlight of the hike was the destination—the teahouse. Visitors can have hot tea and light lunches.

The **Iceline Trail**, completed in 1987, has become very popular. It was designed to replace the eroded **Highline Trail**, and offers spectacular views of Takakkaw Falls, hanging glaciers, and the alpine terrain overlooking the Yoho Valley.

Emerald Lake, Natural Bridge, and Hamilton Falls

The eight-kilometre (five-mile) road into this area begins just two kilometres (1.25 miles) west of Field. Three kilometres along the Emerald Lake road is a large parking area for visiting the **Natural Bridge**. Although the keystone of the bridge has collapsed, you can still clearly see the vertical faulting that is characteristic of the mountains here, and how the enormous force of rivers cuts through them.

Emerald Lake is a major day-use area, and an access point for a number of back-country trails. There is also a short trail leading from the large parking lot to one of the park's major waterfalls, **Hamilton Falls**. You can go another 4.5 kilometres (three miles) of switchbacked trail, steep above the falls, to **Hamilton Lake** itself. It is nestled in a cirque—the characteristic bowl shape that glaciers gouge out of mountainsides.

Emerald Lake is another beautiful, glacially formed lake. A parking lot is located near it, as well as restrooms and a level, self-guiding trail around its five-kilometre (three-mile) perimeter. Emerald Lake Lodge has a terraced cafe with a gift shop for day visitors.

The Trans-Canada Highway

The Trans-Canada Highway follows closely the route of the railway. Several signed points of interest and park facilities are provided along the way. The main park brochure has a map on which each point is marked and coded with brief descriptions. A note of caution here. Because of the number of injuries and deaths that occur on the Trans-Canada in Yoho each year, due to the mixing of through traffic with pleasure traffic, use extreme care when turning on to and off the highway, and when slowing or stopping for any reason.

At the north end of the highway is the **Old Bridge on the Big Hill**, where trains would go out of control and plunge off the tracks on this steepest railway grade in North America. Just down the road is the **Lower Spiral Tunnel Viewpoint**. The park has built a viewing platform in the style of the old wooden trestles that once supported the tracks.

At the southern edge of the highway, just off the Hoodoo Creek Campground, **Deer Lodge Trail** leads to the park's first back-country patrol cabin for wardens.

The three-kilometre (two-mile) trail to the **Hoodoos** begins at the Deerlodge Trail parking area. Hoodoos occur in a number of places where there are steep slopes composed of glacial debris. Over time, water cuts downward through soft layers, which underlie more resistant flat rocks, and carries away the soft material. The flat rocks form a cap, or umbrella, which protects the material directly below, so columns are left, towering over the gutted ravines or valleys around them.

The first part of the trail follows the perimeter road of the Hoodoo Creek Campground to the Hoodoo Creek Bridge. After crossing the footbridge over the creek, the trail climbs quite steeply. There are switchbacks, and the trail surface is level, but it can be wearing, depending on your level of fitness. Several good views are provided along the way, of the river below you and the mountains on the opposite side.

PARK SERVICES AND FACILITIES

Interpretive Program

The park's active interpretive program is well worth attending. Various interpretive events, ranging from guided walks and canoe paddles to evening campfire talks and theatre programs, are offered during the summer months. Watch for advertising in your campground or ask at the Visitor Centre. The Centre has orientation exhibits to help you plan your travels in Yoho, the four-parks block, or Alberta, and interpretive exhibits on the Burgess Shale and Alberta's Dinosaur Provincial Park—both of which have been recognized as World Heritage Sites. You can also watch short films about various aspects of the park on the video monitors provided.

Camping

Kicking Horse Campground is located five kilometres (three miles) from Field. In late July and August, it fills quite early in the afternoon and on weekends. Tent areas are lightly wooded, and the trailer area is a lawned space. The campground is dominated by Mount Stephen, and some sites lie by the river. There are 92 sites, kitchen shelters, flush toilets, showers,

Parks Canada

Elk browsing in the stillness of early evening

trailer sewage disposal, but no hook-ups. Water is provided at washrooms, and from faucets every few sites. Washrooms are wheelchair accessible. Each site has fire grates, picnic tables, and firewood. There is an outdoor interpretive theatre here, and a play area for children. A small grocery store is located just outside the entry kiosk.

Hoodoo Creek Campground, situated near the southern end of the park, is densely wooded. It is the most peaceful and least crowded campground in the park, popular with those who want an old-style forest-camping experience. It has 106 sites, flush toilets, and kitchen shelters. The washrooms are wheelchair accessible. There is trailer-waste disposal, but no hook-ups. Each site has a picnic table and fire grate, with firewood provided. There is an outdoor theatre, and the campground is near the Deer Lodge and Hoodoos Trails.

Chancellor Peak Campground is the southernmost of the campgrounds. It is also a car-based campground, but is more primitive than Kicking Horse and Hoodoo Creek. It is self-registering: you fill out an envelope and deposit your fee. It is located in a lightly treed area, right on Kicking Horse River. The train runs behind it. There are 64 sites, with pit toilets, kitchen shelters, water from faucets, and each site has a fire grate and picnic table. There is an accessible outhouse.

The walk from the parking lot to **Takakkaw Falls** walk-in campground takes about three minutes, along a gravel path. Push carts are available to move gear from car to tent site. The 35 sites are in lightly wooded or open areas. Because of the rocky terrain and sparse plant growth, tents are pitched on large pallets. There are pit toilets, an enclosed kitchen shelter, and fire grates and picnic tables at each site. There is an accessible outhouse. Food storage lockers are available and should be used in order to protect both campers and bears. This self-registering campground has a spectacular location, with a great view of the falls. Because it is at the beginning of the numerous Yoho Valley trails, it is very popular with hikers.

Lake O'Hara Campground is close to 2135 metres (7000 feet) elevation, so it can get snow or sleet at virtually any time of the year. There are 32 sites, kitchen shelters, pit toilets, picnic tables, and fire grates. There is an accessible outhouse. You must reserve at the Information Centre (phone 604-343-6433 for reservations) in Field, and most people reserve a seat on the bus, rather than walk in 13 kilometres (eight miles). Bus reservations are made automatically for campers, when they reserve sites. The campground is just a few steps from the bus drop-off point. There is a fee for the bus.

Primitive Camping

There are six back-country campgrounds—four in the Yoho Valley and two in the Ottertail Valley. A specific number of tents are allowed in each campground in order to control environmental impact. Fires are prohibited—plan to use a backpack stove. Water is from lakes or streams and must be boiled for 10 minutes as a precaution against an intestinal parasite, known as giardiasis. All campgrounds now have high-tech bear poles with pulley systems for suspending food away from bears. A Wilderness Pass is required for overnight stays and can be obtained for a modest fee from the Field Visitor Centre.

Other Accommodation, Gas, Food, and Supplies

The Whiskey Jack Hostel is located 13 kilometres (eight miles) from the Trans-Canada Highway on Yoho Valley Road. The hostel is open from mid-June to mid-September. For reservations, call the Calgary office of Hostelling International at (403) 283-5551.

Several commercially operated accommodation facilities are located in Yoho National Park, ranging from rustic to luxury. A number of bed and breakfast operations are situated in the town of Field. Contact the park for a list of accommodations and their phone numbers, or Discover B.C. (1-800-663-6000) for information and reservations. Plan to book well in advance since Yoho is packed solid through the summer and well into September.

Golden is located 25 kilometres (15.5 miles) from the south gate and Lake Louise is only a 20-minute drive from the north end of the park. Both towns offer a variety of accommodation.

The Alpine Club of Canada operates three huts in the park. These are located in the Lake O'Hara area, the Little Yoho Valley, and on Mt. Daly. Members can make reservations at (403) 678-3200; book several months ahead for summer.

Groceries are available at a small grocery store located just outside the Kicking Horse Campground. Field has a small combined restaurant and grocery store and West Louise Lodge (east of Field) has some camping supplies and groceries. For a larger selection of camping supplies and groceries, you must go to Golden, Lake Louise, or Banff, all within an hour's drive of the park. Gas is available at West Louise Lodge, Golden, and Lake Louise. The lodge is closed for a few months each fall, which means an 82-kilometre stretch between gas stations in Golden and Lake Louise.

Recreational Services

Hiking   Yoho has 360 kilometres (225 miles) of hiking trails—from the very easy, short, self-guiding ones, to trails in the back country, which can be travelled for days. Overnight campers must obtain a back-country use permit. Snow remains on the higher trails into July. Inquire about snow levels, trail conditions, bear sightings, and availability of back-country campsites regardless of the time of year. Check with the Information Centre to see what interpretive walks are being offered during your visit.

Fishing   There is fair fishing for several varieties of trout in the streams and lakes that are not too close to glacial sources. A national park fishing permit is required, and can be purchased at the Information Centre.

Boating   Non-motorized boats are allowed on all waters in the park. People canoe at Lake O'Hara and Emerald Lake; canoes can be rented at the latter. The river is canoeable (Grade II water) between the confluence of the Amiskwi River and the Trans-Canada Highway bridge near Chancellor Peak Campground.

Horseback Riding   There is a stable at Emerald Lake, where rides from an hour to all day can be arranged.

Bicycling   Bicycling is permitted on certain former fire roads. Check with the Visitor Centre for locations and descriptions.

Winter Use   The park offers several designated cross-country ski trails. Ask for the small, free, descriptive booklet. Back-country camping is allowed, but a permit is required. The trails are of varying length and difficulty. The longer ones require considerable skill and endurance, the ability to deal with rigorous winter conditions, and the capacity to judge avalanche hazards. Current snow and avalanche condition information is available at the Information Centre.

Related Activities or Places of Natural or Historic Interest

Discover British Columbia is an excellent information service for all kinds of visitation in the province. Call 1-800-663-6000 (or 663-6000 within Greater Vancouver). The Travel Information Centre in the city of Golden can also provide information on the surrounding area; phone (604) 344-7125.

Related Activities Cont'd

Activities and Places to Consider Visiting:

- The Kicking Horse River provides excellent conditions for whitewater rafting.

- The Columbia River Valley is known as one of the great remaining wetland habitats in the world. You can access the sloughs by canoe or kayak or take one of the wetland float trips offered by local tour companies.

- The B.C. Forest Service manages a network of recreation sites and trails in the area.

- For historic interest, the Golden and District Museum has a variety of displays on the history of Golden and the surrounding area.

FURTHER READING

Handbook of the Canadian Rockies by Ben Gadd (Corax Press, rev. ed. 1995).

For More Information

The Superintendent
Yoho National Park
Box 99
Field, British Columbia
V0A 1G0
Phone: (604) 343-6393
Phone: (604) 343-6324
Fax: (604) 343-6012
TTY: (604) 343-6783

Friends of Yoho
Box 100
Field, British Columbia
V0A 1G0

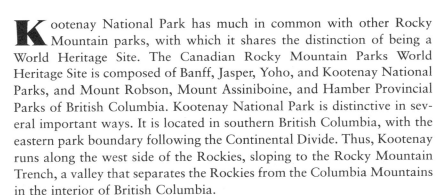

KOOTENAY
National Park

Kootenay National Park has much in common with other Rocky Mountain parks, with which it shares the distinction of being a World Heritage Site. The Canadian Rocky Mountain Parks World Heritage Site is composed of Banff, Jasper, Yoho, and Kootenay National Parks, and Mount Robson, Mount Assiniboine, and Hamber Provincial Parks of British Columbia. Kootenay National Park is distinctive in several important ways. It is located in southern British Columbia, with the eastern park boundary following the Continental Divide. Thus, Kootenay runs along the west side of the Rockies, sloping to the Rocky Mountain Trench, a valley that separates the Rockies from the Columbia Mountains in the interior of British Columbia.

The Rockies comprise three ranges of mountains that are roughly parallel to each other, running north-south; the Front Ranges, Main Ranges, and Western Ranges. Kootenay contains the best representation of the Western Ranges in the Rocky Mountain parks. Characterized by overturned folds, the mountains are geologically complex structures, which are unique in the Canadian Rockies. They are composed of relatively soft shales, with some limestone beds. Craggy, serrated ridge tops alternate with smooth, rounded crests. They form the mountains around Radium Hot Springs.

The extensive faulting in the Rockies makes a fascinating story of the shaping of the mountains. Take advantage of the park's interpretive programs and brochures to learn about their formation. At Kootenay, you can also enjoy a close-up view of some of the smaller-scale results of faulting. Two places are of particular interest. The first is Radium Hot Springs, located at the southern edge of the park. Hot springs are fairly common all along the geologically active western edge of our continent.

The Kootenay Hot Springs have a component of radium that is almost as radioactive as a luminous watch dial. But, in the pre-park days at the turn of the century, many claims were made for the restorative effects of

Parks Canada

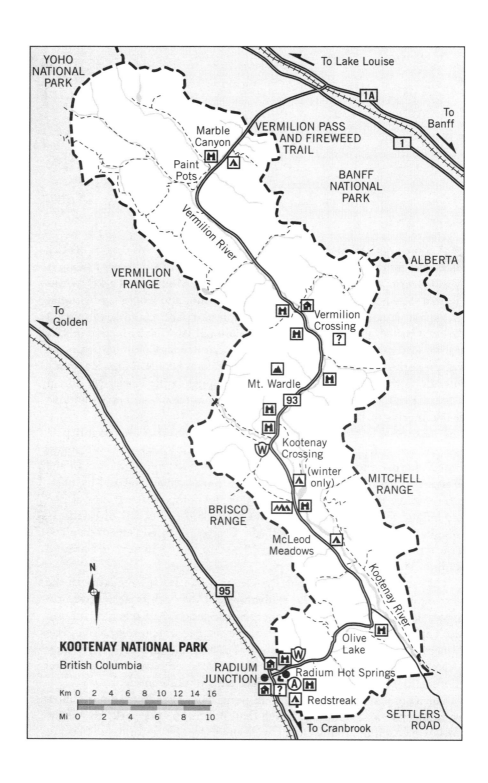

YOHO NATIONAL PARK

To Lake Louise

1A

To Banff

VERMILION PASS AND FIREWEED TRAIL

Marble Canyon

Paint Pots

BANFF NATIONAL PARK

1

Vermilion River

VERMILION RANGE

ALBERTA

To Golden

Vermilion Crossing

?

Mt. Wardle

93

Kootenay Crossing

MITCHELL RANGE

(winter only)

BRISCO RANGE

McLeod Meadows

Kootenay River

N

95

Olive Lake

KOOTENAY NATIONAL PARK

British Columbia

RADIUM JUNCTION

Radium Hot Springs

Redstreak

SETTLERS ROAD

To Cranbrook

Km 0 2 4 6 8 10 12 14 16

Mi 0   2   4   6   8   10

bathing in the hot springs of Kootenay. I think the relaxation of lolling in a hot pool after a chilly hike is sufficient justification for a long soak.

Faulting is easy to see at the Redwall Fault, located half a kilometre north of Radium Hot Springs. Redwall Fault is aptly named, because the oxidation of the iron in the rock has resulted in a brilliant reddish colour. (You can even see it when flying tens of thousands of feet in the air over the area.)

The Paint Pots is another special place in the park. Here an active spring (this time a cold one), with a great deal of dissolved iron in its water, bubbles to the surface, forming muddy beds of reddish ochre.

Kootenay National Park has significant differences between its north and south, because of the effect of the topography of the land to its west. In the south, the air currents are relatively dry. They descend to the Rocky Mountain Trench, having already released a lot of moisture, as rain or snow, on the Columbias. Thus, the forest is predominantly dry interior Douglas fir, and rather patchy at that. As you travel north from Radium Hot Springs, there is a distinct transition to a much moister environment. The highway follows three river valleys. At Sinclair Pass (1486 metres) the forest is in transition from dry interior Douglas fir to sub-alpine (fir and spruce). The highway then descends to the valley of the Kootenay River (around 1200 metres—the McLeod Meadows area)

Parks Canada

Mountain goats at roadside deposits—frequently seen and very vulnerable

where the forest is montane, consisting mainly of lodgepole pine, white spruce and Douglas fir. When you reach the Vermilion River Valley, there is pure sub-alpine forest.

Snow depths are relatively light and winter temperatures more moderate in the lower Sinclair and Kootenay valleys, so winter grazing is easier here. Snow depths are considerably deeper and the temperatures colder in the Vermilion valley. Mountain slopes that are windswept are relatively snow-free, resulting in some slopes and ridges of Mount Wardle providing good year-round habitat for mountain goats. In late spring and early summer goats are often seen beside the road at the mineral lick at the base of Mount Wardle.

Southwest-facing slopes in the Radium Hot Springs area are particularly mild and snow-free in winter. Mostly outside the park boundary, they form the winter range of the Radium band of bighorn sheep.

HOW TO SEE THE PARK

The Park is "organized" by the Banff-Windermere Highway, which stretches its full length. Everything to see and every place to visit starts at the highway. Your first stop is at the Information Centres located at the entry in Radium Hot Springs in the south, or the one at Marble Canyon in the north.

The park also offers a busy interpretive program, which includes guided walks, campground theatre programs, and family activities. Modest user fees are attached to some programs.

There are five self-guiding trails in the park, and several short and fairly easy non-guided trails around the Radium Hot Springs and Redstreak Campground.

The Mountains—East and West

Marble Canyon Trail is a beautiful 20-minute walk, guided by interpretive signs that tell you more about what you're seeing. It is an easy walk, a little uphill, always along the river on one side of the canyon, and then back down the other. It starts just about six kilometres (3.5 miles) from the Banff border.

As you go up, crossing from bridge to bridge, posted signs indicate that the outlines of the canyon are angular because limestone and related rocks crack in a characteristic block fashion. Limestone is easily shaped by flowing water, and it is fascinating to see the scoops and swirls carved in the canyon walls, many metres above where the water now flows.

Plants have taken hold wherever possible in the moist, chill environ-ment of the canyon walls.

The Marble Canyon area has a large parking lot, wheelchair-accessible washrooms, and a picnic area.

The **Paint Pots Self-guiding Trail** is located just south of Marble Canyon. There is a parking lot from which you start the 1.5-kilometre (one-mile) round-trip walk. The first half kilometre of the trail has been upgraded to meet wheelchair-accessible standards. Compacted gravel is used to surface the first section of the trail that leads to a long, low suspension bridge that crosses the **Vermilion River**. From there, the trail surface is natural. The flowers on the far side of the river are very thick.

The Ochre Beds are a flood plain or spillover area of the springs that bring up the iron-laden water and spread it over the surrounding area. The beds are bright brownish-orange, dotted here and there by small islands of grass and small trees.

As you go further up the slight hill, you reach the Paint Pots themselves. Several exit holes for the springs have been formed into "pots," through the accumulation of iron oxide or hydroxide around the rim. Eventually, the rim gets so high that the weight of the contained water forces the spring water to follow a less resistant route, and to form another outlet nearby. When this happens, the pot eventually dries up and forms a "choked cone." Thus, there are a number of pots—three of which are active and others that are just collecting spring water and surface drain-off.

The **Hot Springs** are the centrepiece of the southern part of the park. The general setting of the hot springs is still fairly natural, with rock cliffs and forest, though the spring outlets themselves have been covered by a large pool and are not visible. There are plenty of underwater terrace steps to sit on, or you can just wander around, peering at other equally mellow bathers.

Kootenay—North and South

Marble Canyon is the place to get acquainted with the moist and dense-ly forested area north along the Vermilion River.

In 1968, lightning started a fire near Marble Canyon, and it burned furiously for three days. With a boost from nature's regenerative powers, the park has turned this seemingly unwelcoming environment into a pleas-ant and interesting self-guiding trail. **Firewood Trail** consists of two short loops that begin at the parking lot at the northern border of the park. Interpretive signs guide you along the way. The lower loop is a 0.5-kilometre, wheelchair-accessible trail that has a series of colourful exhibits.

Parks Canada

New growth on the Firewood Trail

For exposure to the drier, Douglas-fir forest of the southern part of Kootenay, a number of short, self-guiding trails wind throughout the Radium Hot Springs area. One is the **Valley View Trail**, which parallels the access road to the Redstreak Campground. A trail also descends from the campground to the back of the Radium Hot Springs pools.

Juniper Trail is somewhat longer, and starts just inside the park gate at the entrance to Sinclair Canyon. It is not a loop trail but rather runs three kilometres (two miles) in length, zigzagging down to **Sinclair Creek**, up to the crest of the canyon, and then gradually down to the motel area across from the Radium Hot Springs pools. Because it gains a bit of altitude, I would suggest that you start from the lower Sinclair Canyon end so that, when you emerge, you can be going downhill, back to your car. Several lookout points with benches survey the Columbia Valley.

Another site worth visiting in the area is **Olive Lake**. This wheelchair-accessible picnic site includes gravel and boardwalk interpretive trails to two viewpoints at the lakeshore. The exhibits include tactile elements (trail map, bear paw print, tree bark, fist) to help people with visual impairments appreciate the site.

PARK SERVICES AND FACILITIES

Interpretive Program

The park offers various interpretive programs including theatre presentations and family activities. There are also excellent self-guiding trails.

Camping

The park offers three campgrounds for car-based campers. Redstreak Campground, located at the southern end of the park in the Douglas-fir forest, is the largest, most developed, and quickest to fill. The Valley View Trail and the trail to the Radium Hot Springs pools run from here. It has three playground areas for children, with swings, slides, teeter-totters, and climbers. There are 242 sites, a number of which are pull-throughs for trailers. There are seven kitchen shelters, as well as flush toilets, showers and trailer sewage disposal. Washrooms are wheelchair accessible. Some sites have full hook-ups. All sites have picnic tables, and most have fire pits. Firewood is available at depots. An outdoor theatre presents interpretive shows on some evenings.

To find Redstreak, you must enter from outside the park, off Highway 95, just southeast of the park entrance on Highway 93. Travel south past the junction, past a few snack bars and shops, and look for the RCMP and Redstreak Campground signs. Both campgrounds are located on the same road.

McLeod Meadows is a smaller campground, situated 26 kilometres (16 miles) north of Radium Hot Springs. There are 98 sites in a wooded area, sandwiched between the Meadow Creek and Kootenay River. The site does not seem to fill quickly and it is quiet. Dog Lake Trail starts from here; naturalist-led hikes sometimes use the trail. This is a self-registering campground; you fill out a permit, deposit your fee in an envelope, and settle in. A picnic area is nearby. All sites have picnic tables, fire pits, and firewood depots. Kitchen shelters are supplied with woodstoves and wood. Flush toilets and cold water are provided and washrooms are wheelchair accessible. A trailer sewage disposal is available, but no hook-ups.

Marble Canyon is a very quiet campground, and is not heavily used. It is located about six kilometres (four miles) from the northern border of the park. There are 66 sites in the fairly open sub-alpine forest. Kitchen shelters provide wood stoves and firewood; flush toilets and trailer waste disposal are available, but not hook-ups. Washrooms are wheelchair accessible. Sites have picnic tables and fire pits, with wood at depots. This campground is well located for the Marble Canyon walks, and is near the

Paint Pots and Stanley Glacier trails. In the evenings in July and August, interpretive programs are offered in the campground's outdoor theatre.

Group Camping

Crook's Meadows, situated 35 kilometres (20 miles) north of Radium Hot Springs, offers private, non-profit group camping on the site of an old homestead. A large log kitchen shelter has a wood stove, picnic tables, and secure food storage. Wood is provided. A hand pump delivers water and there is a large fire circle, many fire grates, and pit toilets. Reservations are required.

Primitive Camping

Along the back-country trails are a number of primitive sites for the overnight hiker. Some have fire grates and wood provided, while others require self-contained pack-in stoves. All have pit privies, and most are located near water. Check the back-country guide brochure, and ask park staff for information on available sites and their condition. A wilderness pass is necessary for overnight back-country travel and camping, and reservations are required.

Other Camping

There are commercial sites at **Radium Hot Springs**, and a provincial park campground at **Dry Gulch**, which is located just to the south.

Other Accommodation, Gas, Food, and Supplies

Radium Hot Springs has a wide variety of motel and hotel accommodations. For information, write to the Radium Hot Springs Chamber of Commerce. Gas and supplies are also available at Radium Hot Springs.

Recreational Services

Hiking   The park has 200 kilometres (125 miles) of hiking trails, ranging from a few kilometres to hikes that can take several days to complete, linking one trail with another. The park provides an excellent back-country trail guide, which has detailed information on elevation gain at a number of points along the trail, and provides an amazing amount of information. Topographic-map use is also recommended. A wilderness pass is required for overnight back-country use. Contact the park for back-country reservations and information on fees. The park encourages spring and fall off-season use, when the park is particularly quiet, although many high-country trails are snowbound until July. For further information, write to the Superintendent.

Swimming   The Radium Hot Springs pools are the most heavily used feature of the park. There is the large shallow "hot pool" that comes directly from the springs, and a "cool pool" that is a regulation swimming and diving pool.

Fishing   Fishing is not particularly good in the park, since so many streams and lakes are glacier-fed, but there are some whitefish, trout, and Dolly Varden. A national park licence can be obtained for a small fee from the Information Centres, wardens, and campground kiosks.

Boating and Canoeing   Non-motorized watercraft are permitted on all lakes and rivers in Kootenay National Park. The Vermilion and Kootenay Rivers can be hazardous, however, so only experienced boaters should attempt them. There are private river-rafting outfits outside the park, which offer trips in the area. Write to the B.C. Rocky Mountain Visitors' Association.

Winter Use   Some cross-country skiing and winter camping are offered in the park. There are no warming huts for skiing, but the area around Dolly Varden picnic area is kept open for campers.

Related Activities or Places of Natural or Historic Interest

Discover British Columbia is an excellent information service for all kinds of visitation in the province. Call 1-800-663-6000 (or 663-6000 within Greater Vancouver).

Activities and Places to Consider Visiting:

- Bugaboo Glacier Provincial Park in the Purcell Mountains, west of the park; Mount Assiniboine Provincial Park to the east.

- Several other hot springs are located in the area. To the south are the Fairmount Hot Springs where there are four pools with an average temperature of 40°, and the even warmer Lussier Hot Springs near Canal Flats.

- For historical interest, you can visit Fort Steele Heritage Town (about 100 kilometres south), where over 60 buildings are restored to their 1890s form.

For More Information

The Superintendent
Kootenay National Park
Box 220
Radium Hot Springs,
British Columbia
V0A 1M0
Phone: (250) 347-9615
Fax: (250) 347-9980
TTY: (250) 347-9615

B.C. Rocky Mountain Visitors Association
Box 10
Kimberley, British Columbia
V1A 2Y5
Phone: (250) 427-4838
Fax: (250) 427-3344

Radium Hot Springs Chamber of Commerce
Box 225
Radium Hot Springs, British Columbia
V0A 1M0
Phone: (250) 347-9331
Fax: (250) 347-9127

WATERTON LAKES

National Park

A t Waterton Lakes, the prairies meet the mountains. This is the southernmost of the Canadian Rocky Mountain parks, but it is also a true prairie park. Nowhere else in Canada is there a place where these two ecological zones are so intermixed. Here, no transition zone of foothills intersects prairies and mountains. On the eastern side of the park, the elevation sometimes soars 1220 metres (4000 feet)—only a kilometre (0.5 mile) from the prairie floor.

Waterton Lakes is located at the southwestern corner of Alberta, where it borders on Glacier National Park in the United States. Waterton Lakes was established in 1895, and its American "sister" was established in 1910. In the years following its creation, members of the Rotary Clubs of Montana and Alberta promoted the idea that, since the natural character of the Rockies here was not changed or severed by a political boundary, the two parks should not be divided either. So, in 1932, the parks were joined in spirit as an "International Peace Park"—the first in the world.

Partly because Waterton Lakes is a small park—just 525 square kilometres (202 square miles)—it is extraordinarily accessible. Prairies fill in many of the canyon and valley floors between mountain ridges, and the three types of mountain habitat—montane, sub-alpine, and alpine tundra—are reached by driving, short walks, or on trails easily covered in a short hiking day.

HOW TO SEE THE PARK

There are three main roadways in the park, and most of the trailheads, viewpoints, facilities, and services are accessible from one of these routes.

For an excellent self-guided walk that introduces all of the major themes of mountain-building and shaping in this area, take the **Red Rock Canyon Interpretive Trail**. The setting is breathtaking: you follow an easy incline along the top of a brilliant brick-coloured canyon. On this walk,

63

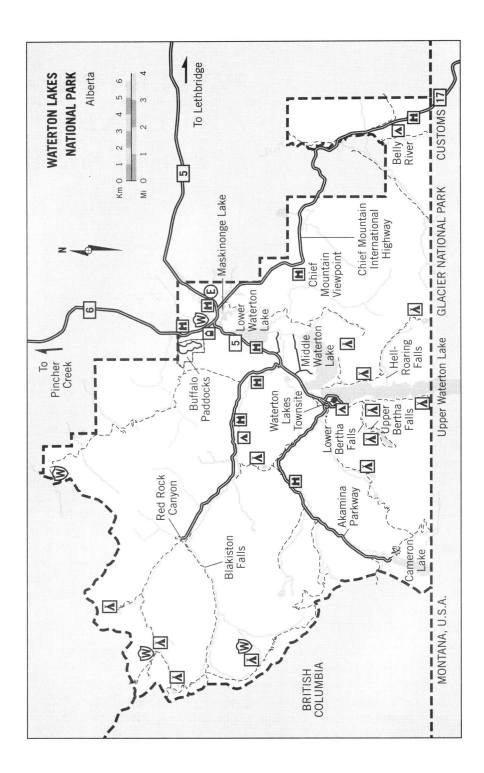

WATERTON LAKES
NATIONAL PARK
Alberta

there are places where hardened ripple marks from the shallow sea that once covered this area have etched the rock, and fossil algae are visible in rocks transported by glaciers from further west. The story of rock formation and erosion here is told by trailside signs.

The townsite area has been greatly shaped by glacial action, and there are signs of it everywhere. First, there are the three Waterton Lakes: Upper, Middle, and Lower. For the most spectacular view of them (and of the townsite), take the short trail to the **Bear's Hump**, located just behind the Information Centre. The trail is one kilometre (0.5 mile) each way, and it is steep, though very wide and smooth.

From the hump, you can see the lakes, which were carved out by glaciers and filled by remnants of ice. **Upper Waterton Lake** extends some 16 kilometres (10 miles), south, about half of it in the United States. As the glaciers melted, they deposited a great deal of debris along their sides and at their toes, forming plateaus or terraces known as kames. The **Prince of Wales Hotel** below is on a kame terrace. **Linnet Lake,** behind the hotel, is also glacially formed.

A number of viewpoints along the roadways provides pull-offs for cars, and interpretive signs to explain topographic features. One of the best ones is the **Chief Mountain Viewpoint** on the Chief Mountain Highway, located about seven kilometres (4.5 miles) southeast of the park entry gate. It has an interpretive display and a free high-power telescope.

The Prairies

There are two particularly good ways to get the flavour of the prairies. One is to drive through the **Buffalo Paddock**. Park your car and walk up the path to a telescope for viewing the buffalo inside the paddock.

Another way to experience the prairies is to walk on them. The **Blakiston Valley/Red Rock Canyon Parkway** has good places to get out, closer to these subtly beautiful sweeps of land. A trail runs along the front of the greenish face of **Bellevue Hill**, eventually going into the park's back country, but the trees to the north, near the paddock, signal the limit of the prairies segment.

The Mountains: Three Life Zones

Mountains and their valleys comprise most of the area of the park. The highest mountain is **Mount Blakiston**, at 2920 metres (9490 feet). Since the park has a well-developed network of walks, and day-hiking and backpacking trails, most visitors can easily experience the two lower life

Marylee Stephenson

Waterton Lakes and the Prince of Wales Hotel from Bear's Hump

zones—the montane forest and sub-alpine forest. Although the alpine zone takes real hiking, I saw some families with young children faring well on the shorter of the day-hike trails.

Montane forest grows on wooded valley floors and the mountain slopes, up to between 1350 and 1675 metres (4500 and 5500 feet). The townsite is located at about 1280 metres (4200 feet) elevation, so the forest around it, and along the lakeshores, is a blend of what is called Canadian forest and true montane forest.

Two walks are excellent for learning about the montane region. One is the trail to **Lower Bertha Falls,** and the other goes the full length of Upper Waterton Lake to **Goat Haunt,** in the United States.

The **Bertha Lake Trail** starts on the south edge of the townsite, and a parking lot is situated off the road to the west. The lower falls are 2.5 kilometres (1.5 miles) away, with an altitude gain of 213 metres (700 feet). A self-guiding trail brochure is available at the Visitor Centre.

The walk to Goat Haunt is rather long, but very interesting. You are advised to take the tour boat on the return trip. A boat runs every two hours from the marina in the townsite at Waterton Lakes, and you can reserve your return space by purchasing your ticket before you start. If you join an interpreter-led group, the arrangements are made for you. The guided walk is known as the International Peace Park Hike and is available for a modest fee.

Parks Canada

Krummholz at the Carthew Lakes

The walk is almost entirely level, and it follows the lakeshore quite closely until it rounds the curve of the south end of the lake. In July, wonderful flowers cover the forest floor.

Near the end of this walk, the trail crosses a river, and hikers walk single-file over a narrow, cable-suspended footbridge. Then the trail passes a marshy area, full of moose tracks, and finally curves back to the lakeshore and the Goat Haunt visitation area.

If you are travelling on your own, the walk takes three to four hours (not including the boat). If you are joining the interpreter-led International Peace Park Hike, it is a full-day event (from 10 a.m. to 6 p.m.).

The **sub-alpine zone** at Waterton Lakes is easily reached by car. Two lakes, linked by trails, are the focal point for visiting and for interpretation of this zone. They are **Cameron Lake** and **Summit Lake**, at the end of the Akamina Parkway. The parkway is 16 kilometres (10 miles) long, and starts just north of the townsite, near the Information Centre. Bear-grass grows in profusion at several spots along the roadside. Watch for bighorn sheep, as well, since a small herd frequents this valley. At Cameron Lake, there is a large parking lot, picnic area, fishing-tackle rental, paddle boat, row boat and canoe rental, and an exhibit centre with interpretive displays and a spotting scope on deck. The 2.5-kilometre (1.5-mile) **Cameron Lakeshore Trail** follows one side of the lake. You will see trees such as Engelmann spruce, sub-alpine fir, white bark pine, and sub-alpine larch that grow in this relatively cool and moist environment—so moist, in fact, that it is snow-covered eight to 10 months a year!

By going left, past the exhibit centre, you will find the trail to Summit Lake. Travelling slowly and peering out at the ever-more-impressive scenery, you can reach Summit Lake in an hour of moderate effort. There are good views of surrounding mountains; the ridge that borders the lake is just at the transition to the alpine zone.

By late June much of the **alpine tundra zone** in the park is clear of snow, and there are a number of good trails to various high mountain areas. The most travelled trails, such as **Carthew Lakes** or **Crypt Lake**, are very well maintained, but they range between 5.5 and 19 kilometres (3.5 to 12 miles) one way, and often have long up-and-down stretches. Again, get the trail guide and speak with park staff at the Information Centre before choosing a trail.

If you are uncertain about your legs, consider one of the horseback rides. You can choose from a number of locations; check at the stables. The **Alderson Lake Ride** traverses montane forest at **Cameron Falls** in the townsite, ascends through sub-alpine forest, decorated with the bright yellow flowers of heartleaved arnica, and emerges at the transition to the alpine zone at Alderson Lake. The round-trip horseback ride, including a lunch stop at the lake, takes about five hours.

You can also walk in the alpine zone. The **Carthew Lakes Trail**, which goes 19 kilometres (12 miles) from Cameron Lake, past Summit Lake, past the Carthew Lakes, down past Alderson Lake and to the townsite, took me seven hours, including many stops for photography and a lunch break at Upper Carthew Lake. This walk was one of the highlights of the trip. First, although the goal is the alpine zone, most of these trails start at montane or sub-alpine levels, so you see a cross-section of all three mountain life zones. Second, the alpine zone shocks the senses with its bleakness on the large scale, and its rich, fascinating life up close.

PARK SERVICES AND FACILITIES
Interpretive Program

The park offers an active and varied interpretive program. Various services and programs are available year-round and personal interpretation programs for visitors are offered from late June through Labour Day. The Information Centre, located at the north end of the townsite, has brochures, booklets, maps, and so forth as well as a schedule of interpretive events. You can visit the exhibit on the sub-alpine area at Cameron Lake, and other on-site interpretive exhibits are provided at Red Rock Canyon and at the Valley Viewpoint. Indoor theatres are located at the townsite campground and at the Crandell Mountain Campground, where slide-show talks are given. Outdoor campfire talks are held at the Belly River Campground on weekends.

There is a very active Waterton Natural History Association, which works closely with the park in helping visitors understand and enjoy the park.

Camping

The park offers three campgrounds for car-based campers. The site that fills first, and has three-way hook-ups for trailers, is located in the townsite. Kitchen shelters, flush toilets, showers, and running water are provided, as well as picnic tables at each site. An interpretive theatre is close, and several trails start nearby.

Crandall Mountain Campground has a more natural setting than the townsite ground. It has 140 sites, in a mixed forest and prairie area. One of its pleasing aspects is that deer regularly browse or rest in the shrubbery between sites. The campground has picnic tables, firepits, firewood, kitchen shelters, a nearby interpretive theatre, and access to several trails.

Belly River Campground is about a 15-minute drive from the townsite, south along the Chief Mountain Road to the United States and Glacier National Park. Its 29 sites are located in a mixed tree and grassland area. This is a small, very quiet campground. Pit and flush toilets, water faucets, picnic tables, and fire grates are provided at each site, and kitchen shelters and firewood are also available. You can fish along the river.

Primitive Camping

A number of primitive campsites are set up along back-country trails. They have pit toilets; water is usually from the nearest lake or stream. Some have kitchen shelters and fire grates for cooking, but since many back-country sites no longer allow fires it is important to bring your own stove. Permits for overnight use are required, which can be purchased for a modest fee from the Information Centre, seven days a week in summer. Ask for the latest trail information, and for maps and brochures on back-country travel.

Other Camping

A large, highly developed commercial campground is located just north of the park on Highway 6. It is situated on the prairies, and is very windy.

Another one is located just east of the park on Highway 5, along the Waterton River. It is sheltered and pleasant. If you arrive at the park near or on a weekend, especially late in the day, these may be the only available places to stay. This happened to me, and it is a reasonable alternative.

Other Accommodation, Gas, Food, and Supplies

Because Waterton Lakes has a small townsite, all types of visitor amenities are available: banks, laundromats, groceries, restaurants, gift shops, camping and outdoor supply stores, gas stations, and so forth. Motels are also available as well as the huge Prince of Wales Hotel, which is a real landmark.

Recreational Services

Hiking   The park has 183 kilometres (114 miles) of excellent trails, with a wide range of location sand skill levels.

Fishing   The park's rivers provide good fishing. Boats are allowed in a few lakes. A National Parks fishing licence is required, which is available for a moderate fee from the Information Centre, Administration Building, some businesses in the townsite, and the fishing tackle/boat concession at Cameron Lake. Fishing tackle may be rented or purchased at the concession at Cameron Lake, and at several stores in the townsite.

Boating   A boat-rental concession is located at Cameron Lake. Rowboats and canoes are available at both lakes. There are cruises on tour boats on Upper Waterton Lake. Visitors can take round-trip tours of Upper Waterton Lake, or be dropped off for the Crypt Lake Trail or at Goat Haunt, at the south end of the lake. You can arrange to be picked up later in the day, or days later if you are back-country hiking.

Golfing   A spectacular 18-hole public golf course is situated just north of the townsite. It is open seven days a week, from May through September. A pro shop provides all services.

Horseback Riding   A commercially operated riding stable is situated just northwest of the townsite. It offers rides of various destinations and durations. Boarding of privately owned horses is available. Horse grazing is not allowed in the park. (People bring food for their horses.)

Winter Use   Although many park and townsite facilities close in winter, an increasing number are staying open. There are opportunities for cross-country skiing and snowshoeing. An excellent pamphlet on winter activities is available on request.

Related Activities or Places of Natural or Historic Interest

Alberta Tourism is a good information service for all kinds of visitation in the province. Call 1-800-661-8888 (or 427-4321 in Edmonton). The Chinook Country Tourist Association can also provide information at 1-800-661-1222.

Activities and Places to Consider Visiting:

- Head-Smashed-In Buffalo Jump, a world heritage site, an hour and 15 minutes drive from the park (phone 533-2731 for more information).

- Alberta-Remington Carriage Centre, located 40 minutes east of the park (phone 653-5139 for more information).

- Frank Slide Interpretive Centre, one hour north of the park (phone 562-7388 for more information).

FURTHER READING

Glacier National Park and Waterton Lake National Park: A Complete Recreation Guide by Vicky Spring (The Mountaineers Publishing: Seattle, Washington).

For More Information

The Superintendent
Waterton Lakes National Park
Waterton Park, Alberta
T0K 2M0
Phone: (403) 859-2224
Fax: (403) 859-2650

Waterton Natural History Association
Box 145
Waterton Park, Alberta
T0K 2M0
Phone: (403) 859-2624

BANFF
National Park

Banff is Canada's most famous national park. Its staggering natural beauty, its location as a key to east-west transportation in Canada, and its value for tourism led to its establishment as our first national park in 1885. Today, all these elements of its beginnings continue to play a vital role in the life of the park.

Banff National Park includes parts of two of the three parallel mountain systems that comprise the Rocky Mountains—the easternmost Front Ranges, with their slanting table-top shape, and the castellate Main Ranges. Mount Rundle, at the Banff townsite, is a classic example of the geology that characterizes the Front Ranges, and Castle Mountain is the most obvious example of the layer-cake or castellate configuration. The park has a complex and fascinating geological history.

There are basically three life zones in the park: the montane forest, sub-alpine forest, and alpine tundra. Each zone is capped by the perpetually frozen world of ice and snow at the tops of the highest mountains. The montane zone is a fairly open forest of Douglas fir, white spruce, lodgepole, and limber pine, with some stands of trembling aspen and balsam fir. The area is home to grazing mammals, such as deer, elk, and sheep, while the wide river valleys at the base of the montane zone provide excellent feeding and nesting areas for many kinds of waterfowl, including wading birds, such as herons, and fishing birds of prey, such as osprey.

The sub-alpine forest is more dense and uniform than the montane forest. It is almost entirely coniferous, with two kinds of spruce, sub-alpine fir, Lyall's larch, and white-bark pine. Many large mammals, including bears, wander through this zone, and seed-eating birds and small mammals, such as chipmunks and ground squirrels, are at home here. Harlequin ducks and Barrow's goldeneye breed in lakes at the border of the sub-alpine and alpine zones.

The alpine tundra area, which occurs above 2195 metres (7200 feet), is viewed by some as a bleak area. However, careful inspection shows that

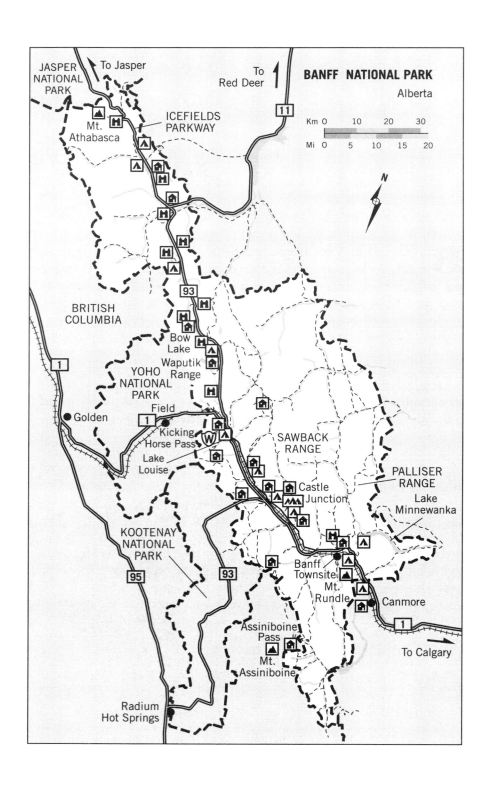

JASPER NATIONAL PARK

To Jasper

To Red Deer

BANFF NATIONAL PARK
Alberta

11

Km 0   10   20   30
Mi 0   5   10   15   20

Mt. Athabasca

ICEFIELDS PARKWAY

N

93

BRITISH COLUMBIA

1

Golden

YOHO NATIONAL PARK

Field

Bow Lake

Waputik Range

1

Kicking Horse Pass

Lake Louise

SAWBACK RANGE

PALLISER RANGE

Lake Minnewanka

KOOTENAY NATIONAL PARK

95

93

Castle Junction

Banff Townsite

Mt. Rundle

Canmore

1

To Calgary

Assiniboine Pass

Mt. Assiniboine

Radium Hot Springs

it is a world of beautiful flowers and intriguing animals—all of which must deal with daily life in a dry, cold, and windswept environment.

Although the icefields and glaciers do not teem with life, as the forest and alpine zones do, they are the source of much of the life-giving water in the park. They drain into beautiful alpine lakes, or tarns, some of which, like Lake Louise, are world famous.

HOW TO SEE THE PARK

One of the first things that is evident to visitors is that Banff National Park has a full-blown, bustling town, from which all activities seem to flow. This town has a year-round resident population of close to 7000 people, but approximately four million more come through in the summer and in the extraordinarily popular winter-sports season.

Some visitors are perfectly happy to stroll along Banff Avenue, peering and being peered at. For these visitors, it's nature enough to be able to do customary things in a very unlikely and dramatic setting.

But, for the visitor who is more interested in peace, quiet, and getting away from it all, there is no reason to be dispirited. It is usually possible to be virtually alone within a five- or 10-minute walk or drive.

In the park, however, remember to respect the wild and unpredictable nature of the wildlife. Large animals in particular, such as bear, elk, moose, deer, and bison, can be aggressive if approached. If you encounter animals at the roadside, remain in your vehicle and do not feed them under any circumstances.

The Town of Banff

A visit to the town of Banff can be an adventure in itself, if only in trying to hold on to your money. There is shopping of any sort, from high-fashion outdoor clothes to rugged jeans, from that camera you forgot to organic or gourmet food.

If your interests include learning more about the park's natural and human history, there are a number of excellent places to do so, right downtown. First, the park itself has a natural history museum, the **Banff Park Museum**, located on Banff Avenue, just north of the bridge across the Bow River. It is western Canada's oldest natural history museum. A short walk from there is the **Whyte Museum of the Canadian Rockies**, which has excellent displays of the human history of the area.

Another museum, located on Birch Street, on the way to the Cave and Basin exhibit, is the **Luxton Museum of the Plains Indians**. There are dioramas and other displays, a gift shop, and special programming in the summer, designed to familiarize visitors with the cultural activities of contemporary aboriginal peoples.

In my opinion, **Cave & Basin National Historic Site** is one of the most striking of all visitor sites in the national parks system. Cave Spring and Basin Spring are the hot springs that placed Banff on the national and international tourism map. They have been restored to their turn-of-the-century state, largely natural with a few added amenities. You will be able to walk into the cave itself, smell the sulphur, touch the water, peer up to the hole at the top of the cave, and picture the rough-hewn men descending into the pool that you now stand beside.

Two interpretive boardwalk trails are situated nearby—the scenic **Discovery Trail**, which leads to the cave hole, and the **Marsh Trail**, which explores the natural history of the Cave & Basin wetlands. Both trails are partially wheelchair accessible. You can also wander farther afield along the **Marsh Loop Trail** or the **Sundance Canyon Trail**, both of which start at Cave & Basin.

Cave & Basin is about a five-minute drive from downtown Banff, on the road past the Administration Building. There is plenty of parking. You can visit the site year-round.

Of course, you'll want to get out into the very nature that you have learned so much about in these interesting places. There are many trails for hiking, driving, horseback riding, canoeing, and bicycling, all of which are all accessible from the town centre; the area around Banff Springs Hotel is a starting point for many of them.

Walking and Driving at Vermilion Lakes

The **Vermilion Lakes** are another easily accessible drive or walk from the centre of town. Vermilion Lakes Drive runs four kilometres (2.5 miles) along the three lakes, and has a number of pull-outs where visitors can park and then easily walk along the flat land by the river or lakes. You may see elk, deer, coyotes, and an occasional black bear. In the summer, bald eagles and osprey nest at the lakes.

Car Tours

The car tours you can take in the park cover a considerable distance, but are very easy to follow. Two are self-guiding. The first is the Bow Valley Parkway, Route IA, which starts approximately five kilometres (three miles) west of Banff Townsite, and is the scenic route to Lake Louise. It is marked by the signs to Johnston Canyon. At either end of the Bow Valley Parkway are signs that orient you to what you will be seeing. Plan to go slowly, and take a picnic.

The other self-guiding drive is along one of the most spectacular stretches of roads in North America—the **Icefields Parkway**. The section within Banff National Park runs 122 kilometres (75 miles) from **Lake Louise** to the **Sunwapta Pass**, at the boundary between Jasper and Banff National Parks. A park brochure lists the points of interest along the parkway, and tells about their natural and human history. Every few kilometres there is another glacier to be seen, or a lookout or turquoise-coloured lake to enjoy and photograph. The major stops along the way are **Bow Summit Lookout** and **Peyto Lake**. An "auto-tape tour," prepared by a commercial enterprise, is available to accompany you on this drive.

It took three and a half hours to travel from Lake Louise to the Banff/Jasper border, stopping at each interpretive display. Several of the park campgrounds are along this route, so you might consider staying in one of them, and taking some of the hikes to the east of the parkway, which offer spectacular overviews.

The **Lake Minnewanka Loop Drive** is about a 24-kilometre (15-mile) round trip. It starts from the Minnewanka Interchange (the more easterly of the two large interchanges) on the main highway, where you enter and

Parks Canada

Rocky mountain sheep by the road at Mount Norquay

exit town. If you take the loop in a clockwise direction, the road follows the base of **Cascade Mountain** and gives marvellous views of the **Palliser Range** mountains just across Lake Minnewanka. The lake is the largest in Banff National Park, and is, in fact, an artificially constructed reservoir, producing electrical power.

The natural resources of Banff haven't been used just for electrical power. Those sedimentary strata contain quite a different source of power—coal. There were two areas where coal mining took place in the park, well after it had been established. These two little towns, Anthracite and Bankhead, had brief booms in the first quarter of the century. The park has turned the remains of the town at **Bankhead** into a fascinating interpretive site.

Mount Norquay Drive is a six-kilometre (3.5-mile) drive up a very steep and winding road, situated at the west exit to the Trans-Canada Highway from Banff. It takes you through the typical montane and sub-alpine forest (watch for the bighorn sheep), to a breathtaking view across the town and to the mountains south and east of there.

At the end of the road, you can park and take one of the trails to the alpine levels. A ski lodge is located at the 2135-metre (7000-foot) level of **Mount Norquay**. The ski hill is open all winter (from November to April).

Halfway There—Walking in the Mountains

If you find that walking or driving, with the mountains towering to either side, is wonderful, but not quite enough, it's time to follow some of the easily accessible trails that take you into the mountains themselves. The Bow Valley Parkway, en route to Lake Louise, and the Moraine Lake area offer several varied and interesting walks of less than a half-day's duration.

Remember that the walks described here are only a few of many similar ones. I chose these ones primarily because they are in well-known areas, but also because I was in the park in mid-June, and many of the higher trails were still under snow.

From the Bow Valley Parkway, you reach Johnston Canyon, which is 18 kilometres (11 miles) west of the town of Banff. It is an extremely popular day-use area, with a restaurant, bungalows, picnic areas nearby, and a well-marked path up the canyon itself.

Johnston Canyon Walk takes you along the pathway of Johnston Creek, starting at a fairly low point and then moving past two major falls and several smaller ones. If you are energetic enough, you can follow the 5.5 kilometres (3.5 miles) up to the broad upper valley, which the stream winds across, as it comes from its source in the snow-laden mountains above. The kilometre to the first viewpoint, at the **Lower Falls**, is the most developed form of park trail; a firm, asphalted surface, with a very gentle slope. When you reach the edge of the canyon, an extremely attractive levered walkway juts out from the sides of the gorge on your left, while the stream rushes below you and out to your right. A very sturdy railing is provided, and you never feel unsafe.

Above the Lower Falls is about another two-kilometre (1.5-mile) ascent to the **Upper Falls**. You can climb above the Upper Falls, and it is very interesting to see how, in a number of other places, the stream is compressed to very narrow widths.

Above the Upper Falls, the path cuts away at a right angle to the river. The first few hundred metres are a catwalk. Then the trail continues for several kilometres along a wide fire road through the forest. One of the lovely sights along the walk, in late June, was of many calypso orchids right along the path. You eventually reach the **Inkpots**, which are cold, mineral, karst springs. Seven small pools are located here, which are most often a beautiful, bright, clear blue. Occasionally, however, with a sudden increase of pressure in this underground system, the water stirs up black silt from below the white limestone surface. The inky darkness in the water has resulted in the name "Inkpots." It's a wonderful place to rest or to cool your feet in the water.

Beyond the large flat meadow of the Inkpots, the land rises a little toward another plateau level, where small conifers are sparsely scattered. This is the nearest of all of the primitive campsites for the back-country packer. It is Johnston Creek 6. It is a five-minute walk from the Inkpots to this campsite, where there are four rustic picnic tables, pit toilets, and open spaces for tents.

No one can go to Banff and not visit **Lake Louise**. In fact, that's the only sight that some travellers see—roll out of the dusty parking lot, ramble up to the lake, stare in amazement for a while, go into the Chateau for tea, and wander on out. Years ago I did that, too, and it was a lovely experience. But this time I took my time, and went on one of the most popular hikes in the park—the **Lake Louise/Lake Agnes Trail**. It was four and a half hours of beauty, new friends, and sweat.

The trail ascends unevenly for the whole four kilometres (2.5 miles) to Lake Agnes. It is forested most of the way, but there are frequent openings where you can get spectacular views of Lake Louise below you. After three kilometres (two miles), you arrive at **Mirror Lake**, a small tarn, which is so protected from wind that it reflects its surroundings perfectly. It is below a major landmark, the **Big Beehive Rock**. Above the lake is the goal of the hikers—**Lake Agnes** and its teahouse.

Another spectacular trail here, also ending at a teahouse, is the **Plain of Glaciers**. Allow a full day to do it.

For another dramatic Main Range setting, with a glacial lake, the **Moraine Lake/Valley of the Ten Peaks** area is a wonderful place to go. I went there to see the Moraine Lake facilities, which include a lodge, picnic area, and interpretive exhibits. This is also the starting point for the trail to **Consolation Lakes.**

The area is reached by a marked road just off the Lake Louise access road on Highway 1A. The drive to Moraine Lake is 12.5 kilometres (7.5 miles) long. Once there, you are met by a view that is as spectacular as that of Lake Louise.

It is well worth strolling around the edges of Moraine Lake. There is a small stand of conifer forest, which has been fenced with rustic rails to preserve its extremely fragile soil.

At the near end of the lake is a huge, imposing rock pillar called the **Tower of Babel**. A number of rock falls have occurred from the tower and from the adjacent slope of Mount Babel. The resultant debris dammed the run-off from the surrounding mountains, and formed Moraine Lake. A very short trail leads to the top of this rock-debris hill. This trail has interpretive exhibits.

The staggering natural beauty of Banff National Park

A number of trails start in the Moraine Lake area, but in mid-June only the ones with the least altitude gain were free of snow. I chose the trail to Consolation Lakes. At the time that I visited, the trail was very damp in places, but quite beautiful.

This short trail is heavily used later in the season, but you can then go farther away to Upper Consolation Lake, or you can choose other trails in the area. For an autumn extravaganza, a trip to **Larch Valley** from Moraine Lake is reputed to be marvellous.

The Back Country—Rocky Mountain High

With all the places to go in Banff, and so many of them easily accessible by car or within an easy walk, it is sometimes hard to realize that most of the park's area is back country. Most of this is also high country—high river valleys, alpine meadows, and windswept icefields. Videos, brochures, and information about back-country travel (and permits) are available from both the Banff and Lake Louise Visitor Information Centres.

If you are interested in this kind of travel in Banff, write to the Superintendent for back-country information. Several excellent books are available on the hiking trails in the park, and these should be studied. Back-country-use permits are required; they can be purchased at the Banff or Lake Louise Visitor Information Centres.

There is one other, very different way to reach alpine altitudes for good views and short walks in a limited area—by gondola. The gondolas are located at **Sulphur Mountain** (a few minutes' drive from downtown Banff) and **Lake Louise**.

PARK SERVICES AND FACILITIES

Interpretive Program

Banff is a large, busy, and varied park. The interpretive program includes theatre presentations and interpreter-led walks. Modest fees are charged for some events. Schedules are available from both the Banff and Lake Louise Visitor Centres, campground kiosks and bulletin boards, and at many of the tourist facilities. The park newsletter, *Banff National Park—Official Visitors Guide,* is an excellent source for all kinds of park activities, as well as the park's history, facilities, and services. Six of the campgrounds have theatres for slide shows. Not every campground has a program every night, but you probably won't be far from one that does. Evening programs are also presented in the Banff Information Centre. Interpreters lead walks in the areas of the communities of Lake Louise and Banff. They can also provide an overview of each hike's difficulty and duration.

The interpretive program also provides excellent signs at places such as Bow Summit and Johnston Canyon, and the informative pamphlets for the Icefields or Cave and Basin Hot Springs, and so on.

The **Lake Louise Visitor Centre**, located beside the Samson Mall, is the place to learn about the area's geology. From an architectural perspective alone, the Centre is worth a visit. The building is designed to repeat and reflect the slanted table-top look of the surrounding mountains. Inside, the Centre houses both information services and interpretive exhibits. There are computer-information terminals and, during regular working hours, you will find helpful staff, a video on back-country use, a trip-planner display, and just about any other information you could possibly want on how to enjoy your visit to the park. The exhibit galleries tell the natural and human history of the area, and a multi-media show traces the geological history of the Rockies. The whole Lake Louise area is an important focal point for trails, accommodation, shopping, and all-round enjoyment of the northern part of the park, so plan to spend some time there—starting at the Lake Louise Visitor Centre.

Camping

Banff has 2448 car-based camping sites, distributed among 12 campgrounds. The largest ones, and the ones that fill first, are located near the towns of Banff and Lake Louise—**Tunnel Mountain, Two Jack**, and **Lake Louise**. There are no reservations for campsites, but you can call ahead to find out whether the park is crowded.

Tunnel Mountain Campground is divided into three sections, all of which have flush toilets, showers, and sewage disposal. **Tunnel Mountain Village** I is situated four kilometres (2.5 miles) east of the town and has 620 sites. **Tunnel Mountain Village II** is located 2.5 kilometres (1.5 miles) east of Banff and has 223 sites—188 with electrical hook-up. There are kitchen shelters with stoves and firewood, and it is wheelchair accessible. **Tunnel Mountain Trailer Court** adjoins Village 1 and has 320 sites with three-way hook-ups. The campgrounds are wooded around their margins, but don't have much privacy. They are well located, if you want to be near town. There are several short trails near the campgrounds, and a car pull-out for a view of the Bow Valley Hoodoos. This spot is also good for learning about the geology and railway history of the area, which the interpretive signs explain.

Two Jack Main is a densely wooded conifer forest area, located 13 kilometres (eight miles) from Banff, on the road to Lake Minnewanka. Although it is not very scenic, the campground offers a sense of visual privacy. There are 381 sites, kitchen shelters, flush toilets, trailer-sewage disposal, and hot and cold water in washrooms. The small lakeshore area at **Two Jack Lakeside** fills up quickly. It has 77 sites, with the usual fire grates, picnic tables, kitchen shelters and flush toilets, and is wheelchair accessible.

Johnston Canyon is set in a fairly mature forest that is not as dense as at Two Jack Main. A number of sites lie along Johnston Creek. It is on Highway 1A, the Bow Valley Parkway, 26 kilometres (16 miles) west of Banff. There are 132 sites, kitchen shelters, flush toilets, showers and trailer-sewage disposal. It is wheelchair accessible. Also on the Bow Valley Parkway, **Castle Mountain** is five kilometres (three miles) west of Johnston Canyon. Forty-three sites are available, with kitchen shelters and flush toilets. The campground at **Protection Mountain** is just over 10 kilometres (six miles) farther west of Castle Mountain on the Bow Valley Parkway. It has 89 sites, kitchen shelters, flush toilets and trailer-sewage disposal.

The **Lake Louise Campground** is a lightly treed, fairly open area located near the main highway and the railway. It is bordered by the fast-flowing Bow River, which provides a nice contrast to the roads and rails. This campground is a 10-minute walk from the village of Lake Louise and is wheelchair accessible. There are 216 tent sites, 189 trailer sites, kitchen shelters, flush toilets, trailer-sewage disposal, and an outdoor interpretive theatre.

Campgrounds North of Lake Louise

Mosquito Creek is located at kilometre 24 (15 miles) of the Icefields Parkway. There are 32 sites and wheelchair access. This is a self-registering campground. It has two sections: a large, gravelly field, and a wooded area with kitchen shelters, pit toilets, and cold water from faucets every few sites. Picnic tables, fire grates and firewood are available, as usual. The Waterfowl Lakes Campground is at kilometre 58 (37 miles) on the parkway. It is a lovely location by a stream and large lake, wooded, with a cleared area at lakeside. Mountains and glaciers are in full view—a good place for easy canoeing. There are 116 sites, kitchen shelters, flush and pit toilets, and water from faucets every few sites. It is only 15 kilometres (nine miles) from Saskatchewan Crossing, with its gasoline, restaurant, and so forth, and has 80 sites with trailer-sewage disposal. Waterfowl Campground has an interpretive theatre for evening programs. Rampart

Creek is at kilometre 88 (54 miles) of the parkway. There are 50 sites, wheelchair access, kitchen shelters, and flush and dry toilets.

Primitive Camping

The back-country areas of Banff National Park have different user categories, in terms of what type of camping is allowed in each area. This distinction is necessary to avoid excessive wear and tear on the land and wildlife. A back-country guide is available at both the Banff and Lake Louise Visitor Information Centres. In both places, you will be able to talk with staff about which routes are best suited to your interests and skills.

There are back-country campsites at about 10-kilometre (six-miles) intervals along the more popular trails in the back country. All have pit toilets, fire grates, wood and small picnic tables. Write to the Superintendent for detailed information, and check at the Information Centres upon arrival for updates on the trail conditions, and to purchase your required back-country permit.

Group Camping

There is a group campground at **Castle Meadows** with 300 tent sites available for non-profit groups. Reservations are required.

Other Accommodation, Gas, Food, and Supplies

There are six hostels in Banff National Park. A minimal fee covers beds and propane cooking. Some have electric light; most are wood-heated. For more information, write to Calgary Office of Hostelling International, 203-1414 Kensingston Road S.W., Calgary, Alberta, T2N 3P9; Phone: (413) 283-5551. It is recommended that you make reservations as early as possible. Most of the commercial accommodation in the park is concentrated at the town of Banff and at Lake Louise, but there is also accommodation at a number of outlying locations. The park has lists of them. Also, you can write to the Banff/Lake Louise Tourism Bureau for a detailed booklet. The town of Canmore, located just outside the east gate of the park, also has a good deal of commercial accommodation and related facilities. Gas, food, and supplies are available in Banff or Canmore. Lake Louise has gasoline, restaurants, and a mall, which includes a sporting-goods store, an organic food store, an excellent bookstore, and more. Saskatchewan Crossing has gasoline and a restaurant.

Recreation Services

Driving   Ask at the Information Centre for pamphlets on drives in the Lake Louise and Banff areas, and on the Bow Valley and Icefields Parkways.

Hiking   The park has phased out its own brochures about park trails, but a number of commercial publications are available. You can find them in many of the gift shops and bookstores throughout the area. Friends of Banff National Park sell topographic maps at their stores in the Banff and Lake Louise Visitor Information Centres.

Boating and Canoeing   Power boats are allowed only on Lake Minnewanka, where there is a boat-launching area and boats may be rented. Canoes are allowed on most of the lakes and rivers, and you can rent them at Lake Minnewanka, Lake Louise, Moraine Lake, and at the town of Banff. Commercial rafting tours are also offered. Write to the Banff/Lake Louise Tourism Bureau, or ask at the Information Centre for further details.

Fishing   Fishing is quite good in some waters. A National Park permit is required. A park brochure lists lakes, limits, and so forth.

Golf   The Banff Springs Hotel offers a 27-hole course, with a driving range next to it. You can rent clubs and electric carts at the pro shop.

Swimming   A dip in the Upper Hot Springs feels good after a day of skiing or hiking. It is open year-round. Check at the Information Centres for the brochure listing the hours of operation and fees.

Horseback Riding, Backpacking and Guided Back-Country Treks   Several commercially operated enterprises offer a full range of these activities. The park has a list (write to the Superintendent), as does the Banff/Lake Louise Tourism Bureau.

Sightseeing Tours, Chair Lifts, Gondolas   Various activities of this kind are provided by commercial operators. For more information, write to the Banff/Lake Louise Tourism Bureau, or ask at any hotel or travel agent in Banff, Canmore, or Calgary.

Winter Use   Cross-country skiing and snowshoeing are very popular in the park. Write to the Superintendent for information, or inquire at the Visitor Information Centres in Banff and Lake Louise. There is an excellent booklet on ski-touring—how to prepare, 20 trails to use, what areas to avoid, and so on. The park has three major downhill skiing areas: Sunshine Village, Mount Norquay, and Lake Louise. These are all commercially run and offer a complement of tows, lodges, rentals, lessons, and so forth. Write to the Banff/Lake Louise Tourism Bureau, or check with your local travel agent for further information.

Related Activities or Places of Natural or Historic Interest

Alberta Tourism is a good information service for all kinds of visitation in the province. Call 1-800-661-8888 (or 427-4321 in Edmonton).

Activities and Places to Consider Visiting:

- There are three provincial parks in nearby Kananaskis Country: Bragg Creek on the east; Bow Valley Park in the north; and Peter Lougheed, a wilderness park to the south.

National Historic Sites:

- Skoki Ski Lodge

- Abbot Pass Refuge Cabin

- Howse Pass

- Sulphur Mountain Cosmic Ray Station

- Banff Park Museum

- Cave and Basin

FURTHER READING

Handbook of the Canadian Rockies by Ben Gadd (Corax Press, rev. ed. 1995).

For More Information

The Superintendent
Banff National Park
Box 900
Banff, Alberta
T0L 0C0
Phone: (403) 762-1550

Fax: (403) 762-3380
TTY: (403) 762-4256

Banff/Lake Louise Tourism Bureau
Box 1298
Banff, Alberta
T0L 0C0
Phone: (403) 762-8421

JASPER

National Park

J asper is the largest and northernmost of the five Rocky Mountain national parks. It lies directly north of Banff National Park and, like Banff, occupies a large part of the eastern slopes of the Rockies in Alberta.

Jasper covers an area of 10 800 square kilometres (4170 square miles). It comprises two of the three ranges of the Rockies—the Front Ranges to the east and the Main Ranges in the remainder of the park. The mountains were built by processes of sedimentation, compression, and uplift. Mountain-building stopped in the foothills beyond Jasper about 40 million years ago, and they have been losing ground steadily since then, as a result of glaciation during the ice ages, and ongoing erosion by wind, water, and frost.

Because the mountains were eroding throughout the period during which they were being uplifted, the maximum height they reached remains open to debate. Today, many of the mountains are over 3350 metres (11 000 feet). The townsite of Jasper is at an elevation of 1058 metres (3472 feet) above sea level. The largest icefield in the Rocky Mountains is here, and 15 to 20 glaciers are visible from the parkway that runs from Lake Louise to the Jasper townsite. The mixed terrain and varied habitat of broad river valleys, wooded lower slopes, alpine tundra above the treeline, and the massive icefields make for a complex and fascinating environment.

HOW TO SEE THE PARK

Jasper has three ecological zones of the Rockies: the montane, with its dry Douglas fir forest and broad river valleys; the sub-alpine forest of Engelmann spruce and alpine fir; and the alpine tundra, with its rocky vastness and miniature plant life, and the awe-inspiring icefields and glaciers. Although each zone is extraordinarily accessible, Jasper is known particularly for offering the opportunity to get away from it all in one of the best and most extensive back-country trail systems in the national parks.

Marylee Stephenson

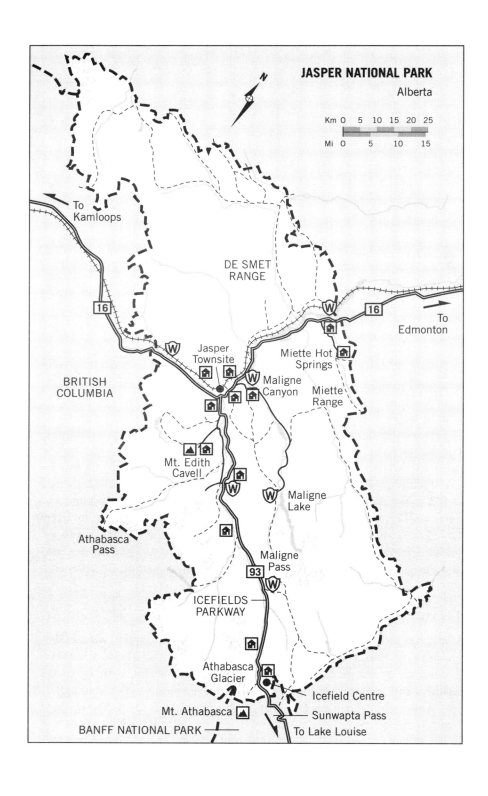

JASPER NATIONAL PARK

Alberta

Km 0 5 10 15 20 25
Mi 0   5   10   15

N

To
Kamloops

DE SMET
RANGE

16

To
Edmonton

BRITISH
COLUMBIA

Jasper
Townsite

Miette Hot
Springs

Maligne
Canyon

Miette
Range

Mt. Edith
Cavell

Maligne
Lake

Athabasca
Pass

Maligne
Pass

93

ICEFIELDS
PARKWAY

Athabasca
Glacier

Icefield Centre

Sunwapta Pass

Mt. Athabasca

BANFF NATIONAL PARK

To Lake Louise

The hub of the park's activities is the townsite; the spokes are the high-ways. There are six main visitation areas: the Icefields Parkway, which highlights the Athabasca Glacier, 101 kilometres (63 miles) south of the townsite at the park's southern border; the 43-kilometre (27-mile) Maligne Lake Road, east of the townsite; the Miette Hot Springs, near the eastern entry to the park; The Whistlers, just south of the townsite; Mount Edith Cavell, about 29 kilometres (18 miles) southeast of the townsite, off alternate Highway 93A; and the Pyramid/Patricia Lakes area, just north of the townsite.

Montane Zone

In Jasper, the **Athabasca** and **Miette River Valleys** represent the montane zone. The typical forest is dry and open. The rivers are wide, and their stream beds change occasionally. Marshy areas in low-lying parts provide excellent habitat for moose, beaver, and waterfowl. The open slopes are ideal for grazing animals, such as mule deer, Rocky Mountain bighorn sheep, and elk. Black bears and coyotes also frequent this zone. Mountain goats come down to the natural salt licks adjacent to the Athabasca River.

The best car-based view of this kind of environment, and the most beautiful drive in the park, is the road north of Jasper on Highway 16, up to **Pocahontas** and the **Miette Hot Springs** turn-off.

For an even closer experience of the montane zone, the **Patricia Lake/Pyramid Lake** road and trails are excellent.

Deer by the roadside, photographed from the car

The Sub-Alpine Zone

Travelling the **Maligne Lake Road** is an excellent way to explore the sub-alpine world. **The Maligne Valley** is a hanging valley. It was carved into its U-shape by a glacier; at the same time, another, much larger, glacier carved its way at a right angle to the Maligne Valley, cutting the wider, deeper **Athabasca River Valley**. The floor of the Maligne Valley is 120 metres (393 feet) higher than the floor of the Athabasca Valley. Thus, the Maligne River, which flows on a very gradual slope for most of its journey, takes a sudden plunge where it joins the Athabasca Valley.

Three major stops are located along the Maligne Valley road, and the site of this precipitous descent at **Maligne Canyon** is the first. The canyon is a spectacular example of the cutting power of moving water.

The second stop up the valley is **Medicine Lake**. It was a mystery lake for a long time: although it does not have a surface river as an outlet, each year it drains out until, in fall and winter, it is mostly exposed mud, with only a few channels and a pond at the north end.

The riddle of this sinking river has only recently been solved. Apparently, a network of caves extends in the valley floor under the lake, to Maligne Canyon. At least two horizontal levels are fed by numerous sink holes in the lake bottom. When the spring run-off is high in the upper Maligne Valley, the lake fills, and so do the caves.

The final stop in the Maligne Valley is **Maligne Lake**, the largest glacier-fed lake in the Rockies. It is 22.3 kilometres (14 miles) long. The lake is bordered by sub-alpine forest; the mountains rising around it show the grey/green shadings of alpine tundra, and then the ice and snow of mountain heights. A network of short trails starts near the boat-launch area. On the **Lake Trail** (east side) an interpretive sign describes glacial remains such as kames and kettles. At the **Schäffer Viewpoint**, the signs tell of intrepid Mary Schäffer, the first white woman to explore the lake, and the mountain climbers, scientists, and adventurous tourists who followed over the years.

Alpine Tundra

If you're a back-country hiker, you'll have no problems reaching this environment. Many of the trails go above the treeline, and wind along ridges and crests for many kilometres. But most visitors will want another way to get there. Here are suggestions.

One option is to hop into the reversible tramway to **The Whistlers** (so named for the hoary marmots that live there). The parking lot is at the end of a short, well-marked access road, just south of the townsite. This is a

Parks Canada

Alpine flowers, mosses, and lichen—low and spreading

commercially operated service, so there is a small gift shop at the bottom terminal and a cafe, restaurant, and gift shop at the top.

The tram ride takes you from 1300 metres (4266 feet) to 2286 metres (7500 feet) elevation. A trail goes to the top of the mountain, and then winds along the ridge to other viewpoints. The path is wide and smooth, but many people are not used to walking uphill, especially at higher elevations. When you arrive, you will be at 2465 metres (8085 feet) elevation.

The other access to the alpine tundra is by the popular **Sulpher Skyline Trail.** Pack a lunch, and plan to spend the day. The trail winds its way up through the sub-alpine forest, past gnarled, stunted trees. At the top, the mountains stretch away on every side, in striking rock formations.

After your return hike, there is no better way to relax than to indulge in a visit to the **Miette Hot Springs,** located near the trailhead in the **Fiddle Valley.**

Icefields and Glaciers

It is artificial to divide the Icefields Parkway into a Jasper stretch and a Banff stretch. But Jasper's section really does stand out, in that it boasts the **Athabasca Glacier.** This glacier is 6.5 kilometres (four miles) long, from the rim of its source in the Columbia Icefield to its terminus, or toe. The glacier is always in motion, always flowing downward and forward, but it has grown shorter because more ice melts each year than is added from the icefield source. It is about 15 metres (50 feet) thick near the toe, and about 300 metres (984 feet) thick at its deepest part, near the icefield rim. You can even drive to a parking lot and walk right up to it. (Walking on the glacier is strongly discouraged, however.) Nowhere else in the world is a glacier this accessible.

There's also a commercially run giant snow-coach service, which takes you a few kilometres on to the main part of the glacier.

The Columbia Icefield Visitor Centre houses the snow coach ticket office, information services, displays, and food services.

Another area of the park complements the Icefield/Athabasca Glacier experience. This is the base of **Mount Edith Cavell**. From the parking lot at the end of the access road, there is a self-guiding trail called **Path of the Glacier**. It follows a lateral moraine, the ridge of debris that accumulates at the edge of a glacier.

One difficulty in reaching this trail is that the road is usually not clear of snow and open to public travel until mid- or late June.

PARK SERVICES AND FACILITIES

Interpretive Program

Jasper has an active interpretive program, with a range of activities offered throughout the week. There are evening programs in the outdoor theatre at Whistlers campground seven nights a week; parking is available near the theatre. Several interpreter-led hikes are offered, of varying degrees of difficulty. There is a junior naturalist program geared toward children aged six to 10 years.

Camping

Ten campgrounds are located in the park, each of which is in a varying stage of development. At smaller sites, fees are collected by a mobile attendant.

Whistlers Campground is right by the townsite, in a lightly wooded area. It has 781 sites, 77 of which have three-way hook-ups for trailers. Forty-three sites have electricity only. There are kitchen shelters, and each car/tent site has a picnic table and fire grate. Flush toilets, and hot and cold water are provided in washrooms, with cold water on the exterior of the washrooms. Showers and toilets are wheelchair accessible. The campground fills quickly.

Wapiti is lightly treed, with 366 sites, 28 of them with electricity only. They are in a paved parking lot at the edge of the campground. There are kitchen shelters, flush toilets, hot and cold water in faucets, and new showers. Water is available from faucets at central locations. This campground is less likely to be full than Whistlers.

At **Pocahontas Campground**, 140 sites, 10 of them walk-in tent sites, are situated in a lightly treed forest. Hot and cold running water, and taps at central locations are provided. There are flush toilets.

Snaring River Campsite has 66 sites, 10 of them walk-in at several hundred metres. There is a kitchen shelter, pit toilets, and water from wells.

Wabasso, a beautiful, lightly wooded location, is accessible from alternate Highway 93A, near the junction of the Athabasca and Whirlpool Rivers, where fur traders used to meet. There are 238 sites, six of which are walk-in tent sites, with flush toilets, cold water at the washrooms and in faucets around campsites. Trailer-sewage disposal is available.

Mount Kerkeslin, along the Athabasca River in a montane forest, offers good mountain views. There are 42 sites, with pit toilets and a kitchen shelter. Water is taken from wells. Swimming is possible here.

Honeymoon Lake Campground, by a small lake, is good for easy canoeing. There is a pump and well-water, or water from the lake, which must be boiled. There are 35 sites, with pit toilets and kitchen shelters.

Jonas Creek is in a wooded area, on a small hillside. The upper section is a short walk in for 12 tents. The lower level has 13 sites, and is very near the highway. There are pit toilets, and kitchen shelters with a water supply.

Icefield Campground is just a few hundred metres south of the Athabasca Glacier, on the opposite side of the road. It is situated by a small creek on a hillside. There are 22 sites, with platforms for tents, a centralized water supply, kitchen shelters, and pit toilets.

Wilcox Creek, the southernmost of the Jasper campgrounds, located just into the park, is lightly wooded and built on several levels. There are 46 sites, with kitchen shelters, pit toilets, faucet water, and trailer-sewage disposal.

Primitive Camping

The park has 1000 kilometres (600 miles) of back-country trails, and the longer ones have primitive campsites along the way. Hikers may stay overnight in these campsites only. A park-use permit and wilderness pass are required. A modest fee is charged for back-country camping. Season passes are available that can also be used at Banff, Yoho, and Kootenay National Parks. Because of the popularity of back-country hiking in Jasper, the park allows reservations for up to 35 percent of a trail's capacity. The remaining 65 percent of the campsites are on a first-come, first-served basis. Write to the Superintendent for further information. When you get to the park, check at the Information Centre or (in summer only) at the Icefields Centre, for the latest trail conditions and to pick up your park-use permit.

Other Accommodation, Gas, Food, and Supplies

Jasper is a townsite of about 4000 permanent residents and hundreds of thousands of visitors, both in the winter and summer. Jasper has all types of indoor accommodation, a full range of restaurants, grocery stores, hardware and supply stores, gift shops, filling stations, laundromats, and so on. In the centre of town is the Jasper National Park Information Centre. There is also gas at a small cafe at Pocahontas, located at the junction with the Miette Hot Springs road. There is a restaurant at Maligne Canyon and Maligne Lake. Bungalows and a restaurant are located at the Miette Hot Springs area.

Recreational Services

Hiking   The park has several short, self-guiding trails, a number of them ranging from four to 12 kilometres (three to eight miles) one way, and many lengthy back-country trails. Ask at the Information Centre for information on day hikes. In the upper elevations the snow does not clear until late June or early July.

Fishing   Most of the glacial lakes are not good for fishing. However, Maligne Lake was stocked years ago, and the fish now maintain their numbers naturally. There is a boat-and-tackle rental there. A National Parks fishing licence is required. A brochure on regulations is available at the Information Centre.

Boating   Motor boats are allowed only on Pyramid Medicine Lake. In most other lakes you can use canoes, rowboats, or kayaks. Electric trolling motors are also allowed. Remember that the waters in Jasper are extremely cold, and accidents can be fatal. Commercially operated rafting tours are offered on the Athabasca and Maligne Rivers. Write to the Chamber of Commerce for more information.

Swimming   Miette Hotsprings is for soaking, rather than swimming. The water is cooled from 54°C to 37°C (130°F to 100°F), for visitor use.

Tennis   Six clay courts are maintained by the park, and are located at the townsite recreational centre. Jasper Park Lodge also provides courts.

Golf   There is an 18-hole course at the Jasper Park Lodge; inquire there about use by non-guests.

Winter Use   Jasper is heavily used for downhill skiing at the commercially run Marmot Basin, and for cross-country skiing throughout the park. Wapiti Campground parking lot, with electrical hook-ups, water, and toilets, is kept open in winter as a self-registering campground. Write to the Superintendent for information on park-run winter use, and to the Chamber of Commerce about downhill skiing.

Related Activities or Places of Natural or Historic Interest

Alberta Tourism is a good information service for all kinds of visitation in the province. Call 1-800-661-8888 (or 427-4321 in Edmonton). The Jasper Park Chamber of Commerce is also a good source of information on the area (403) 852-3858.

Activities and Places to Consider Visiting:

- Nearby provincial parks include Mount Robson Provincial Park, in British Columbia, and William A. Switzer in Alberta

National Historic Sites:

- Jasper House
- Yellowhead Pass
- Jasper Park Information Centre
- Athabasca Pass

For More Information

The Superintendent
Jasper National Park
Box 10
Jasper, Alberta
T0E IE0
Phone: (403) 852-6161
Fax: (403) 852-5601

Jasper Tourism and Commerce
Box 98
Jasper, Alberta
T0E 1E0
Phone: (403) 852-3858
Fax: (403) 852-4932

ELK ISLAND
National Park

W hen I visited Elk Island, I wondered where the island was. I drove past massive bison, went by beaver dams, saw people golfing and canoeing, set up my tent—but still no island.

Staying in the park awhile, walking the trails and talking with the interpreters, I soon learned why Elk Island National Park is an island. First, it is an island in terms of its geological history and present-day topography. It is quite different from the nearly flat plains that spread out on every side. Second, it is an island of protection and preservation. A 2.5-metre (eight-foot) fence surrounds the park; plants and animals can live almost undisturbed by human contact.

Elk Island is oblong in shape, and 195 square kilometres in area (75 square miles). The island is situated 45 kilometres (28 miles) east of Edmonton, in the Beaver Hills, where the terrain is that rather lumpy type called "knob and kettle." Alberta's plains are interrupted in several places by similar hilly land formations, which were formed because glaciers stagnated there. The glaciers would increase slightly in winter, melt somewhat in summer, without much significant movement. At their tips, large chunks of ice would crumble off. When the glaciers retreated permanently, they left great amounts of debris around remaining chunks of ice. This debris formed knobs, and the melting ice chunks eventually formed kettle ponds.

When left to themselves, these hilly areas eventually turn into very rich habitat for plants and animals. Buffalo, elk, moose, deer, and small mammals can have their young here in relative safety, and then range out on the prairies. These mammals, in turn, provide food for predators such as the lynx and coyote.

The kettles play a major role in the life cycle of waterbirds. These birds need lots of aquatic plants and ooze to feed on, and plenty of privacy, among cattails and reeds at the water's edge, in order to raise their young safely. Kettles are extremely rich in plant life, because they are shallow and, in summer, readily warmed by the sun. When plants die, their

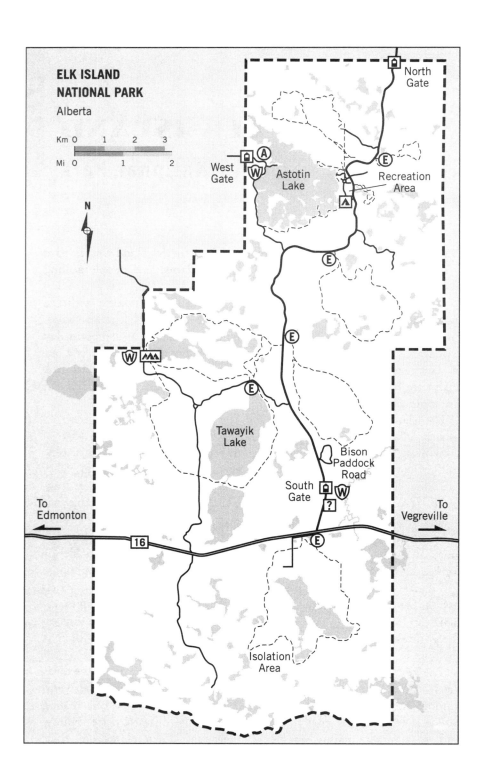

remains stay in the kettles, since few streams feed or drain the ponds. Over time, large amounts of decayed organic material collect so, although kettles have a poor supply of oxygen, they contain rich supplies of nutrients for more plants to grow. These eutrophic ponds form a rather poor environment for fish. In general, the only fish that thrive are minnows and sticklebacks, which are both very small. They are good food for herons, common loons, and grebes, however.

HOW TO SEE THE PARK

Elk Island is a centralized park, with one main road leading from its southern to northern borders. Located about 14 kilometres (8.5 miles) north from Highway 16 is the **Astotin Recreation Area**, with picnicking, camping, canoeing, golfing, the Ukrainian Pioneer Home, the Astotin Interpretive Centre, and the start of several self-guiding trails. The other trails and picnic areas, and the buffalo viewing area, are located just off the highway, north or south of Astotin.

Knobs, Kettles, and Forests

Two trails are particularly good for getting close to the knob-and-kettle terrain, with its multitude of eutrophic lakes and ponds, its poplar groves or small stands of mixed-wood forest. For an easy trek, the best overall trail is **Amisk Wuché**.* This is a self-guiding trail, with boardwalks and signs describing the landscape features of the present-day park.

The lake is a wonderful habitat for animal life of many sorts—the ducks plow through the duck weed, and beavers flood the path in places.

To get a real overview of knob-and-kettle terrain, take the **Moss Lake Trail**. The trail took me four hours, including many stops for taking photos, a lunch break, and a large detour around a basking bull bison. The trail goes up small hills, through small depressions, and past many ponds, meadows, and marshy areas.

Within the knob-and-kettle environment, the water worlds deserve special attention. First, the park has more than 250 lakes, ponds, and wetlands, which occupy 20 percent of its surface area. These ponds are mostly eutrophic. To get an impression of the life and processes of a pond, take the **Lakeshore Trail** north of Sandy Beach, the adjoining **Point of Good Hope Trail/Living Waters Boardwalk** just down the slope from

---

*Pronounced, run on, uhMISK*wushay*. This is Cree for "Beaver Hills."

Parks Canada

Red-necked grebe

the Astotin Interpretive Centre south of the beach, or the paved **Shoreline Trail** that starts just west of the end of the golf course parking lot.

Lakeview Trail is warbler territory, but leads through several habitat types, thereby increasing the opportunity to see a diversity of birdlife. It also traverses an active beaver dam.

Island of Protection and Preservation

The beaver and large grazing animals, such as bison and elk, have a special history here. In fact, several places in the park are devoted to enhancing the visitor's awareness of these animals. As far as beaver are concerned, any pond is likely to have its domed beaver lodge. There's one in the marshy area between the golf course parking lot and the campground access road, for instance. The Beaver Hills Exhibit and Beaver Pond Trail, just a short drive north of the Amisk Wuché, tell the story of the beaver in Elk Island. Be sure to wear waterproof footwear for this and the other trails.

As for bison and elk, the former are very visible and, in August and September at least, the latter are very audible. Herds of over 100 bison can be seen at the south end of the park. Visitors can drive on a loop road through the area and are likely to see some of the bison, unless it's high noon and they are tucked in the poplar stands, avoiding the sun.

The main parkway is a scenic drive that is built lower and for slower speeds than other secondary highways. Its dips and curves give you a clear sense of the rolling landscape, dotted with lakes and ponds. The

Parks Canada

This sculptured mushroom is extremely poisonous

abundance of hoofed animals in the park requires drivers to be extremely cautious when using the parkway, in either the day or night.

Elk are well established in the park but, in contrast to the bison, are quite secretive. As with so many experiences in Elk Island, you need to take time to wander away from the recreation area, or be by the lakeshore at very quiet times, to appreciate the fullness of the natural world, in what is an oasis, even more than an island.

PARK SERVICES AND FACILITIES

An attractive Information Centre is located near the south entrance. Visitors can examine displays on the park, ask staff for suggestions, and pick up brochures, maps, and so forth.

Interpretive Program

The Astotin Interpretive Centre, located south of the beach, opened in June 1984. It has an information desk, a lobby display on various aspects of the park, a theatre seating 100 people, where slide programs, films, and other presentations are offered, and an exterior observation deck with telescope.

Elk Island Radio broadcasts continuously. Dial 1540 AM (English), 1210 AM (French).

Camping

Sandy Beach Campground, located in the Astotin Recreation Area, has 40 multi-use sites, 23 sites for trailers, 17 sites in a walk-in tenting area, and an overflow site nearby. There are centrally located kitchen shelters and firewood, clean washrooms with hot and cold running water and showers, and picnic tables and fire boxes at each campsite (not available in the overflow areas). An additional fee is added to the camping fee for the use of park firewood. No hook-ups are available. The sanitary station is located behind the Snack Bar, south of the main parking lot, by the beach. Back-country camping in the summer and winter is available at the **Oster Lake Group Tenting Area** (a back-country user permit is required). Winter camping is also available in the Astotin Recreation Area, on boulevards surrounding the Boat Launch parking lot.

Group Tenting

Back-country camping in summer and winter is available for groups, individual hikers, and cross-country skiers at the Oster Lake Group Tenting Area, for a modest fee. Write to the Superintendent for information, or call (403) 992-2950. Reservations are required; only tenting is allowed.

Other Accommodation, Gas, Food, and Supplies

Edmonton is a 30-minute drive away, and it provides for all needs. Fort Saskatchewan is 25 kilometres (15 miles) west of the park, and Lamont is five kilometres (three miles) north. Both places offer accommodation, gas, and supplies.

Recreational Services

Hiking   The park offers 14 established trails, which extend 103 kilometres. Check with staff for the condition of the longer ones. You can go completely around Tawayik Lake in the winter only; the narrows are too marshy and wet in the summer. The trails aren't rugged or steep, but they can be mushy. Dogs are not allowed on trails, because of potential conflicts with bison, and elsewhere they must be on leashes at all times.

Boating   No motorized boats are allowed in the park, but canoeing, windsurfing, and sailing are permitted on Astotin Lake. During the nesting season, one arm of Astotin is off limits to boats. It is signed accordingly, and there is still lots of room.

Swimming   You can sunbathe at Sandy Beach, but swimming is not recommended. The water is shallow and warm, and there is swimmer's itch at some times in the summer. This condition is caused by a microscopic, free-swimming larval worm, whose alternate hosts are usually snails, ducks, beavers, or muskrats. The beach area also has a take-out snack bar. Charcoal briquets, ice, and other picnicking supplies can be purchased.

Golf   A nine-hole golf course is located near Sandy Beach. A small fee is required. There is a pro shop, rental of clubs and carts, and a licensed, cafeteria-style restaurant.

Winter Use   The summer hiking trails are used for cross-country skiing and snowshoeing (Amisk Wuché and Lakeview trails) in winter. Winter camping is permitted at the Boat Launch parking lot, in the Astotin Recreation Area (tenters can use the grassed borders of the parking lot), and by reservation at the Oster Lake Group Tenting Area. Chemical toilets are located at several of the trailheads, as well as at the boat launch parking lot. Picnic shelters, with firewood and stoves, are available for winter use at the Tawayik Lake picnic area, and in the Astotin Recreation Area.

Related Activities or Places of Natural or Historic Interest

Alberta Tourism is a good information service for all kinds of visitation in the province. Call 1-800-661-8888 (or 427-4321 in Edmonton). The tourist information zone centre in nearby Edmonton is also a good source of information on the area (403) 426-4715.

Activities and Places to Consider Visiting:

- Cooking Lake-Blackfoot Recreation, Wildlife and Grazing Area (locally called simply Blackfoot) located on the southern and eastern boundary of Elk Island offers a variety of recreational activities. Phone (403) 922-3293.

- The Ukrainian Cultural Heritage Village on the park's eastern boundary. Restored buildings, guided tours, costumed interpreters, visitor reception building, and many special events. Phone (403) 662-3640.

- Miquelon Lake Provincial Park in the southern part of the Cooking Lake Moraine.

FURTHER READING

The Discoverer's Guide to Elk Island National Park by Ross Chapman (Lone Pine Publishing and Friends of Elk Island Society, 1991).

For More Information

The Superintendent
Elk Island National Park
R.R. 1, Site 4
Fort Saskatchewan, Alberta
T8L 2N7
Phone: (403) 992-2950
Fax: (403) 992-2951

KLUANE
National Park Reserve

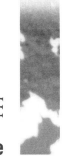

Although there are really two Kluane* parks, only one, the greenbelt of lowland forests and broad valleys, is accessible to general visitors. It is well worth turning off the Alaska Highway and taking a few hours, or even days, to explore this Kluane. The other Kluane, a land of glaciers and mountains, challenges the wilderness traveller, who may have prepared months in advance for an extended visit.

Kluane, a high mountain wilderness park, is located in the Yukon Territory, just two hours' drive west of Whitehorse. Kluane is dominated by the St. Elias Mountains, which run through the park in a southeasterly direction. The St. Elias Mountains consist of two ranges—the rugged Icefield Ranges to the west, where Canada's highest mountains are found, and the Kluane Ranges, a mountain range near the eastern edge.

The mountains of Kluane are the youngest and most active in North America, and the area is the most earthquake-prone in Canada. On average, 1000 tremors occur each year there! Although most tremors are barely perceptible to human senses, a working seismograph is on display at the park's Visitor Reception Centre at Haines Junction.

The shaping of the young, rugged landscape is the theme of the park's interpretive program. The ridges of the Icefield Ranges are covered in snow, compacted over millennia, and linked to form the largest, most continuous icefields outside the north and south polar regions. Extending from these icefields are glaciers: Kluane has 4000 of them. Glaciers have a very active life, as they cut, grind, and tear their way to lower levels. These rivers of ice usually travel very slowly. Occasionally, however, they flow at astonishing rates, becoming what is known as "surging glaciers." In the summer of 1967, Steeles Glacier, on the northwest boundary of the park, began moving at a rate of 12 metres (40 feet) a day! In two years, it travelled more than eight kilometres (five miles) down its valley. Kluane

*Pronounced Kloo-*wah*-nee

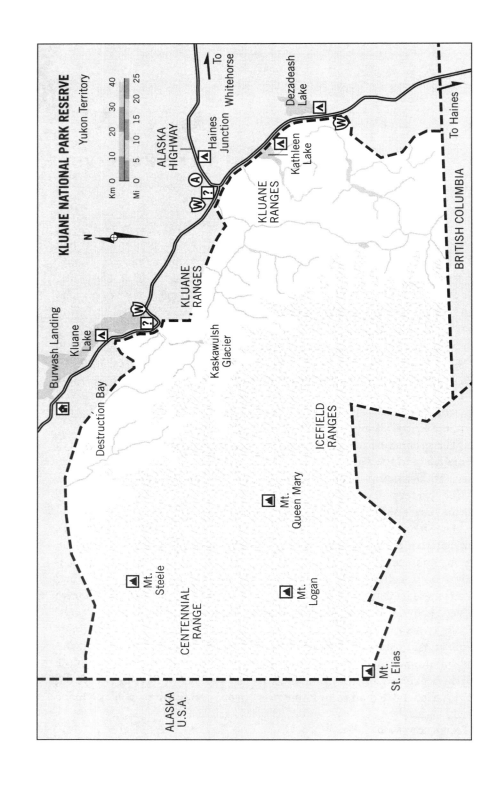

has at least six surging glaciers but, unfortunately, none is accessible to the casual visitor.

Another type of glacier, which is easily seen from the main highway, is the rock glacier. Like an ice glacier, it is a flowing mass, but what moves are rocks that have collected in, and sheared from, high, narrow valleys.

But Kluane is more than just mountains, ice, and snow. The greenbelt area is phenomenally rich in plant and animal life, for several reasons. First, the greenbelt encompasses a variety of habitats, from broad river valleys with gravelly plains sloping upwards, to marshes, dense forest stands, alpine meadows, bare mountain slopes of the Kluane Ranges, and alpine tundra. Second, the greenbelt is relatively narrow, so animals fill every suitable niche. Finally, as the animals are protected against hunters, they reach the maximum numbers that this rich environment can support.

Kluane is famous for having the largest known concentration of Dall sheep. Grizzly bears are also common here; perhaps 250 of them live in the park. A number of black bears also live in the park. They stay fairly close to the patches of forest and are easily displaced by the more aggressive grizzlies, in those lowland areas where they overlap in summer.

Kluane National Park Reserve is part of the homeland of the Southern Tutchone First Nations people who have inhabited this area for thousands of years. The Champagne/Aishihik and Kluane First Nations are two Southern Tutchone groups that are involved as co-managers of Kluane National Park Reserve. The Southern Tutchone have a negotiated right to hunt and fish in the park.

Surveyors and explorers came to this area, especially in the last half of the nineteenth century, but it was the search for gold in the streams, and for adventure in the mountains, that brought the major influx of people. The Klondike Gold Rush of 1897, the Kluane Gold Rush in 1904, and a subsequent rush in 1917, brought many prospectors.

The extreme ruggedness and great height of the mountains of Kluane attract both mountaineers and scientists. In the early mountaineering days, the most famous ascent occurred in 1897, when the renowned Duke of Abruzzi climbed Mount St. Elias. Many of the other peaks of the Icefield Ranges have also been successfully climbed.

Kluane is bordered by the Wrangell-St. Elias and Glacier Bay National Parks in Alaska and the Tatshenshini-Alsek Provincial Park in British Columbia. Together, they form the largest international protected area in the world.

HOW TO SEE THE PARK

When you first enter the park, go to the Visitor Centre at Haines Junction or the Visitor Centre at Sheep Mountain, at the northern edge of the park, on the Alaska Highway. There are many exhibits and displays for visitors, and staff are available to tell you about the park.

The Back Country

The back country at Kluane requires the kind of experience and preparation that most park visitors simply don't have. Back-country visitors must register at either the Haines Junction or Sheep Mountain Visitor Centre, and it's a good idea to write to the park in advance, so that proper planning can be done.

Another option is to visit the back country with a local commercial tour-guiding outfits.

Granted, it is disappointing for car-based visitors to be unable to see, or visit, those massive mountains or great rivers of ice, which this park preserves for us all. The closest that people can come to seeing this area, although relatively few do, is a 27-kilometre (17-mile), two-day walk to the foot of the **Kaskawulsh Glacier**. Another option is to see the region by plane. Several commercial, small-plane touring operators offer flights of varying durations and routes.

Parks Canada

Kaskawulsh Glacier—27 kilometres into the back country

Hiking in the Lowlands

The phenomenon of rock glaciers is easily seen from the road. A 15-minute drive south of **Kathleen Lake** takes you to the **Rock Glacier Trail**. This trail is about 1.5 kilometres (one mile) long, leading over a stream, through a long, damp, wooded area, full of monks' hoods and other flowers, and up on to a rock glacier.

The area east of the Kluane Ranges, running roughly parallel to the Haines-Alaska Highway, is the most travelled part of the park. The campground is here, at Kathleen Lake.

Most of the shorter hiking trails start at the highway. Several are excellent for exploring the greenbelt. You can get a descriptive brochure from the Visitor Centres. Here are descriptions of several trails.*

The **St. Elias Lake Trail** is approximately four kilometres (2.5 miles) long. It is a steady climb to the lake, with a rise in elevation of about 150 metres (490 feet). The trail is an old mining road, which is blocked off to public vehicles. Watch for mountain goats around the lake, and for small mammals and birds.

The **Auriol Range Trail** is the most accessible hiking trail from Haines Junction. The trailhead is five kilometres (three miles) southeast of Haines Junction, on the Haines Highway. Watch for road signs. A parking area is provided. The loop is 15 kilometres (nine miles) long. Allow four to six hours to complete the trail. Although the trail covers easy terrain, it requires steady climbing. In winter, it is recommended for intermediate skiers. From various points along the trail, panoramic views of the frontal ranges and the broad **Shakwak Valley** can be enjoyed.

The **Sheep Mountain Trail** starts just beyond the Sheep Mountain Visitor Centre. From the centre, drive about two kilometres (one mile) down the access road to the gate. You can park there overnight, and a pit toilet is provided. On foot, follow the road 160 metres (176 yards) down, and turn right at the first fork. This mining road climbs Sheep Mountain gradually for eight kilometres (five miles). This path will not take you to the top. You can find your own way up, but it is a long, steep climb! This is the best place to see Dall sheep. Once you are up high, go across **Sheep Creek**—you'll see Sheep Bullion Plateau, known for its brilliant array of wild flowers, and numerous grizzlies.

---

*Because of uncertain weather, I was only able to hike the Auriol Range Trail, so I am indebted to Park Interpreter Allison Wood for these descriptions of trails to St. Elias Lake, Auriol Range, and Sheep Mountain.

Parks Canada

Silver City ghost town

The closest camping to the Sheep Mountain Trail is 9.5 kilometres (six miles) north of the Visitor Centre, on the Alaska Highway at Congdon Creek.

Human History

To appreciate the history of the Native peoples of the area, visit **Klukshu Village**, located outside the southern border of the park. A small gift shop, furnished with antique tools and equipment, sells a modest selection of Native handicrafts.

To get a sense of the gold-mining days, you can visit the ghost town of Silver City, a few minutes' drive along the southern edge of Kluane Lake. This village had a North West Mounted Police station and barracks, a roadhouse, and stables. Many of the buildings remain, though their roofs are caved in and the floors are not in much better shape.

PARK SERVICES AND FACILITIES

Interpretive Program

The summer interpretive program provides the day visitor or car camper with the best introduction to the park. Ask for a schedule from the centre, or check the bulletin board at the Kathleen Lake Campground or picnic area.

Camping

The park has one campground, at **Kathleen Lake**, about a 20-minute drive south of Haines Junction. It has 41 campsites in a lightly wooded area, with trembling aspen and a carpet of flowers between sites. The campground is open from mid-June to mid-September. There are toilets, but no washrooms. Water must be pumped; bring a container with a handle over the top. Picnic tables and fire grates stand at each site; firewood is provided. There is a small, outdoor campfire circle, where evening interpretive programs are often held. The maximum stay is 14 days.

Less than a kilometre from the campsite is the Kathleen Lake Day Use Area, and there is a trail from there, which goes quite a distance around the west side of the lake.

Other Camping

The Yukon Territory has a large network of campgrounds, and several sites are located along the highway, These sites are on the eastern side of the road, which is not parkland. Most of these campgrounds are directly on the shore of a lake or stream, and fishing is a popular pastime. They provide water, pit toilets, and picnic tables. One campground is located just east of Haines Junction, three others lie between there and the northern park boundary, and there is one other at Dezadeash Lake, a 15-minute drive south of Kathleen Lake.

Other Accommodation, Gas, Food, and Supplies

Haines Junction has a range of accommodation, from modest to deluxe. There is a wilderness resort at Dezadeash Lake and several bed and breakfast accommodation. Write to Tourism Yukon for a vacation guide.

Whitehorse is the largest centre for gas, food, and camping supplies. There is a reasonable choice of stores. Prices do not seem to be inflated, considering the transportation distances and short summers.

At Haines Junction, there are several gas stations and a well-stocked general store, with a post office and bank. There are several small café/restaurants at Haines Junction, and another near Kathleen Lake. Gas is available up and down the highway corridor.

Outfitters and Guides

The park has a symbiotic relationship with local back-country outfitters and guides. For some visitors, particularly those from other countries, or those with limited time or experience, hiring an outfitter or guiding service can be very useful. A wide variety of services are offered: hiking, travelling by pack horse, taking day trips, or much longer ones. Write Tourism Yukon for listings, then contact the outfitters directly.

RECREATIONAL SERVICES

Boating Motor boats are allowed on Kathleen Lake and Mush Lake. Because these lakes can suddenly become very rough, experience and caution are called for. Canoeing is not recommended. A number of commercial companies offer rafting trips down the Alsek River, which is a Canadian Heritage river.

Fishing Fishing is especially good at Kathleen Lake, and is reasonable in other lakes and streams. Ask for copies of National Park regulations, and buy the required permit at the Visitor Centres. Catch-and-release fishing is encouraged when possible.

Climbing and Mountaineering For overnight trips or trips of a few days in the back country of the greenbelt, you must register in and out with the park. For a trip into the Icefield Range, you must obtain a permit from the Warden Service of the park, at least three months in advance. The Warden Service must be informed as to the group's skill and experience level as well as its provision for supplies, air, and radio support. Each group member must also have a physician's certificate of health.

Winter Use The park offers seven cross-country and snowshoe trails, a snowmobiling area at Kathleen Lake, and an area for dogsledding. Icefishing and winter camping are also popular activities.

HOW TO GET THERE

It is not particularly difficult to get to Kluane, but the trip can be time-consuming and expensive. You can take the Alaska Highway, or the Alaska or British Columbia auto-ferry system from Seattle or Vancouver. Alternatively, a number of commercial tour buses leave from Prince Rupert, sometimes in conjunction with the ferries.

Related Activities or Places of Natural or Historic Interest

Tourism Yukon is an excellent information service for all kinds of visitation in the territory. Call (403) 667-5340.

Related Activities Cont'd

Activities and Places to Consider Visiting:

- Adjacent to Kluane, in British Columbia, is the Tatshenshini-Alsek Wilderness Provincial Park. This park protects one of the world's greatest river systems, in recognition of which it was declared a World Heritage Site in 1994.

- In Burwash Landing, there is the Kluane Museum of Natural History. As well as a wildlife display, it features Native artifacts and costumes.

National Historic Sites:

- Whitehorse: S.S. Klondike sternwheeler.

FURTHER READING

Kluane Park Hiking Guide, Vivien Lougheed (Repository Press, Prince George, 1992).

For More Information

Kluane National Park Reserve
P.O. Box 5495
Haines Junction, Yukon Territory
Y0B IL0
Phone: (403) 634-2251
Fax: (403) 634-2686
TTY: (403) 634-2133

Tourism Yukon
P.O. Box 2703
Whitehorse, Yukon Territory
Y1A 2C6
Phone: (403) 667-5340
Fax: (403) 667-2634

IVVAVIK[1]
National Park

I vvavik National Park is located at the northwestern boundary of the Yukon Territory, and represents the Northern Yukon Natural Region and the Mackenzie Delta Natural Region. This was the first national park to be established as a result of a comprehensive land-claim agreement. The plan gives full and explicit recognition to the rights of the Inuvialuit people in the use and management of the park's resources, on which they have traditionally depended.

Firth River near Muskeg Creek

---

[1]I was not able to visit the six northernmost (and new) parks. The information here is taken from parks publications and correspondence.

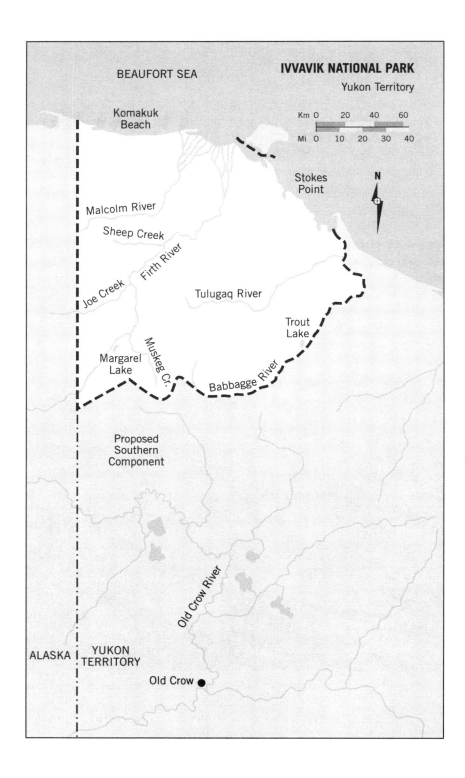

BEAUFORT SEA

IVVAVIK NATIONAL PARK
Yukon Territory

Komakuk
Beach

Km 0   20   40   60
Mi 0   10   20   30   40

Stokes
Point

N

Malcolm River

Sheep Creek

Firth River

Joe Creek

Tulugaq River

Trout
Lake

Margarel
Lake

Muskeg Cr.

Babbagge River

Proposed
Southern
Component

Old Crow River

ALASKA | YUKON
TERRITORY

Old Crow ●

W. Lynch, Parks Canada

The Porcupine caribou are protected by the park

Ivvavik is primarily treeless arctic tundra. The highest points in the park are located on the North Slope, along the western edge of the park, where the British Mountains rise to heights of 1650 metres. From there, the land levels out into a large coastal plain stretching to the Beaufort Sea. Three main rivers—the Firth, Babbage, and Malcom—wend their way across the plain.

Protection of the Porcupine caribou herd, at over 150 000 animals, was of central importance when the park was established. The Inuvialuit and other peoples of the North Slope region have relied on the herd for thousands of years. The Porcupine caribou use the large coastal plain during the summer for feeding and calving, before returning to the forested areas for winter. In fact, Ivvavik means "a place for giving birth—a nursery."

All three species of bear (grizzly, polar, and black) are found here, with grizzlies being the most common and widely distributed type. Other mammals include a small population of Dall's sheep, Arctic fox, and musk oxen. The coastal plain provides a staging, breeding, and migration area for millions of shore birds, geese, swans, and ducks. The park supports a wide variety of fish, with its salt, brackish, and freshwater habitats.

Archeological sites in the park are rich in western Arctic cultural history. Near Engigstciak, on the coastal plain, there is evidence of 5000 years of occupation by nine cultures.

HOW TO SEE THE PARK

The park is located about 800 kilometres (500 miles) northwest of Whitehorse and 200 kilometres (125 miles) west of Inuvik. Primary access is by chartered aircraft from Inuvik, but the trip must be approved by the park beforehand, and aircraft access is restricted to only a few locations in the park. There are no visitor facilities in the park, because it is exclusively a wilderness preserve. Visitors must be prepared to be both self-sufficient and self-reliant, because services and rescue capability are based in Inuvik. No-trace camping techniques must be used. Most visitation occurs through organized tours with outfitters. Whitewater rafting on the Firth is the primary activity, with some backpacking parties each year. There are no roads into the park; the nearest all-weather road ends in Inuvik. Hotels and campgrounds are available in Inuvik.

It is important to come prepared, especially if you are unescorted, because this rugged land has potential natural hazards at any time. Weather is very unpredictable, and temperatures can plunge below zero in any month. The waters are frigid year-round, and the biting insects are daunting. Make sure to write to the park in advance for a list of outfitters, and for other information about visiting the park.

Related Activities or Places of Natural or Historic Interest

The Western Arctic Tourism Association is an excellent information service for this area. Call (403) 979-4321, or write to Box 2600, Inuvik, NWT X0E 0T0

Activities and Places to Consider Visiting:

• Herschel Island/Qikiqtaruk Territorial Park

• Vuntut National Park

National Historic Sites:

• Bar-1 DEW Line Station near Kamakuk Beach

For More Information

Ivvavik National Park
Box 1840

Inuvik, Northwest Territories
X0E 0T0
Phone: (403) 979-3248
Fax: (403) 979-4491

NAHANNI
National Park Reserve

Rivers—raging or calm, flat and meandering or plunging through some of the deepest river canyons in the world—rivers and their mountain context are the basis of Nahanni National Park Reserve. The park is 4766 square kilometres (1840 square miles) in area, encompassing 300 kilometres (186 miles) of the 600-kilometre (373-mile)-long South Nahanni River. The park's setting is in the Mackenzie Mountains, which are situated in the southwestern corner of the Northwest Territories.

The spectacular scenery, distinctive geological history and landforms, rich history and cultural significance to the Dene of the Deh Cho region, wealth of wildlife, and unspoiled character of the South Nahanni/Flat River ecosystem have resulted in Nahanni being named one of the first choices of UNESCO for a World Heritage Site.

HOW TO SEE THE PARK*

Glaciation has played a major and varied role in shaping this park, as it has in the shaping of most of Canada. Glaciers had much to do with the origins of the central feature of the park, **Virginia Falls**—one of the most impressive falls in Canada, if not the world. The falls are over 92 metres (300 feet) high. They are about 200 metres (656 feet) wide, and are broken in the middle by a huge chunk of rock, which seems like a small mountain in itself.

Above the Virginia Falls, the river course is slow and meandering, with only a slight gradient. Below the falls, it begins a steep and winding descent.

---

*I was not able to visit Nahanni. For information on the park, I have relied on interviews with Lou Comin, chief warden of Nahanni for six years, and written material from Parks Canada, and from journals, etc. The writings of Derek Ford and George A. Brook were particularly useful.

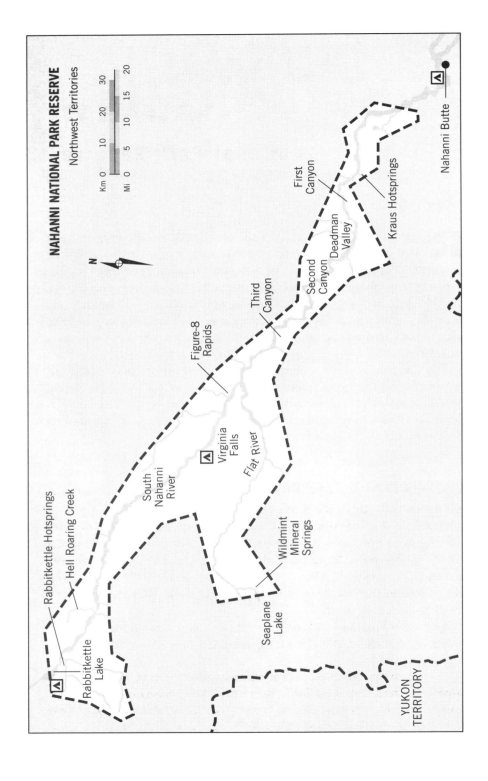

NAHANNI NATIONAL PARK RESERVE

Northwest Territories

Rabbitkettle Hotsprings

Hell Roaring Creek

Rabbitkettle Lake

South Nahanni River

Virginia Falls

Flat River

Wildmint Mineral Springs

Seaplane Lake

Figure-8 Rapids

Third Canyon

Second Canyon

First Canyon

Deadman Valley

Kraus Hotsprings

Nahanni Butte

YUKON TERRITORY

Now and then, the river straightens somewhat, as the rushing water finds an even weaker spot in the rock, and leaps from one curve of a meander to its far side, taking a shortcut and stranding a loop of riverbed. You can see an example of this at the extremely narrow section of the third canyon, called **The Gate**.

At the park's eastern edge, glaciation once again played a role. Here, the glaciers filled the final mountain gateway for the South Nahanni, at what is now called **Twisted Mountain**, and blocked the flow of river water from the west. Over thousands of years, the water built up and flooded backward, making lakes of whole valleys that once had only rivers at their lowest point. Deep gorges have been formed at the centres of the valleys, and forests grow well on the debris of old lakes. This is the story of the **Flat River**. Its rapids at high elevations, and its calm flow and wildlife-rich floodplains, where it meets the South Nahanni, are magnificent additions to the park's amazing diversity.

Although the South Nahanni and Flat Rivers and their immediate environs comprise the central elements of the park, two other places contribute greatly to the park's fascination. One is **Rabbitkettle Hot Springs**, located at the far western border of the park, and the other is the karstlands, which begin at the **First Canyon** and extend north for 50 kilometres (31 miles) in a narrow band from the canyon's north bank.

The 21°C (70°F) water of Rabbitkettle Hot Springs wells up through highly mineralized rock, some of which dissolves and is carried to the earth's surface. Here, the rapid cooling causes the minerals to separate from their watery medium and settle on the ground. This has resulted in a build-up of circular ponds, made up of *tufa*, a brightly coloured calcium carbonate. There are two of these water-soaked mounds. The more distinctly formed **North Mound** rises over the surrounding area about 27 metres (90 feet). Its overall height is achieved by a stairstepping of small, semi-circular terraces, up to circular kettles at the top. Because this area is so fragile, visitors can only reach the kettles when escorted by a warden. A warden is stationed at Rabbitkettle Lake from mid-June through mid-September.

The karstlands of the First Canyon have also formed by interaction between water and limestone rock. Underground streams create caves, sinkholes, and lakes.

Above ground, the action of rain, and of the freezing and thawing of surface water, cuts deep into the earth's crust, forming great citylike mazes of cliffs, ravines, pillars, towers, corridors, and occasional open spaces. The south end of the karst formation can be accessed via a hike

Parks Canada

A shorebird feeds at Rabbitkettle Hotsprings

along Lafferty Creek and canyon. The north karst is accessible by heli-
copter from Fort Simpson, and two lakes in the area (Death Lake and
Mosquito Lake) are accessible by float plane.

Visiting a Wilderness Park

The best time to visit the park is in July and August. The weather is usually more predictable, and the likelihood of snow is minimal. Nahanni is
a wilderness river park. River canoeing and rafting are the best ways to
traverse the park and to see the spectacular environment. A mandatory
reservation system has been implemented in order to evenly distribute visitor use. Only two non-guided departure units are allowed each day to a
maximum of 12 visitors. All visitors must make reservations at the Fort
Simpson park office and register there for back-country use permits before
entering the park. If departing from Fort Simpson, registration is done in
person; if entering the park from any other destination, registration can be
done by phone.

   Some people go down the South Nahanni with an outfitter, by canoe
or raft. Rafting is particularly recommended for those with little boating
experience, or who are limited in physical strength.

   Typically, an independent canoeing trip from Rabbitkettle Lake to
Nahanni Butte will take 10 days, but allow more time, if you can, for hiking and fishing. Two campgrounds are located along the river—one at
Rabbitkettle Lake and one at Virginia Falls. Camping is allowed everywhere else in the park and along the river corridor with the exception of

Virginia Falls

M. Beedell, Parks Canada

the park patrol cabins. The river above the falls is not particularly rough, but below the falls there are sections where the rapids are up to a Class III+ white-water rating, and they require real boating skill and experience. On the Flat River, the first 50 kilometres from the put-in point at Seaplane Lake are almost continuous white water, with a rating of up to Class IV/V.

PARK FACILITIES AND SERVICES

Interpretive Program

Because the park is a wilderness reserve, there is little formal interpretation. Tours to the Tufa Mounds are offered twice a day to any visitor who shows up at the Rabbitkettle Lake warden cabin at the designated departure times (08:30 and 13:30). The park administrative building is located in Fort Simpson, where you can pick up printed information when registering. Videos and interpretive displays can be viewed at the Fort Simpson Information Centre, De Cho tourist association of the Northwest Territories.

Camping

Two designated primitive campsites are located along the river, at Rabbitkettle Lake and Virginia Falls, and parties that stop nearby must use them. Otherwise, any location is fine; dry sandy beaches are recommended.

Other Accommodation, Gas, Food, and Supplies

Most visitors access the park via Fort Simpson, Blackstone, or Fort Liard. For accommodation in Fort Simpson, there is an inn, a motel, and a lodge. Fort Liard has accommodation for 11 and Blackstone for 14. Fort Simpson is now the headquarters for Nahanni National Park Reserve. In Fort Simpson, there are restaurants, stores, a gas station, and hospital. A campground in the community of Fort Simpson has 33 RV/tent sites.

HOW TO GET THERE

There is no direct car access to the park. The usual access is by air, unless you are a hardy adventurer who is willing to paddle in from other connecting rivers far to the west of the park. Air charter companies in Fort Simpson, Blackstone, Fort Liard, and Watson Lake provide air transportation into the Reserve. Charter companies require permits to land in the Reserve and can only land at Rabbitkettle Lake or Virginia Falls. All visitors must register in and out of the park. The only place to make reservations and to register in is at the Fort Simpson park office. De-registration is available at the Nahanni Butte warden station during the operational season, or by calling the Fort Simpson park office.

There is regularly scheduled air service into Fort Simpson from Yellowknife. It is also possible to reach Fort Simpson by road, year-round (barring sudden storms). The Mackenzie Highway, going north from Edmonton, Alberta, and the Liard Highway, which starts in British Columbia, are the two access roads. Many visitors to the north take a circular route, joining the two, for a popular summer trek.

For canoeists, the park destination will be upriver, outside the park at Moose Ponds, at the headwaters of the South Nahanni, or at Seaplane Lake (for the Flat River), or inside the park at Rabbitkettle Lake for the South Nahanni River. Most visitors finish their trips at Blackstone Landing, about a seven-hour paddle down the Liard River from Nahanni Butte. Paddlers should allow extra time as the winds can seriously hinder progress on this stretch of river. Road access at Blackstone Landing allows pick-up by prearranged transportation. Alternatively, both the Nahanni Butte store and the Nahanni Butte band run a boat taxi service between this community and Blackstone Territorial park.

Charter companies can carry canoes and all other equipment, but you must arrange this in advance. No power boats of any kind are allowed in the park.

A number of visitors canoe to the park, through the use of outfitter-guiding enterprises. For the names of current outfitters and operating charter flight companies, write to Visitor Information at the park or the Nahanni-Ram Tourism Association (see addresses below).

Related Activities or Places of Natural or Historic Interest

Northwest Territories Tourism Information is an excellent source of information for visitation in the territory. Call 1-800-661-0788.

Activities and Places to Consider Visiting:

- In terms of historic interest, the Fort Simpson Visitors Centre has displays on the life of the local Dene, crafts, and a reproduction of part of an old Hudson's Bay store.

- Fort Liard occupies a site that has been used by the Dene people for about 9000 years. The town is known for the beautiful birchbark baskets crafted by its residents.

- Blackstone Territorial Park on the Liard River has a campground, picnic area, and staffed interpretive/information centre.

For More Information

Nahanni National Park Reserve
P.O. Box 348
Fort Simpson, Northwest Territories
X0E 0N0
Phone: (403) 695-315
Fax: (403) 695-2446
TTY: (403) 695-3841

Nahanni-Ram Tourism Association
Box 177, Dept. VG
Fort Simpson, Northwest Territories
X0E 0N0
Phone: (403) 695-3182
Fax: (403) 695-2511

WOOD BUFFALO

National Park

W ood Buffalo is Canada's largest park. At 44 807 square kilometres (17 300 square miles), it covers an area larger than Switzerland. The park straddles the border between Alberta and the Northwest Territories, with two-thirds of the park on the Alberta side.

Wood Buffalo was established as a national park in 1922 to protect the remaining herds of wood bison in northern Canada. Between 1922 and 1926 the slightly smaller plains bison were brought into the park from southern Alberta and the two groups have since hybridized. Today, these wood/plains hybrids comprise the largest free-roaming bison herd in the world. Besides protecting the bison herd, Wood Buffalo encompasses the only natural nesting site of the whooping crane in the world. This magnificent and reclusive bird migrates yearly from its wintering grounds in the Texas wetlands, to lay its precious eggs in the interior of what is now not only a Canadian National Park, but also a UNESCO World Heritage Site. Although the park was initially created to preserve the bison and protect their habitat, over the past 70 years there has been a growing awareness of the importance of protecting the ecological integrity of the area. The park is an example of a massive tract of the northern boreal plains, which are threatened by logging, dam building, and activities associated with petroleum extraction and mining.

HOW TO SEE THE PARK

The landscape can be divided into four major units: the Caribou and Birch Uplands, the Alberta Plateau, the Slave River Lowlands, and the Peace-Athabasca Delta.

The **Caribou and Birch Uplands** comprise a very small portion of the park, and are virtually inaccessible to visitors. The uplands are sedimentary rocks of the Cretaceous age, and they have yielded fossils

R.D. Muir, Parks Canada

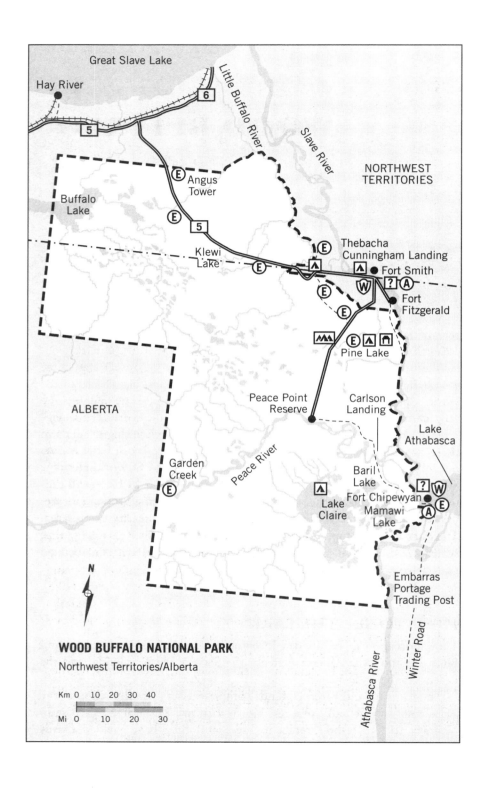

Great Slave Lake

Hay River

Little Buffalo River

Slave River

6

5

Buffalo
Lake

E Angus
Tower

E 5

NORTHWEST
TERRITORIES

Klewi
Lake

E

E

Thebacha
Cunningham Landing

E

A

A ● Fort Smith

W

? A

E

Fort
Fitzgerald

E

ALBERTA

Peace Point
Reserve

E A 🏠
Pine Lake

Carlson
Landing

Lake
Athabasca

Garden
Creek

E

Peace River

Baril
Lake

? W

Fort Chipewyan ●

A

E

A
Lake
Claire

Mamawi
Lake

N

Embarras
Portage
Trading Post

WOOD BUFFALO NATIONAL PARK

Northwest Territories/Alberta

Athabasca River

Winter Road

Km 0   10   20   30   40

Mi 0   10   20   30

R.D. Muir, Parks Canada

The endangered whooping crane breeds here, far from visitor access, though a few visitors glimpse them from their nesting sites

including, in localized areas, great densities of fish scales, which are of great paleontological interest.

The **Alberta Plateau** covers most of the park. It is land with huge rivers, great swathes of muskeg, and countless bogs, swamps, and meandering streams. One of its most distinctive features is the **karstlands**. Karst occurs where groundwater dissolves pockets of soft bedrock—in this case the bedrock is gypsum—creating caves and sinkholes. "Collapse" sinkholes are formed by underground water gradually carving out a cave below the surface. Park visitors can see an example of a large collapse sinkhole at Angus Tower, located just off Highway 5. "Solution sinkholes" are caused by surface water pooling and then draining into cracks and dissolving the soft bedrock. Most individual solution sinkholes are quite shallow but some of the largest sinkholes in the park are solution sinkholes. For example, the **Rainbow Lakes** are stream-fed solution sinkholes and **Pine Lake**, the main recreation area in the park, was formed when two sinkholes merged. Visitors can see examples of both solution and collapse sinkholes on the **Karstland Trail** at the Salt River day-use area.

The **Slave River Lowlands** occupy two narrow strips of the park, along its eastern border. The lowlands mark the end of the boreal plains, for they abut the granite-based hills of the Canadian Shield. As well as the underground rivers that create karstland, other rivers seep out to the surface at the base of a low escarpment. The underground water passes through a layer of salt, deep beneath the surface and, when it reaches the surface, it deposits the salt, sometimes as a sheet, which glistens in the sun or in mounds almost two metres (six feet) high and six to nine metres (20 to 30 feet) long. This action has created the Salt Plains area, with its distinctive landscape and plant life.

The park's rivers are responsible for the formation of the fourth sub-area of the park—the **Peace-Athabasca Delta**—one of the largest inland freshwater deltas in the world. The Delta is located in the southeast corner of the park, where the **Peace, Athabasca, Slave,** and **Birch Rivers** flow toward the **Great Slave Lake.** The rivers carry enormous loads of silt, which they drop in the Delta each year. This annual renewal is very important for maintaining the richness of the environment. In spring and fall, waterfowl by the millions converge on the Delta; some come to nest, others are on their way to and from their nesting grounds.

All of this life depends on a delicate ecological balance. The construction of the Bennett Dam, on the Peace River in British Columbia, has dramatically altered the seasonal run-off that had set the rhythms of plant and animal life. The area no longer has dramatic periodic flooding, as it used to, and is slowly drying out. Much of the wildlife is losing its habitat; the richness of life has definitely decreased.

Visiting a Wilderness Park

The main visitation of the park's special features is through back-country hiking and canoeing. Because mosquitoes can be a trial, the best times to

B. Lewis, Parks Canada

The Peace-Athabasca Delta. Will dams further erode the richness that remains?

visit are in May and June, and in late August to early October. You may choose to participate in some of the guided hikes, such as the "bison creeps," conducted by park client services to get a close look at the imposing beasts, or to take a trip to the salt deposits. Or you may choose to hire a licensed guide to accompany you on your travels. Please note that you must register if you will be staying overnight in the back country.

Fort Smith

Fort Smith is located on the Slave River, and is actually about 20 kilometres (12 miles) outside the park. It is the park's administration centre. Upon arriving at Fort Smith, you should speak with the staff at the Visitor Reception Centre about where to go, and inquire about road conditions.

Just 25 kilometres west of Fort Smith is the beginning of the Salt Plains. One of the best ways to see this area is from the **Salt Plains Overview**. The Overview is most easily accessed from Highway 5. The Salt Plains are one of the few places where you may see the whooping cranes, because they feed here now and then, far from their breeding grounds in the far north of the park. You might also see white pelicans and sandhill cranes here, as well as large mammals such as bison, moose, bears, and wolves, which are attracted by the salt mounds.

The Salt River day-use area, located between Fort Smith and Pine Lake, offers two short walks, and two longer hiking trails. The two short walks are **Karstland** (0.7 kilometre, and wheelchair accessible) and **Salt Meadow** (1.3 kilometres). Both trails provide a very good sense of this distinctive area—a typical karst topography, with sinkholes and crevasses etched in the limestone soil. The Karstland Interpretive Trail has one of the most striking sights you could hope to see. It has a hibernaculum of the red-sided garter snake. In late April, dozens of these snakes come out of a sinkhole at one time. They form "mating balls," as they carry out this essential springtime rite, and then separate and go to the nearby marsh, to eat frogs all summer.

Both hikes are part of the **Salt River Loop Trail** system. The terrain varies, with the trail winding in and around sinkholes (some of which have long ago filled with bush and trees), climbing the Salt River Escarpment and crossing salty streams. The north loop is 7.5 kilometres (4.5 miles) long and passes by Salt Pan Lake. The south loop is nine kilometres (5.5 miles) in length and takes hikers by Grosbeak Lake.

The **Rainbow Lakes Trail** can be accessed by either the Pine Lake Road or, during the summer season, by Parson's Lake Road, a wilderness drive that is only passable when dry. This 13-kilometre (eight-mile) trail provides excellent views of sinkholes (the Lakes themselves are solution sinkholes) and bison wallows.

Fort Smith offers the most direct access to **Pine Lake**, located 65 kilometres (40 miles) south, the only road-accessible campground in the park. The campground has 36 sites (two of which are wheelchair accessible), with fire pits and picnic tables. Firewood is available, and a playground, water, and pit toilets are also provided. The Pine Lake day-use area has a cook shelter, picnic tables, change rooms, pit toilets, a beach and recreation area, and a boat launch. The **Lakeside Trail** follows the shore of Pine Lake from the day-use area to Kettle Point on the opposite side. A group campground is located at Kettle Point, as well as a day-use shelter.

The final trail in the Salt Plains area is the **Lane Lake Trail**, which can be accessed either by the Lakeside Trail or from the parking lot three kilometres (two miles) down Kettle Point Road, south of the Pine Lake turn-off. This 13-kilometre (eight-mile) return will take you past three smaller lakes and several ponds, providing sights of beaver dams and sinkholes, before arriving at Lane Lake itself.

Fort Chipewyan

One of the best ways to visit the park from Fort Chip is with a park-licensed guide. Services include specialized boating and sightseeing trips.

A popular back-country destination near Fort Chip is **Sweetgrass Station**, a cluster of old cabins and remnant corrals built in the mid-1960s during the round-up of the bison herds for anthrax vaccinations. Sweetgrass is located west of Fort Chip near the shores of Lake Claire. A visitor cabin there has bunks for six as well as a wood-burning cookstove. Water in nearby Sweetgrass Creek (800 metres from the cabin) is *not* potable. A bug jacket and repellant spray are necessary if you are visiting in June or July. The best way to get there is by motor boat from Fort Chip to Sweetgrass Landing on the Peace River (this journey will take two hours). Then it is a 12-kilometre (7.5 mile) hike through a boreal forest to the open meadows of Sweetgrass (this part of the trip will take three hours). The meadows are an excellent place for seeing bison and wolves. The shores and marshlands of Lake Claire are also an excellent location for viewing waterfowl.

PARK FACILITIES AND SERVICES

Interpretive Program

The park offers a variety of events during the summer seasons. A maximum of 8000 visitors come to the park each year, so the staff can adapt

their programs to visitor interest. The only event that interrupts programming, or curtails full use of the park in summer, is fire.

Camping

There is a 36-site campground at **Pine Lake**, with water, chemical toilets,
fire grates, and firewood. Back-country camping is allowed throughout
the park, except in special protection zones. Back-country registration
permits are required. A wilderness campground is located at Rainbow
Lakes. There is a pit privy, an anti-bear food cache, fire grates, and water
from the lake. It is entirely a pack-in/pack-out situation.

Group Camping

Kettle Point Group Camp, located on the shores of Pine Lake, offers a log
shelter and tenting area, fire circle, firewood, picnic tables, outhouses,
and playground. The camp is wheelchair accessible. Reservations are
required and groups must have at least eight people.

Other Accommodation, Gas, Food, and Supplies

Fort Smith offers the Queen Elizabeth campground, a 45-room motel, and
a small hotel. At Fort Chip there is the 10-room Fort Chipewyan Lodge.

Gas and other supplies are available at Fort Smith and Fort Chip,
although no auto propane is available in Fort Chip. Prices are generally
higher than in southern Canada, because of transportation costs.
Camping equipment, cross-country skis, boating equipment, and raingear
can be rented in Fort Smith.

Recreational Services

Hiking   Three types of hiking are offered in the park. The first is day hiking on the park's short trails, to specific points of interest, such as Pine Lake
to Lane Lake. No permit is required for day hikes. The second type is
overnight hiking. For overnight hikes in the back country, such as Rainbow
Lakes, a back-country permit is required. If you are going out on your own,
make sure to familiarize yourself with the area prior to departure, take
along extra food and clothing, and carry a map and compass. The park does
not sell topographical maps. Do not follow bison trails unless you are confident that you know where you are going and how to get back. The third
option is to go on a guided hike with a licensed park guide or outfitter.

Winter Use   The park may be used in the winter; however, currently no
guides or outfitters are licensed for winter use and few people are suffi-

ciently skilled and well equipped to go into the park on their own. Snowshoeing and cross-country skiing are permitted, but recreational snowmobiling is not allowed.

Boating Boating is a popular activity in the park. Canoes, for use in lakes and deeper streams, can be rented at Fort Smith. Outfitters also provide canoe tours. Motor boats are allowed on the major rivers—the Slave, Peace, and Athabasca. Rafting is increasingly popular with tour groups in Fort Smith. There are five rapids along the Slave River, between Fort Smith and Fort Fitzgerald, though this area is not actually in the park. These rapids are not suitable for canoes, and fatal canoeing accidents have occurred here.

Fishing Fishing is not particularly good in most park waters due to the silt load. Pine Lake is stocked with rainbow trout, but they are very difficult to catch; the other lakes and rivers yield pike, pickerel, whitefish, and suckers. A National Park fishing permit is required and can be obtained at either Visitor Reception Centre.

Flightseeing Getting an overview of the park from a small airplane is becoming increasingly popular. Flights are available in Fort Smith, both in the winter and summer, and in Fort Chip in the summer only.

HOW TO GET THERE

The easiest way to reach the Wood Buffalo area is by air. Flights leave Edmonton for Fort Smith six days a week. Flights come into Fort Chipewyan from Fort McMurray (with good connections from Edmonton) six days a week, two flights each day, with reduced service in winter. Check with your travel agent for details. You can rent a car in Fort Smith. Some summer visitors drive to Fort Smith; it takes two long days' driving from Edmonton, sometimes on packed-dirt roads. In winter, from mid-December to mid-March, ice bridges and a winter road are constructed, connecting Fort Chip with Fort McMurray and Fort Smith. The roads are long, with no services in between, and motorists are advised to carry survival equipment in case of vehicle breakdown.

Related Activities or Places of Natural or Historic Interest

Northwest Territories Tourism Information (1-800-661-0788) or Alberta Tourism (1-800-661-8888) can provide information on other sites in the area.

Related Activities Cont'd

Activities and Places to Consider Visiting:

- In the Northwest Territories, nearby parks include Little Buffalo River Falls Park and Queen Elizabeth Park. In Alberta, near Fort Chipewyan, is the Dore Lake Recreation Area.

- For historic interest, in Fort Chipewyan there is the Bicentennial Museum and in Fort Smith, the Fort Smith Mission Historic Park and Northern Life Museum.

National Historic Sites:

- Fort Chipewyan: Monument Hill National Historic Site (site of the original Hudson's Bay Company fort)

For More Information

Please note that, since this is a wilderness park, it is particularly important to write or phone ahead, to see whether the park will meet your interests and experience. Also, facilities and services, particularly commercial ones, are subject to sudden change, and planning ahead is essential to a fulfilling trip.

Operations Manager
Wood Buffalo National Park
Box 750
Fort Smith, Northwest Territories
X0E 0P0
Phone: (403) 872-2349
Fax: (403) 872-3910
TTY: 872-3727

Area Manager
Wood Buffalo National Park
Box 38
Fort Chipewyan, Alberta
T0P 1B0
Phone: (403) 697-3662
Fax: (403) 697-3560

PRINCE ALBERT
National Park

Endless plains, wind-blown snow, or grain waving in the blistering August sun—that's Saskatchewan's image. The map shows Prince Albert National Park located close to the geographical centre of the province, so that's what the visitor expects to see. On arrival, however, there's not a plain in sight.

The park is a protected area of 3875 square kilometres (1496 square miles) of parkland and boreal forest. In the parkland, segments of grassland are mixed with many stands of aspen forest. There are a few sections of fescue and other grasslands where a herd of plains bison roams freely. The boreal forest is damp, pocked by bogs and dominated by evergreen trees, particularly the moisture-loving black spruce and tamarack.

Prince Albert National Park is a transition zone, from more southern aspen parkland to the edge of the boreal forest that covers so much of northern Canada. Transition zones are always rich in plant and animal life because, in one relatively limited area, the life forms of two different environments succeed side by side.

Prince Albert was established in 1927, as a public recreation area and to preserve its rich natural history. However, it has also had a distinctive human history. The park's most famous resident was Grey Owl—the Englishman, Archie Delaney—who lived here from 1931 until his death in 1938. He became a park naturalist, using Prince Albert as a home base for his vigorous campaigns to conserve animal life, particularly the beaver. His cabin still survives, and the many beaver throughout the park are a tribute to his work.

The park is a vertical oblong, looking rather like a miniature version of Saskatchewan itself. The transition from parkland to boreal forest occurs roughly along an east-west line, halfway up the length of the park, with Waskesiu Lake marking the change. Waskesiu townsite is the focal point for services and facilities available for park visitors. Some include the car campgrounds, a number of recreational facilities, the park's interpretive

143

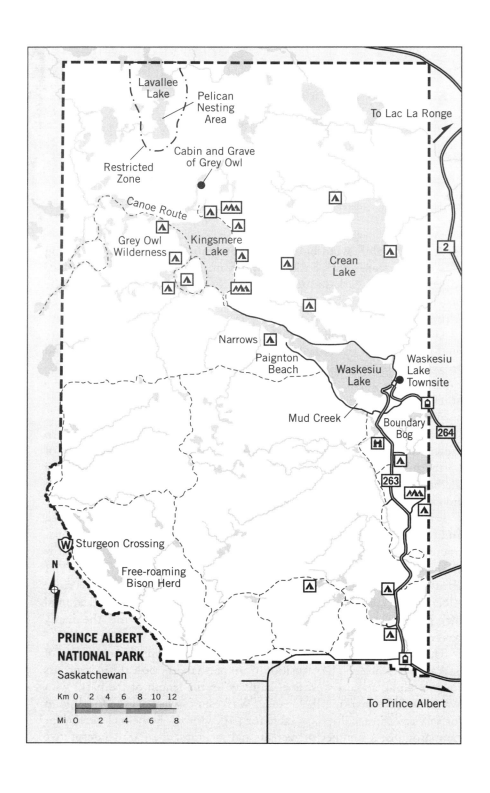

Lavallee
Lake

Pelican
Nesting
Area

To Lac La Ronge

Cabin and Grave
of Grey Owl

Restricted
Zone

Canoe Route

Grey Owl
Wilderness

Kingsmere
Lake

Crean
Lake

2

Narrows

Paignton
Beach

Waskesiu
Lake

Waskesiu
Lake
Townsite

Mud Creek

Boundary
Bog

264

263

Sturgeon Crossing

N

Free-roaming
Bison Herd

To Prince Albert

**PRINCE ALBERT
NATIONAL PARK**

Saskatchewan

Km 0   2   4   6   8 10 12

Mi   0   2   4   6   8

and information centres and administrative headquarters, and the shops, cabins, and other services of a small townsite.

HOW TO SEE THE PARK

There are outdoor theatre programs at the Beaver Glen campground, guided walks, self-guided trails, and informative roadside stops. There is also a special interpretive feature at Prince Albert, which has been designed to give car-based visitors the most exposure, in the easiest manner, to the diversity of the park environment. This is the self-guiding auto tour.

A special publication, *Driving to the Narrows*, is sold at the Friends of the Park bookstore. This brochure guides the visitor by car from the townsite, along the south shore of **Waskesiu Lake**, to the **Narrows** day-use area. The suggestions contained in the brochure will make this two- to four-hour excursion the highlight of your visit.

THE LAND FORMS

Prince Albert National Park owes its soil type, its myriad lakes and streams, and flatness to two factors. One is that the bedrock has never been pushed, squeezed, or broken by the great internal pressure of the earth's crust that formed mountains near the edges of the continent. The other, more recent, cause is glaciation. The entire area was under as much as 1600 metres (one mile) of glacial ice during the three main periods of ice advance, the last of which retreated about 10 000 years ago. Advancing glaciers dug out the beds of some of the major lakes, such as **Waskesiu, Crean,** and **Kingsmere.**

If you drive along Highway 263, a little farther south than Shady Lake, you will reach the **Height-of-Land Tower.** You can see several lakes, and King Island, in Waskesiu Lake.

The cutting action of the glacial melt water is easy to see from the **Spruce River Highlands Tower,** situated just north of the Spruce River, about 12 kilometres (seven miles) north of the park's southern entrance. The trail to the lookout is a 10- or 15-minute walk on good gravel, and a few places along the way have benches and attractive interpretive signs. Keep to the right of the fork at the beginning of the trail. The river meanders in what was once a very wide channel, carved out by the glaciers.

Land shaping did not stop with the end of the glacial periods, of course. Ice continues to play a role, when it builds up in large lakes and then begins to break up in the spring. Blocks of ice are pushed by strong winds up on to land. The front edges of ice hit the shallow bottom of the lake, close to shore, and actually push some of the lake bed up out of the water, forming a low ridge. Plants often colonize the new surface and stabilize it, making it less vulnerable to wind and water. In this way, a small new land form is created. The place to see this is the **Ice Push Ridge** display area, located about halfway along the road to the Narrows day-use area.

The Transition Zone: Aspen Parkland to Boreal Forest

If you can distinguish trembling aspen, with its straight, white trunk and twinkling, triangular leaves, from the Christmas-tree look of a conifer, the drive along Highway 263 from the southern entrance of the park, northwards 41 kilometres (26 miles) to Waskesiu Lake, affords an excellent overview of the change from the southern aspen parkland to the boreal forest.

If you choose to go at your own speed, two trails are particularly good for experiencing the transition. An attractive brochure maps the self-guiding two-kilometre (one-mile) trail to **Mud Creek,** and tells you about 13 points of interest along the way. The walk is extremely pleasant, moving from the aspen woodlands over to a damp area, where the creek flows into the lake. There are several beautiful viewpoints of Waskesiu Lake, and of the areas where the beaver are busy.

At this point the trail gains some height—just enough, in fact, to provide an overview of the melt-water valley in which Mud Creek meanders slowly toward the lake.

Kingfisher Trail, also situated along the south shore of Waskesiu, is the other trail to take if you choose to explore on your own. It is about 17 kilometres (10.5 miles) long, and will take about four and a half hours to complete at a fairly steady pace. Bird-watching is very good from this trail.

One area of particular interest on this walk is a clearing that opens out very near the shore. There is a natural animal lick, a large patch of open, grey, sticky mud, which you pass on the wooden boardwalk. When I was there, it was completely covered with the hoof-prints of animals—probably moose and elk.

The Boreal Forest

The boreal forest flourishes in Prince Albert National Park, because the park area has more rainfall than the surrounding prairies, and has a lower average temperature, with less evaporation. The northern half of the park has particularly moist conditions, with many more lakes, ponds, and streams than the southern part. Bogs form in any area that has poor drainage, but the most common place for them is the boreal forest, which grows in areas where glaciers scooped out millions of bowls that collect water that cannot drain.

The park has another self-guiding trail, **Boundary Bog**, which takes you through the surrounding spruce forest, by a glacial kettle, past a wolf rendezvous site, to a bog where you'll learn a lot about the geological history, and plant and animal life here. This is one of the best-designed self-guiding walks I have ever been on.

Human History

Grey Owl's Cabin, on **Ajawaan Lake,** exists today, and the beaver lodge that once reached into its interior is still there. Car-based visitors cannot

Parks Canada

Grey Owl beside his favourite tree—the Jack Pine

reach the cabin; it is a 19.5-kilometre (12-mile) hike, one way. The walk is an easy one, along the shore of **Kingsmere Lake**, and campsites are situated along the way. Of course, you can canoe or boat across Kingsmere, and walk the last three kilometres to visit the cabin.

Special Preservation in the Park

The park preserves three important types of life. One is the breeding colony of the rare white pelican, located at the northwestern edge of the park. The only people who visit are those involved in monitoring the pelicans' status. But keep your eyes open, when you canoe or walk by any lake in the park, and you may see a flock dipping their bills in unison, as they herd fish and scoop them up. The park also preserves an area of true prairie—the fescue grasslands. These grasslands occur in the southern portion of the park, and are most concentrated more in the southwestern corner. Finally the park protects a herd of free-roaming plains bison in the park's southwestern corner.

Other mammals thriving in the park are wolves, bear, moose, fox, otter, and fisher. Do not expect to see many of these animals, however, since they are so wild.

Parks Canada

Visitors and residents can view each other on quiet evening walks

PARK SERVICES AND FACILITIES

Interpretive Program

In the summer, there are guided walks along short, but interesting, trails; outdoor theatre programs are given in the Beaver Glen Campground and special events are offered, such as wolf howls or star gazing. Special family programs are also provided. The park offers an annual Waskesiu Children's Festival. The park newsletter, *Wolf Country*, provides interesting short articles on the park's natural or cultural history. A monthly Park Activity Schedule is published in July and August.

Camping

The park provides several campgrounds, which offer visitors a full range of options, from fully serviced sites to wilderness camping.

The largest and most developed campgrounds are Beaver Glen and the Trailer Park. **Beaver Glen** is a short drive from the townsite, and about a 10-minute walk from the main beach. It offers 213 sites (76 electrical, 137 non-electrical), located in a densely wooded area. It has kitchen shelters, with wood stoves and wood supplies. There are washrooms, with showers, and also separate water faucets, although I found that they were located quite a distance from each other and served an unusually large number of sites per facility. Fire hibachis and picnic tables are provided at each site, and firewood is available at several enclosures. Although there are no hook-ups for trailers, a waste-disposal station is provided for them. The **Trailer Park** has 152 pull-through sites available, all with water, power, and sewer hookups. Spaces are available in a variety of settings, ranging from open lawn to very treed and private. The campground seems to fill very quickly.

Narrows Campground is about a 30-minute drive from the townsite, on the south shore of Waskesiu Lake. It is a much more natural setting than Beaver Glen. Some sites are located very close to the shoreline. It is lightly wooded, with the campsites located fairly close to each other. There are flush toilets, with cold running water there, and faucets around the campsites. Fire grates, picnic tables, and firewood are available. The Narrows marina is nearby, with canoe and boat rentals, a lawned picnic area, and lots of shoreline fishing.

Namekus is a car-accessible campsite, located just east of Highway 263, 10 kilometres (six miles) south of Waskesiu. Twenty-one campsites are situated along the lakeshore, six of which are walk-in sites. Drinking water comes from the lake. There are pit toilets, fire hibachis, picnic tables, and firewood. **Sandy Lake Campground**, situated on the west side of Highway 263, six kilometres (four miles) north of the South Gate entrance, has 31 sites, six of which are walk-in sites, about 150 to 300 metres from the parking area. All have picnic tables, fire hibachis and firewood, pit toilets, lake water, and camp kitchens.

Trapper's Lake Campground, east of Highway 263 and just south of Namekus, offers five primitive sites, with firewood, fire grates, pit toilets, and picnic tables. A number of primitive sites are accessible by hiking and motorboat travel. The most easily reached sites are at the south end of **Kingsmere Lake**, only a 30-minute walk from the nearest parking lot. The other marked sites are along the back-country canoe and hiking routes. Most have pit toilets, firewood, fire grates, and bear-resistant food-cache platforms. All are located on lakeshores. Users must register with the park information office, and pack out all garbage.

Group Camping

Vehicle-accessible group camping is available near the **Trapper's Lake** camping area. Groups must reserve in advance, by writing to the park. Two group camping opportunities that are non-vehicle accessible are offered on Kingsmere Lake: **Westwind** (three kilometres up the east side along the hiking trail) and **Northend** (17 kilometres along the trail). Both areas are very popular for hiking or canoeing groups heading to Grey Owl's cabin.

Other Accommodation, Gas, Food, and Supplies

Waskesiu has a full range of motel, hotel, and cabin accommodation.

There are restaurants, a laundromat, gift shops, gas station, post office, accommodations, grocery stores, and movie theatre. There is no bank or automated teller in the park. Prince Albert is located only 100 kilometres (56 miles) away, and caters to a full range of shopping needs.

Recreational Services

Facilities for People with Disabilities   Waskesiu River Trail is a short, scenic trail, beside the Waskesiu River, designed for wheelchair use. Ask staff for exact directions. Also, the park rents one "all-terrain wheelchair."

Hiking   Along with the trails used for interpretation, or for walking along Waskesiu Lake, there are many kilometres of back-country hiking, particularly in the southwestern section of the park. Check with the staff for the conditions of the trails. Three trails have self-guided brochures to accompany them: Boundary Bog, Mud Creek, and Treebeard.

Canoeing This is a very good park for short or long canoe trips. Canoes can be rented at the Hanging Heart Lakes and Narrows marinas, and at the Main Marina.

There are canoe routes going from Kingsmere Lake to several loops through small lakes and over portages, and in Crean and Hanging Heart Lakes. Canoeing is also allowed in Namekus, Trapper's, Shady, and Sandy Lakes.

Boating Motor boats, with a maximum of 40 horsepower, are allowed on Kingsmere; there are no restrictions on Waskesiu, Hanging Heart, Sandy or Crean Lakes. At each of the three marinas, you can rent 20- and 25-horsepower motor boats. You can take tours from the main beach area on a paddle-wheel launch.

Swimming In the summer months, there is swimming at all day-use areas on Waskesiu Lake. Swimming is allowed in all lakes, except Lavallee.

Golf There is an 18-hole golf course in the townsite, with a pro shop, equipment rental, and restaurant. Another 18-hole course is located just outside the park's east gate.

Bicycling Bicycles can be rented at a local business. Watch for signs.

Fishing A national parks licence is required to fish within the park. Inquire from the staff at the Information Office as to limits, open lakes, and so on.

Winter Use The park has a very active winter season. Camping is possible in several sites, where winterized kitchen shelters and toilets are provided. There are snowshoe trails, and over 150 kilometres (90 miles) of cross-country skiing trails. Skiers must register in and out, on back-country overnight treks. Write to the Information Office or Client Services for the winter-use brochure, or call for up-to-date information, at (306) 663-5322. There are commercial accommodations and a restaurant in the townsite.

Related Activities or Places of Natural or Historic Interest

Tourism Saskatchewan is an excellent information service for all kinds of visitation in the province. Call 1-800-667-7191.

Activities and Places to Consider Visiting:
- Nearby provincial parks include Candle Lake, Clarence-Steepbank Lakes, and Narrow Hills.

Related Activities Cont'd

- The city of Prince Albert provides several sites of historic interest, including Diefenbaker House and the Buckland Heritage Museum.

National Historic Sites:

- Battleford: Fort Battleford

- Batoche: Batoche National Historic Site

For More Information

Client Services
Prince Albert National Park
Box 100
Waskesiu Lake, Saskatchewan
S0J 2Y0
Phone: (306) 633-5322
Toll-free phone: 1-888-333-7267 for Beaver Glen and Trailer Park campground reservations (beginning of April to the end of August)
Fax: (306) 663-5424
TTY: (306) 663-5384

Waskesiu Chamber of Commerce
Box 216
Waskesiu, Saskatchewan
S0J 2Y0
Phone: (306) 653-7510 (winter)
        (306) 663-5410 (summer)

GRASSLANDS
National Park

S ince the mid-nineteenth century, almost all of Canada's prairies have been drastically altered—Euro-Canadian settlement and accompanying farming, cattle-raising, and wholesale slaughter of large mammals, such as the bison and antelope, have permanently changed them.

However, a pocket of mixed-grass prairie in southwestern Saskatchewan has been left relatively undisturbed, and two sections of land located near Val Marie and Killdeer on the Saskatchewan/United States border have been designated Grasslands National Park.

Unlike most of the other national parks, which were established as complete park areas, Grasslands is being assembled gradually as land becomes available for purchase. Although the initial agreement to establish the park was signed by Canada and Saskatchewan in 1981, and the first two blocks of land were purchased (totalling 140 square kilometres), it was not until 1988 that the two governments reached a workable agreement resolving the issues of management of water and mineral resources.

The grasslands are the home of these burrow-dwelling prairie dogs

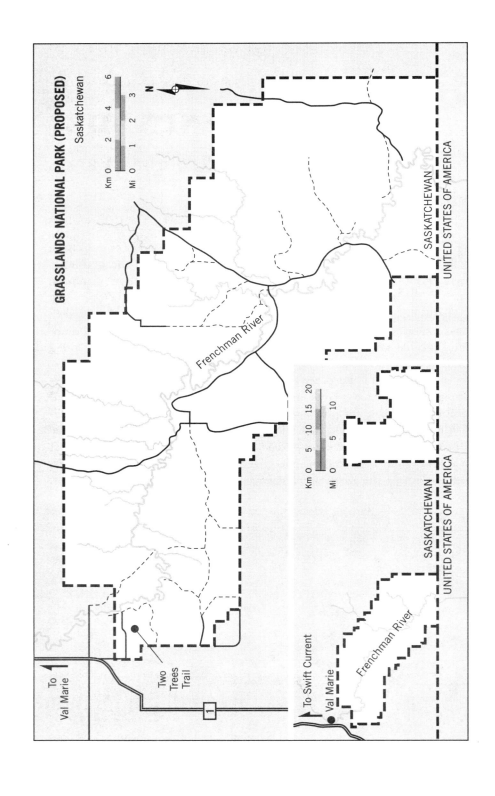

GRASSLANDS NATIONAL PARK (PROPOSED)

Saskatchewan

Km 0   2   4   6
Mi 0   1   2   3

N

Two Trees Trail

Frenchman River

To Val Marie

Km 0   5   10   15   20
Mi 0   5   10

SASKATCHEWAN
UNITED STATES OF AMERICA

To Swift Current

Val Marie

Frenchman River

SASKATCHEWAN
UNITED STATES OF AMERICA

This agreement identifies two blocks of land totalling approximately 900 square kilometres (350 square miles), which may eventually constitute Grasslands National Park. Because the purchase of land is on a voluntary basis (no land will be expropriated), it will be years before the park's final boundaries are set and visitor facilities and services are fully established.

HOW TO SEE THE PARK

The Park Information Centre is located in Val Marie. The Centre offers some displays and videos, which tell about the park's natural and human history. Several brochures and maps are also available.

The West Block

The dominant feature of the West Block is the Frenchman River Valley. Ten thousand years ago the valley was carved out by a glacial stream, and the resulting large runoff created coulees, buttes, and creeks. The highest point of land in the area is 70-Mile Butte in the far west of the park, rising 100 metres above the valley floor. The West Block is accessible by one main dry-weather road and several secondary dry-weather roads. Visitors can explore the West Block on their own by using the self-guided Frenchman River Valley Ecotour brochure or by using the self-guided audio cassette tour. The 1.5-kilometre (one-mile) Two Trees Interpretive Trail is the only designated hiking trail, although visitors may choose to explore the park on their own by hiking the valley and coulees.

W. Lynch, Parks Canada

West Block of Grasslands National Park

The East Block

The park's East Block encompasses diverse natural features including deep wooded coulees in the north, extensive grasslands of the open prairie to the south, and the Killdeer Badlands in the east. The Badlands were unglaciated and centuries of erosion have produced a dramatic landscape. Access to the East Block is limited, with only a small portion accessible in dry weather. It is recommended that you start a visit to the East Block at the Rodeo Ranch Museum in Wood Mountain Regional Park. Check with park staff before starting out.

Natural History

Canada's twenty-ninth national park preserves a rich and complex ecosystem. The park supports an incredible diversity of plant and animal forms, although many species are rare or endangered.

As the park's name suggests, the main plant forms are grasses—over 40 different varieties are found in the park. In the valley floors and coulees where there is more moisture, trees and shrubs such as aspen and buffalo berry flourish, while drier areas support sage and cacti. Lichens and mosses thrive and can survive for long periods with little moisture. Wildflowers provide for a succession of colour.

Birdlife is plentiful. Commonly seen species include horned larks, Sprague's pipits, lark buntings, and black-billed magpies. Several rare species are found in the park, including long-billed curlews, and great grey and short-eared owls. Endangered or threatened species still found in the park include the peregrine falcon and ferruginous hawk.

Commonly seen mammals include the pronghorn antelope, mule deer, and white-tailed deer. The Frenchman River Valley is the only place in Canada where you can still see the black-tailed prairie dog in its natural habitat.

Reptiles and amphibians found here include painted turtle, the eastern short-horned lizard, and the prairie rattlesnake.

Human History

Aboriginal habitation dates back 10 000 years. In the 1600s, this area was the hunting ground for the Gros Ventre and more recently the Assiniboine, Blackfoot, and Cree Peoples. Evidence of campsites, tipi rings, vision quest sites, medicine wheels, and bison drive lanes are found in the buttes.

PARK SERVICES AND FACILITIES

Because park management is focused on its priorities of the acquisition of new parklands and resource management to restore newly acquired lands to a more natural state, visitor services and facilities are still very basic.

Interpretive Program

Check at the Information Centre for schedules of events, celebrations, and heritage presentations. Sunday hikes led by an interpreter occur during July and August.

Primitive Camping

Only no-trace primitive camping, one kilometre off roads and away from old ranch yards is allowed. Campers must register at the Information Centre or the Rodeo Ranch Museum. Open fires are not allowed.

Other Accommodation, Gas, Food, and Supplies

Fuel, food, and retail services are available in the local villages of Val Marie, Mankota, Glentworth, and Wood Mountain. Mankota supports a motel and a campground is located in Val Marie.

Related Activities or Places of Natural or Historic Interest

Tourism Saskatchewan is an excellent information service for all kinds of visitation in the province. Call 1-800-667-7191.

Activities and Places to Consider Visiting:

- Wood Mountain Post Provincial Historic Park, located east of Grasslands. The park consists of reconstructed buildings with displays on the North West Mounted Police and Sioux Indians. There is also the Rodeo Ranch Museum, operated by the Wood Mountain Historical Society.
- Notukeu Heritage Museum in Ponteix, situated north of the park, houses one of the largest collections of Native artifacts in southwestern Saskatchewan.
- Gravelbourg, located north of the park, known as the French cultural, educational, and religious centre of Saskatchewan. There is a museum with early pioneer items.

For More Information

Canadian Heritage
Parks Canada
Grasslands National Park
Box 150
Val Marie, Saskatchewan
S0N 2T0
Phone: (306) 298-2257
Fax: (306) 298-2042
TDD: (306) 298-2217

RIDING MOUNTAIN

National Park

iding Mountain is a meeting place and a refuge. The park is situated in south-central Manitoba, near the geographical centre of Canada, and covers 2978 square kilometres (1150 square miles). Plants and animals from three ecological zones are found in the park, and they all are protected here, safe from the radical changes wrought upon most of southern Manitoba.

Riding Mountain is located on the Manitoba Escarpment, a tilting shelf of siliceous shale—a form of sedimentary rock that is harder than the surrounding limestone. The escarpment extends into northern Saskatchewan, where it forms similar upland areas but, here in Manitoba, it has its own character and its own name—Riding Mountain. Relative to the plains that stretch away from it on all sides, it is a mountain. At its highest edge, on the northeastern side, it is 756 metres (2480 feet) high—the third-highest point in Manitoba.

HOW TO SEE THE PARK

The park comprises three ecological zones: the eastern deciduous forest, with its Manitoba maples and bur oaks; the aspen parklands of mixed forest and grassland; and the boreal forest, with its white spruce and balsam fir. Each zone is accessible by car. There are self-guiding trails, roadside signs at car pull-offs, and a Visitor Centre in the community of **Wasagaming**.

It is important to remember that the three ecological zones of Riding Mountain intermix. So, although each trail or location may be largely one type or another, you will see a range of habitat while visiting each zone.

The Boreal Zone

You can reach areas that are mostly boreal forest by travelling north from Wasagaming on Highway 10, or east on Highway 19. If you take

Marylee Stephenson

163

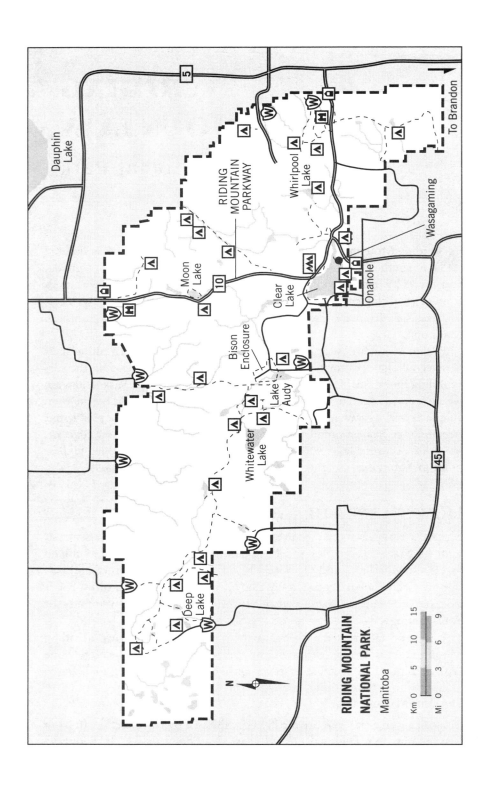

RIDING MOUNTAIN
NATIONAL PARK

Manitoba

Parks Canada

Prairie rose

Highway 10, stop at Moon Lake. A small campground is located there, in case you want to stay awhile. This is the heart of the boreal forest zone, in the north of the park.

East of the townsite, two trails cut through boreal growth. Arrowhead and Brûlé Trails are located near the Shawenequanape Kipichewin (formerly Lake Katherine) Campground. **Arrowhead** is less than three kilometres (two miles) long, and shows the progression of spruce superseding aspen. You can see evidence of the area's glacial history. There are exposed granite rocks, and the ponds in the area are kettles, also known in prairie areas as potholes, formed by melting chunks of ice, which were left behind by retreating glaciers.

On **Brûlé Trail**, you can see how boreal forest recovers from fire. The trail passes through an area of spruce and jack pine that was burned completely in 1929 and 1957, and burned again in smaller areas in 1971. If you take the short side trip to **Kinosao Lake**, you will find more boreal forest, some of which is charred. The lakeshore is quiet and beautiful.

The **Rolling River Trail** brings you even closer than the Brûlé Trail to the experience of fire. In 1980, there was a major burn, over 186 square kilometres (72 square miles), in the park's eastern segment. On this short trail, you can study the pictures and texts that explain fire-fighting techniques.

To get a really good idea of the terrain and habitat variation of the Manitoba Escarpment, which is the basis of the boreal zone, take one of the guided events to the **Wilson Creek** area.

Eastern Deciduous Forest

The best walk through this kind of forest is the Burls and Bittersweet Self-guiding Trail. Very few stands of eastern deciduous forest are left in southern Manitoba, because most have been destroyed in clearing land for agriculture. But here you see a rich remnant of this complex ecological zone. The trail is oriented to Dead Ox Creek, a stream far more lovely than its name. In the surrounding forest, there is an understory of vines, berry bushes, mushrooms, fungi, and flowers.

The **Oak Ridge Trail** and **Beach Ridge Trail** also have significant deciduous growth.

Aspen Parkland and Prairie Potholes

Open, rough fescue grasslands, with stands of aspen and mixed boreal forest, edge the eastern side of **Lake Audy**. A campsite is situated in this area, as well as a plains-bison enclosure, where a small herd of about 30 bulls and cows are kept for breeding and display purposes.

The edge of the fescue grassland—the transition from prairies to forest

Although there are no established trails in this immediate area, you can wander over the prairie area on your own. There are car caravans or interpreter-led walks there, at least once a week.

If you want an overview of what has happened to the expanse of prairie land that surrounds the park, visit the **Agassiz Tower**. It is located about 6.5 kilometres (four miles) from the park's northern boundary, on Highway 10.

Manitoba is famous for thousands of prairie potholes—lakes of all sizes that were left as glaciers retreated. These lakes are havens for waterfowl, fish, bird life, and insects. There are dozens of potholes at Riding Mountain; the park is one of the few places in habitable parts of Manitoba where they have not been drained off and plowed under. The best place to see one is at **Ominik Marsh**, located at the edge of the community, off Wasagaming Drive, on the south side of Boat Cove Road. A floating boardwalk creates an unforgettable experience of the heart of a prairie marsh. Before you go out on it, sign out an Ominik Marsh Discovery Kit, which is available at the Visitor Centre.

PARK SERVICES AND FACILITIES

Interpretive Program

At the core of the Riding Mountain summer interpretive program is a weekly slate of several interpreter-led outings. These are off-trail walks to intriguing places, such as bear and coyote dens, or the remains of old lumber mills.

Riding Mountain has paid a lot of attention to facilities for the disabled. Most of the picnic and day-use areas, the campgrounds at Moon Lake, Lake Audy and Whirlpool Lake, and the group camps at Kipichewin and Ma-ma-o-pe are wheelchair accessible. As well, the Lakeshore Trail along Clear Lake and the one-kilometre (0.6-mile) Boreal Island Trail are suitable for wheelchair use.

The park has a varied and full schedule of interpretive events. Schedules are provided at entry kiosks, the Visitor Centre, and on bulletin boards at campsites. The events occur at various locations in the park, so most visitors' interests and schedules can be met. The Visitor Centre is situated in the centre of Wasagaming. It has been declared a heritage building and has been restored to its original condition. The Centre has a movie theatre, where you can choose films from their listing and have them projected.

Camping

The park offers five car-based campsites and one walk-in campground. **Wasagaming Campground** is located right downtown, and offers a full range of facilities. There are 86 sites with three-way hook-ups for trailers, 74 sites with electricity and water, and 72 sites with electricity only. There are 279 other sites that have picnic tables, fire grates, water from faucets, firewood, and washrooms with flush toilets and showers. Kitchen shelters are also provided. This campground now has a toll-free reservation line, 1-800-707-8480.

Moon Lake Campground is located near the northern boundary of the park, on Highway 10. There are 29 sites, in a mixed-forest environment. This campground has cold-water faucets, flush and pit toilets, picnic tables, fire grates, and firewood.

Lake Audy Campground is located west of Wasagaming on Lake Audy. It offers 34 sites, with kitchen shelters and pit toilets. The campground is close to the Bison Enclosure and several hiking, cycling, and riding trails.

Deep Lake Campground is situated at the far western area of the park. There are 12 sites, well water, and pit toilets.

Shawenequanape Kipichewin (formerly Lake Katherine) Campground is located five kilometres (three miles) east of Wasagaming, on Highway 19. This campground is now operated independently by the Anishinabe First Nation and has a different fee schedule than the park's campgrounds (phone 204-947-3147 for details). Various interpretive programs, cultural experiences, and day tours are offered, providing visitors with a glimpse of the life of the Anishinabe People.

Whirlpool Walk-in Campground is located in the eastern part of the park, on Highway 19. The parking area is only about 100 metres (325 feet) from the grassy camping area at the lake's edge. This seems to be a little-used, and very quiet, campground. There are just 15 sites. There is a kitchen shelter, pit toilets, fire grates, and firewood. You can use lake or well water.

Primitive Camping

There are 11 back-country trails, with primitive campsites. Most have water, and are provided with fire grates and firewood. All have pit privies. Registration in and out is required, if you are planning to stay overnight. Check with staff regarding trail conditions, fire-hazard levels, bear occurrences, and so on.

Group Camping

The park offers two group campgrounds. Write to the Park to find out about the facilities in detail or call 1-800-707-8480. You must reserve in advance.

Other Accommodation, Gas, Food, and Supplies

Because Riding Mountain is a park with a townsite, a wide range of cottages, trailer sites, motels, hotels, restaurants, grocery stores, gas stations, shops, and so on are available. The park can send you a complete listing of the facilities in Wasagaming.

Recreational Services

Hiking   The park offers a variety of hiking trails, from short, self-guiding trails to slightly longer walks around lakes, to lengthy, back-country treks. Park maps are provided as a centrefold in the park newsletter, *The Bugle*. In addition, Parks Plus People (the park's cooperative association) sells trail guide books.

Swimming   The park's numerous lakes offer many opportunities for unsupervised swimming. Note, however, that some lakes have the parasite that causes swimmer's itch.

Boating   Motor boats are allowed on Clear Lake and Lake Audy, both of which have launching ramps. Water skiing is allowed on both lakes. Boats can be rented at Clear Lake, which is situated behind the park administration office.

Canoeing   Many of the park's lakes are good for canoeing, but the rivers are often dammed by beavers, and are less suitable.

Fishing   Although fishing is allowed in all lakes, the major ones are Clear Lake, for pickerel, pike, whitefish, and a few lake trout, and Lake Audy, for jackfish. A National Park fishing licence is required, which may be purchased at the Visitor Centre and park entrance kiosks, from some park wardens, and at numerous sales outlets in the hamlets of Rossburn and Lake Audy, just outside the park.

Golf   There is an 18-hole golf course in Wasagaming with pro shop, rental clubs, and carts. There are washrooms and a licensed restaurant. Another 18-hole course is located in Onanole just south of Wasagaming, and a nine-hole course is situated at Sandy Lake, southwest from Wasagaming.

Tennis The park offers six hard-surface courts, and washrooms. A moderate fee is paid to an attendant, at an hourly, weekly, or seasonal rate.

Horseback Riding   Several licensed outfitters rent horses and conduct trail rides. Watch for signs.

Winter Use The park is open for alpine skiing at Mount Agassiz ski hill. There is a lodge, cafeteria, equipment rental, chair lift, T-bar and rope tow, and snow-making. Hotel accommodation is available in the nearby towns of McCreary and Onanole.

Cross-country skiing is a major winter use. There is extensive trail-grooming and, if you register, you can strike out into the back country. A number of warming huts are provided, each with stove, wood, and axes.

Ice fishing for jackfish, pickerel, perch, and whitefish is possible on Clear Lake.

Vehicle camping is permitted at the main parking lot in Wasagaming, Lake Katherine and Moon Lake day-use areas, and Camp Ma-ma-o-pe. Winter camping requiring an overnight backcountry permit is allowed at Whirlpool Campground, Cairns Cabin (requires reservations) on the Ochre River Trail, and at primitive campsites on other trails in the Park.

Related Activities or Places of Natural or Historic Interest

Travel Manitoba is an excellent information service for all kinds of visitation in the province. Call 1-800-665-0040 (or 945-3777 in Winnipeg).

Activities and Places to Consider Visiting:

- Nearby Provincial Parks include Duck Mountain to the north, which encompasses Baldy Mountain, Manitoba's highest point; Asessippi to the west; Rivers to the south; and Spruce Woods, southeast of the park, which contains the desert-like area known as the Spirit Sands.

- For historic interest, Dauphin, situated just north of the park, is home to the Fort Dauphin Museum, a replica of a North West Company trading post, and the Ukrainian Heritage Village. Several of the small towns near the park support local museums. Contact Travel Manitoba for details.

- Neepawa, to the southeast, is the site of the girlhood home of author Margaret Laurence. The home is designated as a

Related Activities Cont'd

provincial heritage site and is open daily from May to mid-October and then on weekends only from October to December.

National Historic Site:

• Riding Mountain Park: East Gate Complex (entrance to Riding Mt Park on Hwy 19).

For More Information

Riding Mountain National Park
Wasagaming, Manitoba
R0J 2H0
Phone: (204) 848-7275 or 7272 or 1-800-707-8480
Fax: (204) 848-2866
TDD: (204) 848-2001

PUKASKWA

National Park

Pukaskwa* National Park covers 1880 square kilometres (725 square miles), along the northern shore of Lake Superior. Most of the park's area is wooded wilderness and icy water; the park's theme is "Wild Shore of an Inland Sea." Canoe the wild rivers or the length of the coastline, or walk along the Coastal Hiking Trail, and Pukaskwa's special character will emerge clearly and impressively.

Pukaskwa has two main types of environment: the water of Lake Superior and the rivers that flow into it; and the forests, which are boreal and mixed-wood deciduous. Lake Superior is the largest body of fresh water in the world. Its depth and northern location make it extremely cold. A lake of this size behaves as a small ocean would at this latitude, except that it has no tides. Its weather is highly erratic. Terrifying storms and fogs appear in minutes, seemingly out of nowhere, and then calm returns just as suddenly. The cold water has enormous effects on the land: the lake chills the air above it, and moist air that seeps inland helps to determine the kinds of plant and animal life that can survive.

The boreal forest at Pukaskwa has been greatly affected by the cold lake. In July and August, average temperatures range from 7°C (45°F) to 15°C (60°F). There *are* hot, sunny periods, but the pervasive coolness, and thin soil on the Canadian Shield have created the primary conditions for the dense, scrubby spruce forests of the boreal zone. Parts of the park are so exposed to cold winds, and so lacking in soil, that species of arctic-alpine plants, usually found at least 1000 kilometres (600 miles) north, grow there.

Not all is thin soil and blowing wind, however. Fault lines in the rock can result in surface depressions, where soil collects. This has happened around Hattie Cove, where patches of mixed coniferous and deciduous forest of balsam fir and white birch have taken hold.

*Pronounced Puck-a-saw

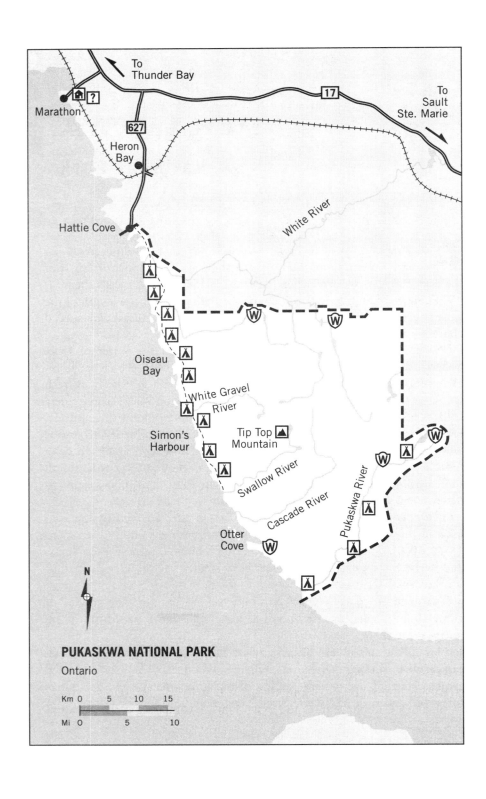

To
Thunder Bay

17

To
Sault
Ste. Marie

Marathon

627

Heron
Bay

Hattie Cove

White River

Oiseau
Bay

White Gravel
River

Simon's
Harbour

Tip Top
Mountain

Swallow River

Cascade River

Pukaskwa River

Otter
Cove

N

PUKASKWA NATIONAL PARK

Ontario

Km 0   5   10   15

Mi 0   5   10

There is little history of human use in the area, but it is believed that people living here 5000 to 10 000 years ago made the mysterious Pukaskwa Pits. These stone pits range from 1 to 2.5 metres (three to eight) in length, and have walls about 1.5 metres (four to five feet) high. Were they observation posts, or shelters for fishing or hunting? No one knows for certain.

HOW TO SEE THE PARK

Despite the wildness of this park, a non-hiker can learn a great deal about the lake, the wilderness, and how people travel it, by visiting the Interpretive Centre at Hattie Cove. There is also a campground, with nearby trail access to sandy beaches, the Southern Headland Walking Trail, the Halfway Lake Trail, and a protected inlet for family canoeing. But, if you are visiting specifically for the wilderness, come with lots of previous canoeing or hiking experience, plenty of time, good equipment, and a full share of mental and physical endurance.

The Hattie Cove Visitation Centre

Hattie Cove is located just 20 kilometres (12.5 miles) south of the town of **Marathon**. At Hattie Cove, there is a parking lot and a beautiful Interpretive Centre.

The **Southern Headland Trail** focuses on the fascinating geological history of the headland. Starting outside the Centre, it takes you through small stands of the mixed forests, and out to the shoreline. Farther along, the trail leads to a beach at **Horseshoe Bay**, and back through a strip of boreal forest. Most interesting were the small, fresh-water pools that collect in the protected parts of shoreline rock during storms. Here, you can see dragonflies, water striders, and plant forms that live in the still water, warmed by the summer sun. The **Halfway Lake Trail** is a short, two-kilometre walk along the shoreline of the small, boreal, rock-rimmed Halfway Lake (formerly known as Beaver Lake). Self-guiding interpretive signs have been placed along both trails.

The Coastal Hiking Trail

The Coastal Trail, as it now exists, runs 57 kilometres (36 miles), from the **Hattie Cove Nature Centre** and registration site to the **North Swallow River**. For a day-hike, you can walk the first leg of the trail, from the Hattie Cove Campground to the first primitive campsite, at the junction with White River. This hike takes three to four hours each way, and will provide a good sense of the shoreline, lake, and bordering forest. More

Parks Canada

Plant life survives on soil caught in cracks in the rocks

intrepid visitors can get a full-fledged wilderness experience by hiking the length of the trail—which takes seven days, on average.

The Coastal Canoe Trip

The full trip covers 180 kilometres (112 miles), through **Lake Superior,** starting north of the park at **Marathon,** and ending at **Michipicoten Harbour,** just outside of **Wawa.** Many people choose to start at Hattie Cove, where they park and register for the trip. At Michipicoten Harbour, a short road leads from there to the Trans-Canada Highway. Some people hitchhike back to the park or, if the canoe party has two cars, a vehicle can be left at each end of the route. Alternatively, the bus service between Wawa and Marathon can be used. The Coastal Canoe Trip is potentially risky; cold, fog, and wind must always be guarded against.

Because the shoreline is filigreed, there are many places to camp, or wait out the wind. In fact, canoeists are advised to expect to be grounded by wind for one day out of three. All of the skills of the wilderness canoeist are required for this trip—orienteering, endurance, good planning, and appropriate equipment.

The White River Canoe Route

This is the way to experience the forests and rivers of Pukaskwa. The full route is 184 kilometres (114 miles) long, starting above White Lake.

However, most paddlers choose to do the lower third, from **White Lake** to **Lake Superior**, near Hattie Cove. The White River was a route of voyageurs, and it passes through muskeg, past boreal forests, and through bare expanses of the Canadian Shield. There are many portages, as rapids, dams, and falls impede progress. On average, the trip takes five to seven days.

PARK FACILITIES AND SERVICES

Interpretive Program

The interpretive program includes guided hikes, slide and film shows, prop talks, and special events, which run from late June through to Labour Day.

Camping

A 67-site campground is located at **Hattie Cove.** There are 29 sites with electricity only. There are showers, flush toilets, and hot and cold water in washrooms. Unserviced sites have picnic tables, fire grates, and a tent-pad area. The campsite is densely wooded, with a good vegetation screen between sites. Expect many biting insects.

Parks Canada

Filigreed shoreline at Hattie Cove

Primitive Camping

There are frequent designated primitive camping sites along the **Coastal Hiking Trail** and **White River Canoe Route**. They have pit toilets, and fire rings may be set out. Use of your own camping gas stove is the most dependable source of heat, because wood may not be dry.

Other Accommodation, Gas, Food, and Supplies

The small village of Heron Bay, situated five kilometres (three miles) north of the park, on Highway 627, has a general store and gas station. The town of Marathon, on Highway 626, off Highway 17, has a variety of stores, hotels and motels, gas stations, restaurants, and so on.

Recreational Services

Hiking   There are the short walks around the Hattie Cove area, and the lengthy Coastal Trail. Back-country and canoe trip/boating registration boxes are present, and registration is strongly encouraged, due to the rugged and wilderness aspects of the park.

Canoeing   Although the major canoe routes are the Coastal Canoe route and the White River, some people also canoe the Pukaskwa River to Otter Cove on Lake Superior. In Hattie Cove, the inexperienced canoeist can spend a safe, easy hour or two, paddling in sight of the Centre and by the campground. For the long routes, however, canoeists must register.

Fishing   Lake Superior and the rivers provide good fishing for trout, pike, pickerel, salmon, and whitefish, depending on the season. A national park licence is required.

HOW TO GET THERE

You can reach Pukaskwa by private car from the Trans-Canada Highway, or by Greyhound Bus and then taxi. The drop-off point for the bus is Marathon. Commercial boat services operate to drop-off points for the Coastal Hiking Trail, although most people walk the entire distance. With park permission only, canoeists who have taken the Pukaskwa River to Otter Cove can be picked up there. Write to the Superintendent for information on transportation operators.

Related Activities or Places of Natural or Historic Interest

Ontario Tourism can provide information for all kinds of visitation in the province and direct you to local Travel Information Centres. Call (416) 314-0944.

Activities and Places to Consider Visiting:

- Provincial parks nearby include Neys Provincial Park, at Marathon, 25 kilometres west of the park; Rainbow Falls and Slate Islands, at Terrace Bay/Schreiber, 96 kilometres west; White Lake, at White River, 95 kilometres east.

- There are also several other provincial parks and places of interest bordering Lake Superior. Excellent guides for this area are the *Lake Superior Circle Tour* and the *North of Superior Guide*.

For More Information

The Superintendent
Pukaskwa National Park
Hwy 627, Hattie Cove
Via: Heron Bay, Ontario
P0T 1R0
Phone: (807) 229-0801
Fax: (807) 229-2097
TTY: (807) 229-2191

Friends of Pukaskwa
General Delivery
Heron Bay, Ontario
P0T 1R0

BRUCE PENINSULA
National Park

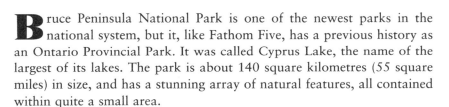

Bruce Peninsula National Park is one of the newest parks in the national system, but it, like Fathom Five, has a previous history as an Ontario Provincial Park. It was called Cyprus Lake, the name of the largest of its lakes. The park is about 140 square kilometres (55 square miles) in size, and has a stunning array of natural features, all contained within quite a small area.

Several of the park's easily accessible trails wind along some of the most spectacular shorelines in Canada. And not far from all this natural beauty is the multitude of activities and facilities provided for visitors to the area—the very popular tourism destinations of Bruce and Grey counties.

Bruce Peninsula National Park preserves a part of the West St. Lawrence Lowlands Natural Region. This is a limestone-based area, with a dramatically varying topography, and a rich natural and human history.

At one time, this area was covered by an inland sea, which was present during the Silurian Period of the Palaeozoic Era. The sequence of events that resulted in today's landbase is very complex but, in essence, the skeletons of the underwater corals and other sea creatures formed layers of calcium-based sediments, as they collected on the sea floor. These layers were compressed at the lower levels by the weight of the layers above them. This pressure, and various chemical reactions, created a type of limestone rock, called dolomite, out of the sediments.

The fact that the bedrock of the Bruce Peninsula is dolomite also contributes greatly to the dramatic character of the area. Dolomite tends to break down in straight lines—either vertical or horizontal. Water seeps down through vertical cracks, and then flows along horizontal spaces. When a rock is weakened by thousands of years of flowing water, or by the pressures of that water freezing and then thawing and freezing again, the rock tends to break in straight lines. Where there is a thicker dolomite caprock, as is true for the whole of the Niagara Escarpment, the water action undermines the softer lower rock, and huge segments of rock may

Parks Canada

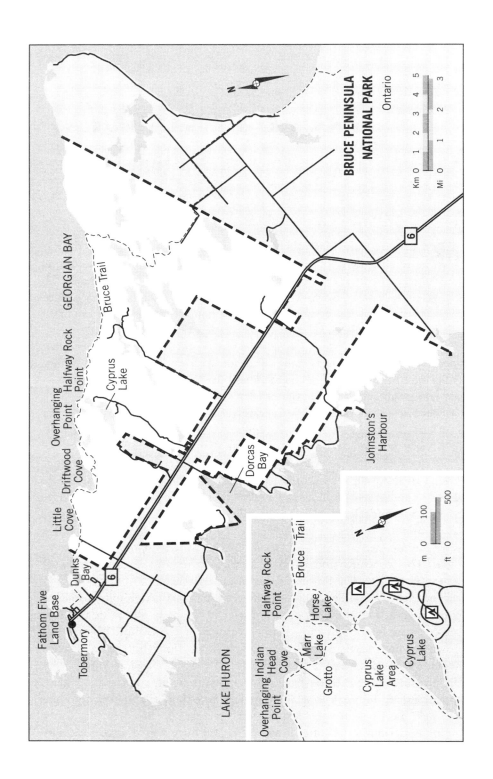

BRUCE PENINSULA
NATIONAL PARK

Ontario

Km 0   1   2   3   4   5

Mi 0   1   2   3

GEORGIAN BAY

Bruce Trail

Overhanging
Point   Halfway Rock
Point

Cyprus
Lake

Driftwood
Cove

Little
Cove

Dorcas
Bay

Johnston's
Harbour

Fathom Five
Land Base

Dunks
Bay

Tobermory

6

LAKE HURON

N

6

Overhanging Indian
Point   Head
Cove

Halfway Rock
Point

Bruce Trail

Marr
Lake

Horse
Lake

Grotto

Cyprus
Lake
Area

Cyprus
Lake

m 0   100

ft 0   500

N

fall abruptly away along a fault line, making massive topographic features like the Escarpment itself. This process is seen on a smaller scale in the flowerpot, or pillar, formations that are found along the shoreline of the park.

The geology of the area is just one aspect of its distinctiveness and interest. Although the Peninsula may be far from the ocean, it has a maritime climate, because of the huge body of water that cradles it. The relative mildness of the climate, and the abundance of moisture, provide a rich environment for plant and animal life.

HOW TO SEE THE PARK

Because Bruce Peninsula National Park is a park in transition, not all of the visitor sites are clearly defined or fully developed for use. As in any national park, it is wise to start your visit at the Visitor Centre. Bruce Peninsula National Park and Fathom Five share the Visitor Centre at Little Tub Harbour in Tobermory.

Cyprus Lake offers both a campground and a day-use area. On its eastern edge, along the shore of Georgian Bay, is one of the most spectacular walks in the national park system. There is also a very interesting complex of lakes, forests, and bogs in the Cyprus Lake area.

Marylee Stephenson

Halfway Rock Point on Georgian Bay

The Cyprus Lake visitor area is situated about seven kilometres (four miles) south of Tobermory. The entrance is from Highway 6, and is clearly marked. Since this is the only campground for the park, it is easy to combine a camping trip with easy hikes along the lakes or the shoreline.

The walk that you should not miss is a circle trail, which starts out from the parking lot at the east end of Cyprus Lake. You can choose to follow the **Horse Lake, Marr Lake,** or **Georgian Bay** trails, to start. The first part of the circuit takes less than an hour, and you will wind your way through the conifer forest, and pass along the shores of the inland lake. Then you will emerge along the shoreline of Georgian Bay. Here, you join the **Bruce Trail,** that famous trail that runs 730 kilometres (456 miles) along the Niagara Escarpment, from Niagara Falls right into Tobermory, at the tip of the Bruce Peninsula.

The story of this circle trail is very much the story of the geology of the limestone landscape that the park epitomizes. The park has an excellent map of the whole trail complex at Cyprus Lake, and it helps you to identify and understand key points of interest. The boulder beach that separates Marr Lake from Georgian Bay is a great place to see how active the interaction between water and land can be. The beach is constantly changing, as storms throw up rocks that have broken off from the cliffs and fallen into the water. Caves and grottoes are situated along the trail.

You can also look up at the cliffs, and clearly see the various layers of sedimentary rock. Then, as the trail ascends to the top of the cliffs, you will be treated to vista after vista of brilliant blue water far below, green forest running to the edge of the cliffs, white shorelines, and turquoise shallows.

The trail has a few places, however, where you will cling to roots and rocks to help you along. It's not too strenuous; you just have to watch your step and not hurry.

Even though the lakes nestled in the network of trails aren't as immediately spectacular as the walk along Georgian Bay, they are well worth a leisurely stroll, especially if you take the time to look closely at the varied "micro-habitats."

Singing Sands

A visit to the Singing Sands is a dramatic contrast to the rugged cliffs, convoluted shoreline, and imposing forest of the Cyprus Lake area.

The Singing Sands visitation area has two distinct areas. One is the beach itself. It is a very firm, flat beach, which is perfect for wading. The water warms up considerably on sunny days, because it is so shallow.

As you move back from the shoreline, at the northern edge of the beach are several terraces of low rock perpendicular to the shore. There are low, parallel rock ripples, about five metres (15 feet) from crest to crest. The glaciers made these grooves more than 10 000 years ago.

The other part of the Singing Sands area is the **Dorcas Bay Nature Reserve**. Visitors are asked to be especially respectful of this fragile area, parts of which should be avoided, because regeneration projects are under way. (These are noted at the site.)

The Dorcas Bay area is the wooded backdrop to the Singing Sands beach. It starts with the wet bog/fen areas that are home to orchids and insectivorous plants, including pitcher plants, sundew, and butterworts.

Beyond the wet bog/fen area is the sandy forest, with stands of red and white pines. Streams meander down to the beach. A trail leads away from the water, and into the woods to the east. There is dense cedar bush, with occasional clearings with low domes of rock, where soil has been unable to develop. These clearings are good places to see various types of lichen—which manage to take hold where little else can. Deep cracks also cut through the rock and, as you look down into them, you will see ferns and mosses, which have been able to use the moisture and small amounts of soil that collect there.

Marylee Stephenson

Singing Sands in Dorcas Bay area

The signs for Dorcas Bay were not fully in place when I visited, and it is very easy to become lost in this terrain. Consequently, make sure to inquire at the Visitor Centre about the status of the trail and its signs, before you stray far from the shore.

PARK SERVICES AND FACILITIES

Because this park is so new to the system, and a number of issues must be resolved in the years to come, the park facilities and services are not as comprehensive and well established as they are in most of the other national parks. As with a visit to any park, start your visit at the Visitor Centre, at Little Tug Harbour in Tobermory.

Interpretive Program

Most of the park's interpretive programming is provided out of the Cyprus Lake Campground, from June to September. Programs are offered at the outdoor amphitheatre, which is located at the western edge of the campground complex, near Cyprus Lake itself. Interpreter-led walks are provided in the Cyprus Lake area, along the Georgian Bay trails, and at the Dorcas Bay Reserve location.

Some interpretive walks start in the Visitor Centre at Little Tub Harbour in Tobermory. These are explorations of the natural and human history of Fathom Five National Marine Park. The administration, and a number of visitor activities, for Fathom Five and Bruce Peninsula are combined, because of Tobermory, and because the two parks are so closely related, in location and in their natural and human histories.

Camping

The park provides one campground, with three sections, at the Cyprus Lake area. There are 242 sites in all. **Birches**, with 98 sites, is designed with room for trailers to pull in. No services are provided for trailers.

A pumping station for trailers is situated just before the campground office. The **Poplars** campground, with 63 sites, and **Tamarack**, with 81 sites, are tent-camping areas. Each site has a picnic table and fire grate. There are toilets and water taps for every few campsites. There is no electricity. Firewood can be purchased in the evenings, from a woodlot across from the Birches campground. When the woodlot is closed, campers can obtain wood from businesses situated along Highway 6.

In July and August the campground is usually full, so it is important to reserve well in advance. Reservations are made by phone only: (519) 596-2263.

Other Accommodation, Gas, Food, and Supplies

Because Bruce Peninsula is such a well-developed tourism area, an abundance of services and facilities are provided for visitors. At least 25 commercial campgrounds, some bed-and-breakfasts, and several motels are located along Highway 6. Restaurants, gas stations, and stores that carry any camping supplies or emergency items you may need, are readily accessible.

Many businesses have racks of brochures, with pamphlets listing local services and attractions. The regional tourist association offers excellent publications. These sources will tell you anything you need to know about visiting the area. The Park Visitor Centre is also an excellent source of information.

Recreational Facilities

Swimming　Two swimming areas are offered at Cyprus Lake. The day-visitor beach is located just to the left of the campground office. Campers may also use it. The other beach is for campers, and it is situated in front of the Poplars site.

Boating　Non-powered boats are allowed on Cyprus Lake at any time. However, motorboats are prohibited from June 15 to September 15. There is a great deal of powerboating and sailing around the Bruce Peninsula. Most of this activity occurs in Tobermory, where a marina is located.

Fishing　Bass, perch, and yellow pickerel are found in Cyprus Lake. Some trout live in nearby streams, and good fishing can be found in some of the coves in Georgian Bay. Fishing is allowed under provincial regulations. Ask at the Visitor Centre in Tobermory for further information.

Winter Use　There is limited winter camping, snowmobiling on the Tobermory Ski and Snow Association Trail in the park, and cross-country skiing. Ask at the Visitor Centre, or call the park in advance to determine the status for any of these activities—snow conditions, trail quality, and so forth.

Related Activities or Places of Natural or Historic Interest

Ontario Tourism can provide information for all kinds of visitation in the province and direct you to local Travel Information Centres. Call (416) 314-0944.

Activities and Places to Consider Visiting:

- The Bruce Trail, which passes through the park, is well worth exploring. The northern end of the trail follows the Georgian Bay shoreline from Wiarton to Tobermory.

- There are several provincial parks in the area. On the shores of Lake Huron you will find Sauble Falls, MacGregor Point, and Inverhuron; on Georgian Bay there are Craigleith and Wasaga Beach; just south of Georgian Bay is Devil's Glen.

- For historical interest there is the Bruce County Museum, located in Southampton and the Country of Grey Owen Sound Museum in Owen Sound.

National Historic Site:

- Point Clark Lighthouse (on Lake Huron at the southern end of Bruce County)

For More Information

The Superintendent
Bruce Peninsula National Park
P.O. Box 189
Tobermory, Ontario
N0H 2R0
Phone: (519) 596-2233
Fax: (519) 596-2298

Bruce Peninsula Tourist Association
R.R. #2
Hepworth, Ontario
N0H 1P0
Phone: (519) 422-2114

The Bruce Trail Association
P.O. Box 857
Hamilton, Ontario
L8N 3N9

FATHOM FIVE
National Marine Park

Many of Canada's national parks protect the shorelines along our oceans and gulfs. They offer the opportunity to camp by the sea, or to hike for days along trails that follow "inland seas," such as Lake Superior. But, in fact, the water is not included within the protective mantle of these parks (with the exception of Pacific Rim) because, until very recently, Canada had no marine parks. This omission was corrected in 1987, with the designation of Fathom Five as Canada's first national marine park.

Fathom Five is located at the tip of the Bruce Peninsula, which juts out into Lake Huron, separating Georgian Bay in the east and the larger portion of Lake Huron on the Peninsula's western side. Visitors come here to don their diving gear and explore shipwrecks, some of which are situated just a few metres from shore. They come to visit islands that were once the floor of a giant inland sea. They peer at rare orchids, and wander around old lighthouses. All of these activities can be found in one park—well within a half day's drive of Toronto.

The Park preserves a beautiful example of the Georgian Bay marine natural region, which is one of the five Great Lakes marine natural regions (and one of 29 marine regions throughout Canada). The water surface area of the park is about 130 square kilometres (50 square miles). There are three main areas to visit: the water environment itself; the islands located to the north and east of the tip of the Bruce Peninsula; and the small segment of the rugged Georgian Bay coastline situated at the eastern landbase of the park.

The aquatic environment is a mixed one, because the park is located at the meeting place of the relatively warm water of Lake Huron and the colder, and less biologically diverse waters of Georgian Bay, the eastern segment of Lake Huron. For visitors, one of the most attractive features of the waters of the park is their clarity and brilliant colour. Hikers can peer down from cliffs into waters that are reminiscent of pictures of tropical

Marylee Stephenson

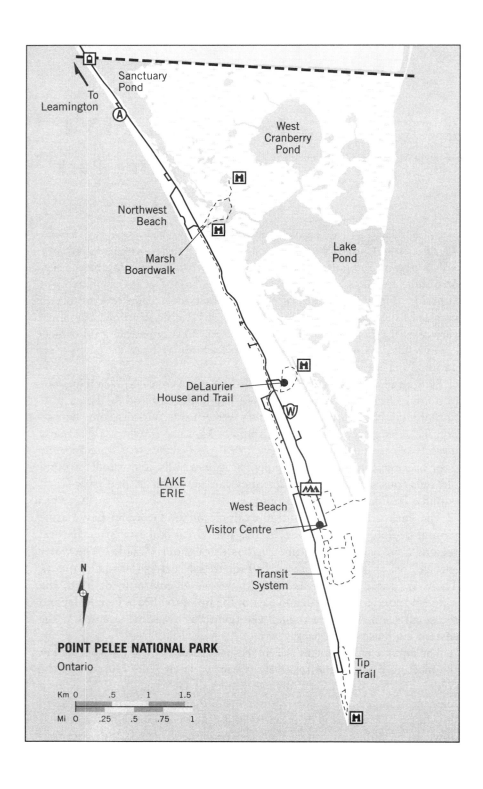

Sanctuary
Pond

To
Leamington

West
Cranberry
Pond

Northwest
Beach

Marsh
Boardwalk

Lake
Pond

DeLaurier
House and Trail

LAKE
ERIE

West Beach

Visitor Centre

Transit
System

N

POINT PELEE NATIONAL PARK

Ontario

Km 0   .5   1   1.5

Mi 0 .25 .5 .75 1

Tip
Trail

islands, with shorelines of the palest grey bordering turquoise shallows and vibrant blue depths. For divers, the water's clarity makes for some of the best diving in North America. The rugged underwater topography is fascinating but, for many, the greater appeal is the human history of the area, as evidenced by the remains of 23 shipwrecks, scattered across the lake bottom within the park boundaries.

Because of its strategic location in the Great Lakes shipping lanes, the waters of what is now Fathom Five have been a busy place for ships for 150 years. The sudden squalls that characterize the area, and the cliffs and canyons of the lake bottom, which create irregular wave patterns, combine at times to create very hazardous conditions for boats. These storms have left a ghostly underwater heritage. Although divers can glide among the skeletons of these wrecks, the location of some of them, in shallow water right in Tobermory's two coves, makes it possible for visitors to get a good look at several of them without ever having to dive in.

The landforms of the mainland part of Fathom Five are part of the famous Niagara Escarpment, a rocky ridge stretching from Niagara Falls, becoming the backbone of the Bruce Peninsula, and dipping underwater at the Peninsula tip. Then bits and pieces of the Escarpment appear as the many islands in this part of Lake Huron.

The bedrock underlying Fathom Five (and nearby Bruce Peninsula National Park) is limestone—sedimentary rock formed from warm inland seas that covered the area more than 400 million years ago. The seas retreated and the sea floor was uplifted, only to be scoured and eroded by the action of weather, rivers, and repeated glaciation.

The human history of Fathom Five's land and waters is long and intriguing. Archeological evidence shows that aboriginal people have visited the area—trading, fishing, hunting, and camping—for at least 3000 years.

HOW TO SEE THE PARK

With all its distinctive aquatic and land features, and wonderful opportunities for enjoying them, it is important to know that Fathom Five is an integral part of one of the most popular tourism areas in Eastern Canada.

Some 300 000 people pour through the tiny town of Tobermory each year, mostly during June, July, and August. The choice for travel is the car ferries, M.S. Chi-Cheemaun and M.S. Nindawyama, which carry about 260 000 of these visitors between South Baymouth, on Manitoulin Island, and Tobermory. Often, ferry passengers circle Georgian Bay, stopping at points of interest along the way. Fathom Five, and the two other national parks on Lake Huron—Georgian Bay Islands and Bruce Peninsula—also play a significant role in attracting visitors to the area.

The Land of Fathom Five

Very little of the land base of Fathom Five is on the mainland around Tobermory. These areas are in a transition period, with ongoing discussions between local residents and the park regarding possible changes to visitor facilities, the marina, local roads and parking, and so on. As a result, by the time you visit the park the information provided here may be outdated. If this is the case, the park publishes a map and newsletter, as well as other brochures that provide up-to-date information.

Tobermory has two harbours—**Little Tub** and **Big Tub Harbours**—around which most of the land-based visitor activities happen. A temporary Visitor Centre is situated at Little Tub, as well as a Diver Registration Centre. On weekends, volunteers from the Ontario Underwater Council assist in the diver-safety program. Strolling in the town is very enjoyable in itself, and there is an excellent boardwalk now, along the southeast shore of Little Tub, which was built by the Friends.

At the northern side of the mouth of Big Tub Harbour is the **Big Tub Lighthouse**, which was built in 1885. This is a very small area, but it is always enjoyable to be so close to a real lighthouse. You may also be mingling with divers, because they come here for the easy access to the water—one of the popular shore-accessible dive sites.

The best-known part of Fathom Five's terrestrial area is an island, known as Flowerpot. It can be reached by private boat—overnight mooring is provided there—and by a range of water taxis, which can be boarded in Tobermory.

Flowerpot Island

Flowerpot is a popular destination for visitors to Fathom Five. Flowerpot is an enchanting island—its geological history readily evident in its limestone cliffs, caves, and "flowerpots." A three-kilometre (1.75-mile) walk starts at the docking area at **Beachy Cove**, and a self-guiding brochure explains the island's natural history. If your time is limited, be sure to see the flowerpots—the tapered columns at the water's edge, for which the island is named.

On the north side of the island, caves are situated high in the cliffs above the trail. Visitors may view the main cave, which has a stairway and observation platform; however, access to the other caves is prohibited.

Further evidence of earlier high-water levels is the cobblestone corridor that you cross on the 10-minute walk from the main trail to the marl beds. The cobblestones, rounded by lapping waves, were the beach of a small bay, which once filled the indentation in the land.

The plants of Flowerpot Island depend, of course, on the type of soil available—its chemical and organic composition, depth and slope, moisture content, and so on. The cool, moist, shallow soils create a boglike habitat that is ideal for plants such as orchids.

The Water World of Fathom Five

For a more than superficial view of the marine element of this national marine park, it is necessary either to take a boat or take a dive. If you travel on the "Chi-Cheemaun," you'll get a good overview of the expanse of water leading to the tip of the Bruce Peninsula. There are also tour boats to Flowerpot, as well as charter boats for divers, for fishing, for nature lovers, and general sightseers.

A distinctive feature of the local boating services available to visitors is glass-bottom boats. They are not the glass-bottom boats that are found in the calm waters of Florida tourist attractions, however, because the waters of Lake Huron are too powerful for that type of boat. But they have windows along the hull, below the water, and you lean over and peer down through them to the shipwrecks or natural life of the underwater.

For more than 9000 visitors each year, scuba diving is the big draw of the waters of Fathom Five. They come for the human history and the natural history of the underwater world of the park.

The human history is evidenced in the remains of 21 shipwrecks within the park boundaries (though only 19 have been identified). Some, like the Sweepstakes, in Big Tub Harbour, are in very good condition, while others are just collections of lumber and other debris. There are schooners, steamers, tugs, barges, barques, and motor ships. Depths range from a few metres to the deepest, which lies in 45 metres (135 feet) of water.

The natural history of the marine element of Fathom Five is also fascinating and readily accessible to divers. Diving in designated areas provides visitors with an opportunity to gain a stronger sense of the geological forces that shaped the Bruce Peninsula. It's easy to see the action of glaciers, including huge underwater boulders—the glacial "erratics" that have been carried by the sheets of ice far from their original locations, in the north. Pitting and scouring are evident, and there are also underwater caves.

Other Places of Interest

Because there are several islands in Fathom Five, it is a good idea to ask at the Visitor Centre about other sites. For example, **Cove Island** has the oldest lighthouse in the Upper Great Lakes, built in 1856—one of six Imperial Towers built during that period.

PARK SERVICES AND FACILITIES

Because Fathom Five has so little land base, and much of that is island and rather fragile, there is relatively little park development of the sort that land-based parks tend to have. A small, temporary Visitor Centre is located at Little Tub Harbour.

Interpretive Program

The interpretation of Fathom Five's natural and human history is achieved mainly through the Visitor Centre displays, an attractive newsletter, trail brochures for Flowerpot Island, and interpretive signs at Flowerpot itself. During July and August, interpreter-led hikes are conducted on Flowerpot Island. If you are staying at Bruce Peninsula

Marylee Stephenson

Visual displays at the Visitor Centre

National Park, the interpretation there often addresses some aspects of Fathom Five, and they have offered walks along the Tobermory harbour shoreline, as part of the interpretive programming of Fathom Five.

Camping

The park offers just six campsites, all of which are on wooden decks, slightly above the shoreline on Flowerpot Island. Sites are available on a first-come, first-served basis. You must pack everything in and out. Camp sites have wood fireplaces and pit toilets. The closest other camping in a national park is at Bruce Peninsula National Park. There, three camp-grounds offer 242 sites.

Other Accommodation, Gas, Food, and Supplies

The whole Bruce Peninsula, and the areas to the south and east (Owen Sound, Grey County) bordering Lake Huron, are a wonderful combination of rural, nearly natural, and moderately urban life. At least 25 commercial campgrounds are located within a one- or two-hour drive from Tobermory, and a 242-site campground is situated at Bruce Peninsula National Park. The area also has many motels, restaurants, and gas stations.

People with trailers will find a number of facilities welcoming them, and I even saw one brochure for a mobile sewage-disposal service!

Recreational Services

The park itself does not provide recreational services, such as patrolled beaches. A ski route is provided on the land base, and there are many recreational opportunities within the park boundaries, because of the commercial services available.

Boating As noted, there is a municipal marina with full services in Tobermory. If you are unfamiliar with the waters of Georgian Bay, it is essential that you familiarize yourself with local conditions. Wind and weather are extremely unpredictable, and the thousands of islands strewn throughout the area must be taken into account at all times. If you do not have a boat, you are likely to find exactly the kind of commercial service you want—from taking the "Chi-Cheemaun" to going out for a few hours in an afternoon, or being dropped off at Flowerpot to camp, and being picked up on schedule a couple of days later.

Diving Fathom Five offers a wide range of diving opportunities, and peo-ple with novice to very advanced skills will find something suited to their interests and experience. All divers must register at the Diver Registration Centre, at the waterfront of Little Tub Harbour. Upon registration, divers receive annual dive tags, which show that they have received the safety message. All divers must observe standard safety and courtesy requirements, and the park urges divers to be particularly sensitive to the needs of local residents and boaters in the harbour areas, which can become rather crowded. There are three dive shops with air in Tobermory.

Swimming Despite all the water of Fathom Five, there are no designated swimming areas, and few places along the shores with safe or easy access to swimming. Your best bet is to visit the Cyprus Lake Campground or Singing Sands of Bruce Peninsula National Park, for swimming at the beaches there.

Winter Use   People visit Tobermory year-round, and the Park Administrative Office is open throughout the year. Boat services and diving, however, run from late April to mid-October. This means no access to the islands, as well.

Related Activities or Places of Natural or Historic Interest

(See previous chapter on Bruce Peninsula.)

For More Information

The Superintendent
Fathom Five National Marine Park
P.O. Box 189
Tobermory, Ontario
N0H 2R0
Phone: (519) 596-2233
Fax: (519) 596-2298

Bruce Peninsula Tourist Association
R.R. #2
Hepworth, Ontario
N0H 1P0
Phone: (519) 422-2114

Friends of Fathom Five National Park
P.O. Box 214
Tobermory, Ontario
N0H 2R0

The Bruce Trail Association
P.O. Box 857
Hamilton, Ontario
L8N 3N9

GEORGIAN BAY ISLANDS
National Park

The best publicists for the Georgian Bay Islands were the artists of the Group of Seven. The windswept trees, bare, pink rock of the ancient Canadian Shield, trees with branches flagged out in the prevailing winds, jagged coastlines, and clear blue water—all are known to most Canadians from the paintings.

Three geological factors have shaped the 59 islands (or parts of islands) that comprise the 12 square kilometres (4.6 square miles) of Georgian Bay Islands National Park. To understand how the islands came to have their exotic variety of shapes and sizes, it helps to imagine the park area as divided from north to south. The islands on the east side of Georgian Bay are based on exposed Canadian Shield rock, which is composed of quartz, granite, and gneiss. The northern part was heavily glaciated, with the great masses of ice scraping down to the bedrock of the Canadian Shield, and leaving its now-gentle contours exposed. Here, stunted, windswept trees cling to the edges of rocky inlets—the environment that entranced artists of yesterday and visitors of today. The southern part was the recipient of the debris of retreating glaciers—debris that formed the soil that supported the forest growth. Here, aboriginal peoples lived off the richness of the forest and the lakes, and archeological remains of these cultures show habitation as long ago as 11 000 years.

HOW TO SEE THE PARK

North/south differences are quite easily seen by visiting several of the major camping or day-use areas of the park. All of the regions must be reached by boat but, with the extensive water-taxi services available, and some visitors using their own boats, it is possible to see key parts of these fascinating variations in just a one-day visit, though you'll be glad if you stay longer.

Marylee Stephenson

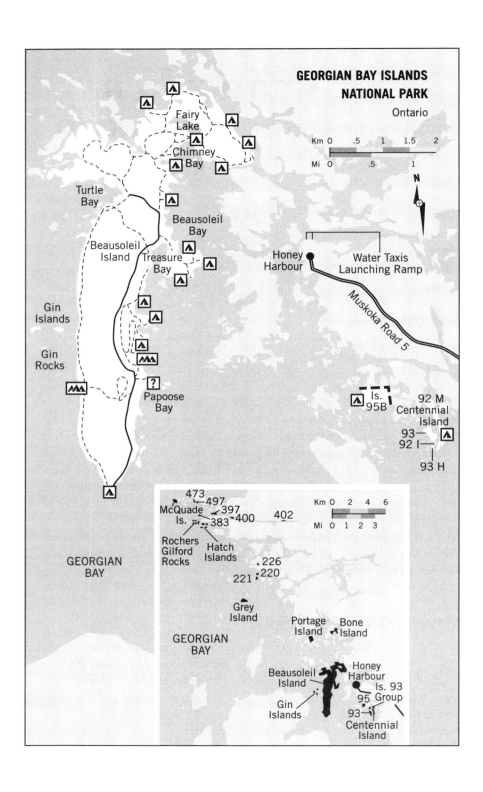

GEORGIAN BAY ISLANDS
NATIONAL PARK

Ontario

Km 0 .5 1 1.5 2
Mi 0   .5   1

N

Fairy Lake
Chimney Bay
Turtle Bay
Beausoleil Bay
Beausoleil Island
Treasure Bay
Gin Islands
Gin Rocks
Papoose Bay

Honey Harbour
Water Taxis
Launching Ramp

Muskoka Road 5

Is. 95B
92 M
Centennial Island
93 —
92 I —
93 H

473
497
McQuade Is.
397
400
402
383
Rochers Gilford Rocks
Hatch Islands
226
221 220

Grey Island
Portage Island
Bone Island

GEORGIAN BAY

Km 0 2 4 6
Mi 0 1 2 3

Beausoleil Island
Honey Harbour
Is. 93 Group
Gin Islands
95
93
Centennial Island

GEORGIAN BAY

The park has one main access point: Honey Harbour. It has a marina, water taxis, and boat-launch facilities for private boats. If you want to visit Bruce Peninsula National Park or Fathom Five National Park, located on the western side of Georgian Bay, it is advisable to trailer your boat from Honey Harbour to Tobermory unless you're a very skilled sailor. The drive is about four hours.

Beausoleil Island: South and North

I started out at Honey Harbour, and was taken to the park's headquarters on Beausoleil Island, where you can see the finest example of the difference between the northern and southern variations of the Canadian Shield. The southern end is composed of glacial till—basically gravel deposits that form a glacial remnant, known as a *drumlin*. In contrast, in the northern part of the island, the glaciers scoured the rocks, and did not leave sand or gravel to form the basis of soil.

Two drumlins comprise **Southern Beausoleil Island.** They are the source of some fascinating Indian legends, about the founding and shaping of the area by an ancient giant. Two trails in the southern part of Beausoleil are very good for seeing the area's geological history, and the life that has formed there.

The **Fire Tower Trail** begins a five-minute walk from the Visitor Centre. It is approximately one kilometre (0.6 mile) long, and takes 30 to 45 minutes to complete at an easy pace. There is a beautiful view into the hardwood forest on the left, as the trail approaches the Fire Tower clearing, and then as the trail descends to lake level. At the bottom of the slope, watch for the glacial erratics—the large stones and boulders that were left here by glaciers.

The **Circuit of the Southern Tip** has a number of names that change as the trail progresses—the first section, leading out from behind the Visitor Centre, is called **Christian Trail.** The last leg of the trail, returning on the eastern edge of the island up to the Visitor Centre, provides the most intense experience of a hardwood forest that I believe is available in the eastern national park system.

But, with all this richness of forest and water, Southern Beausoleil also has a long human history. Early Native people camped on the island from spring to fall, hunting and fishing for their livelihood. Archeological remains attest to this for the whole Georgian Bay area, though little archeological exploration has been conducted in the park itself. However, the Visitor Centre area is a good place to learn more about the more recent human history of this area, where a number of Native families farmed and fished from 1842 to 1858. Then, as the difficulties of farming on land that was better suited to trees than to corn became almost insuperable, most of the families moved to the Christian Islands Reserve.

Northern Beausoleil Island is the scoured, craggy land portrayed by the Group of Seven. Vegetation takes hold here by sending roots into cracks in the rocks, or into crevices created by glaciers, or by wind, ice, or water erosion. The largest plants are the white pines—gnarled and often reaching their branches out on their leeward side, like bizarre flags. The irregular shoreline, with its many inlets, makes excellent mooring for the hundreds of boats that visit here on busy summer days.

For a two- or three-hour walk, there is one main trail, with some off-shoots that lead out from several of the campgrounds: Honeymoon Bay, Sandpiper Bay, and Chimney Bay. The primary trail is a circle around **Fairy Lake** and the smaller lake nearby, called **Goblin Lake**. The trail meanders over scoured rock, which shows signs of glacial movement. The trail is not easy to follow, particularly over the exposed rock areas; watch out for the small cement pylons with the yellow-painted caps.

You can also reach this trail from the campsites located much farther south, along the eastern side of the island, all the way down to the Cedar Spring Campground. This would be a four- to five-hour round trip.

Parks Canada

Lady's slipper orchid

Marylee Stephenson

The ruggedness of the Canadian Shield at Northern Beausoleil

Other Places of Interest

Since Georgian Bay Islands National Park stretches over 50 kilometres (30 miles) of the Georgian Bay coastline, there are many other places to visit. Ask park staff for information on other areas suitable for visitor use.

PARK SERVICES AND FACILITIES

Interpretive Program

The park has an active interpretive program, which runs from mid-June through Labour Day. Often, outdoor theatre presentations and children's programs are provided in the Cedar Spring area, but heritage educators also travel to other camping areas and give talks, or meet people informally to answer questions about the park's natural and human history. Each July, special events are held to celebrate Canada Day and Parks Day.

Camping

All camping in the park is tent only; visitors cannot drive within the park. The only access is by boat—either privately owned or water taxi. There are many places to drop anchor, to tie up next to a dock, or to pull up on shore, and docking facilities are provided for boats with self-contained accommodations.

Cedar Spring Campground is the largest campground, with 87 semi-serviced sites along the eastern shoreline of southern Beausoleil Island. Fees are collected by self-registration here, and throughout the park. Security staff are on hand at Cedar Spring during the summer months. Access is from Honey Harbour, located about 20 minutes away by boat. There are two docks, and the sites are situated just behind the narrow sandy beach. Large, wheeled carts are available for off-loading camping supplies from the boat, and for rolling them to the campsites. Fire grates are provided at each site, and picnic tables, flush toilets, hot showers, water from several faucets, and kitchen shelters, each with several large cookstoves and picnic tables, are also available. The park sells bagged firewood at the campground kiosk during posted hours.

Many of the trails can be taken from the Cedar Spring area, and the Interpretive Centre is there, with its small museum and theatre for slide shows. There is a playground area for children.

The park offers accessible facilities for the physically challenged at Cedar Spring, including a wheelchair-accessible dock, trails, two campsites, picnic area, and washroom/shower facilities. The Visitor Centre and Outdoor Theatre are also wheelchair accessible.

The Cedar Spring area is excellent for bird-watching. The variety of bird life in June is fantastic. Watch out for mosquitoes and poison ivy in your rambles, however.

Primitive Camping

The park offers 14 primitive campgrounds, all of which have pit toilets. Water comes from the lake. There are fire grates with firewood, cleared tent-pad areas, picnic tables, and most areas have kitchen shelters.

The largest area is **Tonch North, South,** and **East**—three spots situated close to each other, and joined by paths—which has 25 sites in all. All campgrounds, except two, are located on Beausoleil Island. Each area has either docking or beach pull-up areas for boats. Fees are collected by self-registration.

Group Camping

Beausoleil Island offers two group-camping areas. Occupation is by reservation only; write to the Superintendent in advance. Access is by canoe, or hiking in from Cedar Spring—water taxis do not serve the Christian Beach area because of the shallow waters. The Cedar Spring group campground has flush toilets and showers.

Other Accommodation, Gas, Food, and Supplies

Because Honey Harbour and all of Georgian Bay is a major tourist and recreation area, numerous motels and private campgrounds and some hotels are available. Gas, food, and supplies are available in Honey Harbour, and in the other towns and villages in the area. A store and marina are located on Picnic Island (not within the park), which is a short motorboat ride from the Cedar Spring docking area.

Water Taxis   You can be dropped off at any campsite or picnic area by water taxi, from Honey Harbour.

Recreational Services

Hiking   A special word of caution: this park has quite a complex network of trails, which pass through varying terrains, including wetlands, shield country, and hardwood bush. Sturdy boots are recommended. Trails often cross over large, open expanses of rock outcrops, where paths are not easily delineated. Hikers must be ever-watchful for the colour-coded stone cairns, because in these areas it is easy to wander off the trail and become lost. Although distances on the islands are not great, hikers should carry a compass. This is particularly true for Beausoleil Island. Pick up a *Trail Hiker's Guide* from park staff, and become familiar with the maps, marking system, and trail names, before heading out.

Mosquitoes can be a real trial, particularly in wooded areas in early summer (June).

The northern half of Beausoleil Island is also a refuge of the Eastern Massasauga rattlesnake. These snakes are small and non-aggressive, but they are poisonous. If you encounter one along a trail, note the snake's location and give it a wide berth.

Boating   Boaters are encouraged to use local nautical charts, available from marinas, or by writing to the Canadian Hydrographic Service, Department of Fisheries and Oceans, 1675 Russell Road, Ottawa. Caution is advised, because there are 90 000 islands and thousands of underwater shoals to dodge around, distances can be great, and the weather is extremely changeable and often hazardous.

However, this must be one of the most beautiful places to boat in North America. Several marinas and sailing or motorboating clubs are located in the area. Marine fuel, oil, boat repairs, and rental facilities are available in Honey Harbour, located near Port Severn, Midland, and Penetanguishene. The park itself offers many designated loading and unloading areas for camping or day use, and boaters should not obstruct these places. Camping or overnight docking is allowed only at designated areas, and overnight docking is limited to 78 hours. Bilge water must not be discharged anywhere in or near the park, since the lake is the source of drinking water for all areas.

Swimming   One area for toddlers is located at Cedar Spring, where some shallow water is roped off. There is no supervision, but the rope does keep the boats out. Changing houses are situated at Cedar Spring. Otherwise, unsupervised swimming is allowed anywhere in the park. There are many appealing coves and sandy beaches.

Winter Use   Beausoleil Island is increasingly used for winter recreation. There are cross-country skiing, groomed snowmobile trails, and snowshoeing (you can borrow snowshoes at the Visitor Centre on Beausoleil). The Visitor Centre is open weekend afternoons in winter for information on trail conditions. It is also a good place to warm up in front of the fireplace. All primitive campgrounds are open for winter camping, with picnic shelters at Cedar Spring and Chimney Bay. Contact the park before arriving, to ensure that ice conditions will allow you to cross safely from the mainland. Usually, mid-January to early March is a good time to visit.

Related Activities or Places of Natural or Historic Interest

Ontario Tourism can provide information for all kinds of visitation in the province and direct you to local Travel Information Centres. Call 416-314-0944.

Activities and Places to Consider Visiting:

- Provincial Parks: Awenda near Penetanguishene offers an excellent opportunity to experience the thick glacial till and hardwood forests of Southern Ontario; Massasauga, north of the park, for wilderness camping; Algonquin west of the park.

- For bird-watchers, the Wye Marsh Wildlife Centre at nearby Midland offers an excellent interpretive program.

- For historic interest, St. Marie Among the Hurons at Midland and Discovery Harbour at Penetanguishene.

Related Activities Cont'd

National Historic Sites:

* Gravenhurst: Bethune Memorial House

For More Information

The Superintendent
Georgian Bay Islands National Park
Box 28
Honey Harbour, Ontario
P0E 1E0
Phone: (705) 756-2415

POINT PELEE

National Park

Point Pelee National Park is a jewel of nature: small, rare, valuable. A thin triangle jutting into Lake Erie at the southernmost point of Canada, this spit of land stretches as far south as the border of northern California. Location, latitude, and the surrounding water create a setting for plant and animal life that is unique in Canada. Point Pelee is one of the most visited parks in Canada, and one of the most famous parks in North America.

HOW TO SEE THE PARK

Point Pelee is a tiny peninsula, stretching only 10 kilometres (six miles) in length, and four kilometres (2.5 miles) across. It is bordered on the east side by a marsh, which comprises most of the park area.

The land base of Point Pelee is quite young in geological history—only about 10 000 years old. It has a sand and gravel base, with some top soil to support woodlands, and some grasslands. Because of its exposure to the lakes, currents, and fierce winds, the land is ever-changing, especially at its fragile tip. The beaches that rim the park may be flat, wide, and clear one day, but steep, narrow, and awash with flotsam of many sorts, following a storm.

Access to all the park's habitats is by trails, boardwalks, or picnic areas, with parking close by.

Plant Life

Because of its variety of habitats, Pelee is a feast for those interested in plant life. Over 700 species of flowering and non-flowering plants are evident, some of which are only found here or in nearby southern areas of Canada.

In the dry forest area, the predominant tree is the hackberry. The sycamore, black oak, and black walnut are also found here. The low

211

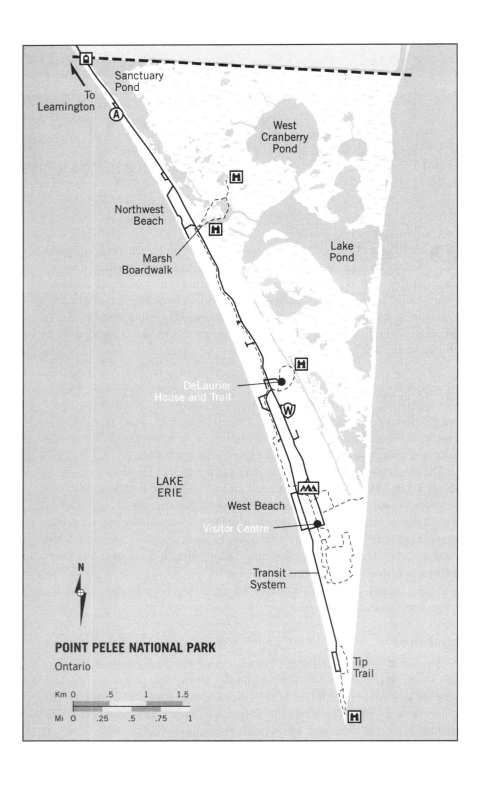

Sanctuary
Pond

To
Leamington

Ⓐ

West
Cranberry
Pond

Ⓗ

Northwest
Beach

Ⓗ

Marsh
Boardwalk

Lake
Pond

Ⓗ

DeLaurier
House and Trail

Ⓦ

LAKE
ERIE

West Beach

Visitor Centre

Transit
System

N

POINT PELEE NATIONAL PARK

Ontario

Km 0   .5   1   1.5

Mi 0   .25   .5   .75   1

Tip
Trail

Ⓗ

elevation and shallow, often soggy, soil of the swamp forest produce the right conditions for the silver maple. A leisurely walk along the **Woodland Nature Trail** clearly demonstrates the relationship between the dry and swamp forests.

The flowers of the woodland are some of the earliest to be seen in spring in Canada, because of the temperature, the moderating effect of the lake, and the southern latitude of the point.

The grassland and savannah areas are interesting, for being the habitat of the prickly pear. These are some of the few places in eastern Canada where this cactus is found. As the grasslands age, the red cedar, staghorn sumac, and dogwood move in.

The marsh habitat shows the changes in plant life that occur at varying water levels. At the north end, visible from the park entrance and from the boardwalk, are cat-tails. In the open-water areas, water lilies decorate the dark water with their glazed, round surfaces and brilliant, white flowers. The damp soil of the land that borders the southern end of the marsh supports water-loving plants and trees, such as the willow, cottonwood, dogwood, and silver maple. The place to see these is along the trail to the **East Beach**.

The beaches dramatize the story of plant succession: the plants that are swept on to the beach, or whose seeds are dropped by wind or birds, begin to colonize the land above high-water marsh. The rotting, beached

Marylee Stephenson

The birds of Point Pelee are its glory, and its fame

plant and animal matter enriches the sand. A few metres further from the water's edge, the enriched sand slowly becomes soil. Here, grasses such as lime grass, beard grass, and witch grass put down their lengthy and hearty roots, as they contribute to an increasing stability and growth of the soil. A large storm may wipe out months or years of growth at the interface between water and vegetation, but neither the plants nor the wind and water ever surrender. Further inland, forests and dry fields become established.

Birds

The birds of Point Pelee are its glory, and its fame. No other place in North America is so ideally located for the presence of great concentrations of such a wide variety of bird species. This is especially true in mid-May and, to a somewhat lesser degree, in the fall.

Birds migrate along fairly wide, and very long "flyways." Birds that have flown the long, foodless trip over the expanse of Lake Erie, virtually tumble on to the mainland—tiny, windswept Point Pelee.

Since the turn of the century, about 350 bird species have been recorded at Point Pelee. Almost 100 species nest there, and about 50 remain over the winter. On a very active day in the spring, bird-watchers have reported seeing nearly 200 species. An individual bird-watcher, or two or three observing together, may see as many as 100 species in a day.

J. Pamela Sachs, Parks Canada

A warbler along the damp woodland trail

Bird-watchers refer to such a day as a "century day," which means that, of all the kinds of birds in North America, the bird-watcher has seen more than one species out of six.

In order to achieve a "century day," however, requires some effort on your part. First, you must catch the train to the point, from the Visitor Centre, at around 6:00 a.m. Then you work your way back up to the Centre; perhaps follow the **Woodland Trail**, or those seasonal trails that are open only during spring migration. Then drive to the **Marsh Boardwalk**, maybe walk through the wooded paths, or picnic on the west side along the entry road, and, as the day closes, watch the woodcock display, near the Centre, in the fading evening light, and listen for the whip-poorwill's repetitive call.

Mammals

For the casual observer, the mammal most likely to be seen is the grey squirrel. Deer are visible in the day, or at night, and they are always a pleasant surprise. Raccoons are also common. Weasels, mink, skunk, and even coyote are present in the park, although they are not often seen. Five species of bats also live here. Although the bats can move in and out of the Point Pelee region, the other mammals are almost marooned. They are hemmed in by water on two sides, and by the built-up area of Leamington, a town of considerable size, located on the park's northern boundary.

Reptiles and Amphibians

A large and varied number of species of reptiles and amphibians can be found at Point Pelee. There are also several uncommon, and even rare, species. In the marsh area, or in the swamp areas along the Woodland Trail, you might see or hear the bullfrog. The somewhat smaller green frog and northern leopard frog are also found there. Reptiles in the marsh area include six species of turtle: snapping, musk, spotted, map, painted, and Blanding's turtles.

Swampy areas are home for that tiny, vocal frog, the spring peeper, and the western chorus frog. Although you are more likely to hear frogs than to see them, they add much to the experience of woods or marsh regardless.

Snakes inhabit the woods, as well as the marsh or swamp areas. The eastern garter snake lives here, and there is a population at Pelee that is entirely dark, instead of having the familiar three light stripes on a dark body. The marsh area is also home to the northern water snake, which eats fish, frogs, or even small mammals. The eastern fox snake—

brownish-yellow, with dark spots—is often mistaken for a rattlesnake, but is harmless. No poisonous snakes live in the park: the last sighting of a Timber rattlesnake was in 1895.

Insects

We often think of insects simply as creepy-crawly creatures to swat as we walk along a trail. The role that insects play as a central food resource for other animals is often overlooked. Unfortunately, the array of insects at Point Pelee—the result of the rich, relatively warm and varied habitat—is often not seen by the casual observer. But there are exceptions, such as dragonflies. You see these insects around the beaches, marshes, and in open fields. Their crystal-clear, veined wings, and colourful bodies (green, purple, yellow, and black, all in one species) are quite striking.

Underfoot in the fields, a wide variety of grasshoppers, crickets, katydids, and walking sticks abound.

The better-known insects are butterflies and moths. Point Pelee is famous for concentrations of monarch butterflies, which gather on certain trees near the tip of the land, from mid-September to early October.

A word about mosquitoes is in order. They certainly exist at Point Pelee, but during the summer, in open areas of the trail, or in fields, or over the marsh when it's bright and hot, they do not pose a problem. Stable flies and horse flies can be annoying anywhere in the park.

Fish

Even though Lake Erie has a wide variety and a fair number of fish (both changing and declining), in general, park visitors only catch smelt. The park is not open for smelting at night and a federal licence is required. There is usually a peak one-week period, during the nine days when the park is open for smelting, where the catch can be really rewarding.

The marsh is another place where fish are an integral part of park life. The marsh is shallow and reed-clogged in most areas. Of the 26 types of fish recorded here, two are "sport fish"—the northern pike and large-mouth bass, both of which are fairly common. Carp are so adaptable to these conditions that they flourish, as do yellow perch, bluegill, and pumpkinseed.

Fishing is allowed in the seasons appropriate to the type of fish. You will need a licence to fish in the marsh. Speak with park staff at the entrance for further details.

PARK SERVICES AND FACILITIES

Interpretive Program

Walking is the key to seeing Point Pelee. Cars are allowed along the main road; you can pull off in the Marsh Boardwalk parking lot, at some of the picnic grounds, and at the main lot at the Visitor Centre. The brochures, available at the entry gate, clearly show these areas.

The Visitor Centre is an excellent place to start your visit. It has informative displays and daily showings of nature-oriented slide shows and films. Special birding hikes are offered in the spring.

The wonderful **Woodland Nature Trail** starts behind the Centre. If you have time for just an hour or two of walking, this is your best choice. The main trail is three kilometres (1.5 miles) of the most concentrated exposure to the wide variety of habitats in the park. Few signs mark the way, so you should bring the informational material you received from the Centre, as well as your own bird or plant guides, camera, and binoculars.

After the Woodland Trail, try the train ride to the point. The train will pick you up at the Visitor Centre, and drop you off at the new facilities, directly north of the **Tip Boardwalk Trail**. These facilities consist of a washroom/fountain building, and an open-concept building to house interpretive displays.

The Marsh Boardwalk is also fascinating. It is now over a kilometre (0.5 mile) in length, and forms a circle with a spoke off it at the farthest end. During July and August, staff operate a daily live interpretive exhibit at the boardwalk, known as the Marsh Cart, to introduce visitors to the life of the marsh. The most activity occurs in the marsh during the early mornings and early evenings, when there are fewer people.

The **DeLaurier Trail**, located halfway between the Visitor Centre and the Marsh Boardwalk, is a delightful 20- to 30-minute walk through old fields, forests, and irrigation canals. The trail leads through **DeLaurier House**, the original, refurbished home of the first squatters on the Point. Parts of the house and barn are open to visitors, with displays and taped commentary.

Across the road from the Visitor Centre is the **Tilden Woods Trail**. This is a short version of the Woodland Trail, with a swamp/forest habitat, and is a favourite with birders.

Camping

No individual camping is allowed in the park. There are three group campgrounds, which you must book ahead with the Superintendent.

Other Accommodation, Gas, Food, and Supplies

Several towns are situated near the park, of which Leamington is the closest. A number of modest, comfortable motels, and even quite a luxurious one, are located just a few minutes from the entry gate. If you plan to visit in mid-May, and want to stay in Leamington or Kingsville, you usually must book a motel by December. Windsor is about a 40-minute drive, and because it is a city with a population of over 200 000, finding year-round accommodation should not be a problem.

The park offers one fast-food concession, which is located at the Marsh Boardwalk. It is open from April 6 to October 29.

Gas is not available in the park, but there are a number of stations in the nearby towns.

Recreational Services

A number of facilities are available in the park. Always check with the entry person or the centre staff for the most current information.

Canoeing   A rental concession is based at the Marsh Boardwalk. You can bring your own canoe, and park there.

Bicycling   The park has a bike concession, which is open in the summer. Some people prefer to bring their own bikes. The existing bike trail is in very good condition, and bicyclists are encouraged to use it. Bikes are allowed as far as the facilities at the Tip.

The Tram   From April until Thanksgiving, there is transit service from the Visitor Centre to a point just north of the tip. At the height of the spring bird migration, this service runs from 6:00 a.m. to 9:00 p.m.

Winter Use   When there is enough snow, some trails are open for cross-country skiing. An area near the Marsh boardwalk is kept clear, and is flooded for ice skating throughout January and February, or as long as the ice lasts.

Related Activities or Places of Natural or Historic Interest

Ontario Tourism can provide information for all kinds of visitation in the province and direct you to local Travel Information Centres. Call (416) 314-0944.

Activities and Places to Consider Visiting:
- There are many birding sites in Essex County, including

Related Activities Cont'd

conservation areas, bird sanctuaries, and nature reserves. Visitor services can provide you with more information.

- For historic interest: Heritage Village, near Harrow; John Freeman Wall Historic Site; North American Black Historical Museum, in Amherstburg.

- Wheatley Provincial Park, located one kilometre east of Wheatley; Rondeau Provincial Park at Morpeth.

National Historic Sites:

- Amherstburg: Fort Malden, Bois Blanc Island Lighthouse

For More Information

The Superintendent
Point Pelee National Park
R.R. I
Leamington, Ontario
N8H 3V4
Phone: (519) 322-2365/322-2371 (recorded information line)

ST. LAWRENCE ISLANDS

National Park

I slands always have an aura of adventure. It is exciting to spend a few hours "marooned" on an island, even if you can walk its length in 10 minutes. Islands aren't the only feature of St. Lawrence Islands National Park, but they are what makes it distinctive.

This park, with about nine square kilometres (3.5 square miles) of land area, is the smallest in the Canadian system. Nevertheless, the 21 islands and numerous tiny islets that comprise the area stretch for 80 kilometres (50 miles) west from Brockville along the St. Lawrence River. The Thousand Islands Parkway runs the length of the park, offering a spectacular view of the myriad islands that dot the St. Lawrence. A raised bicycle path runs parallel to the Parkway and river shoreline for 38 kilometres (24 miles).

All of the 21 islands have some part that is park area, and 16 islands offer boat tie-ups, picnicking, and/or camping facilities.

The Thousand Islands are actually the worn-away roots of an ancient mountain range, over which the St. Lawrence River flows. The mountains formed a bridge of rock that stretched between the southern edges of the Canadian Shield, which underlies much of Canada, and the area that is now the Adirondack Mountains of New York State. This bridge is called the Frontenac Axis. When the glaciers retreated from this area, and the St. Lawrence River became established, the high points of this rocky link remained evident as islands.

Broad-leaved forests are the dominant landscape, with breaks for open fields, many of which have been cultivated over the years, and are now abandoned to their own regrowth. The islands are, characteristically, a meeting place for northern plants that find here the southernmost place where they can survive, and plants from the south that cannot exist farther north. Even from island to island, there is often quite a difference between those plants that thrive at either the northern or southern end of the land. Prevailing winds and protective locations, in relation to other islands, have a decided effect.

221

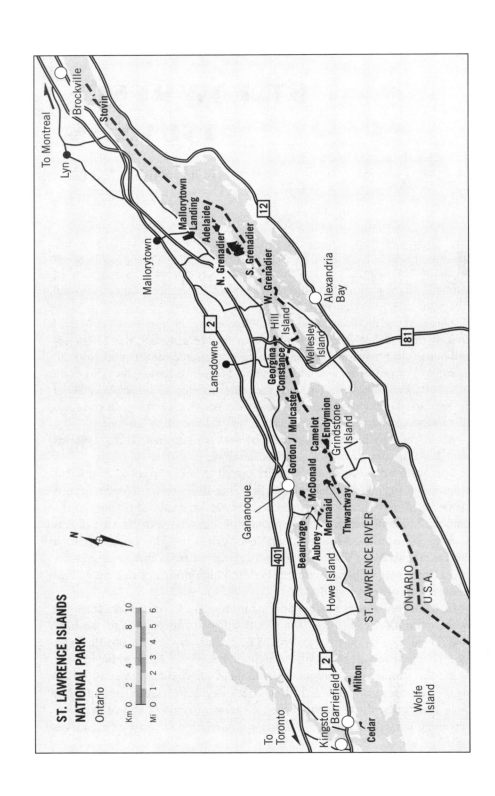

ST. LAWRENCE ISLANDS
NATIONAL PARK

Ontario

Km 0 2 4 6 8 10
Mi 0 1 2 3 4 5 6

N

To Montreal

Brockville

Stovin

Lyn

Mallorytown Landing

Adelaide

Mallorytown

N. Grenadier

S. Grenadier

W. Grenadier

12

Alexandria Bay

Lansdowne

2

Hill Island

Wellesley Island

81

Georgina

Constance

Gordon

Mulcaster

Camelot

McDonald

Endymion

Grindstone Island

Gananoque

Beaurivage

Aubrey

Mermaid

Thwartway

401

Howe Island

ST. LAWRENCE RIVER

ONTARIO

U.S.A.

To Toronto

Kingston

Barriefield

Milton

Cedar

2

Wolfe Island

Animal life differs from mainland to island. Animals that hibernate, such as chipmunks, never cross over the ice to the islands in winter, nor do they swim there in summer. But squirrels, some kinds of mice, and some shrews are active all winter and therefore can be found living on both the mainland and many islands. Larger animals, such as the deer or porcupine, fox, and even coyote, can also wander among the islands.

HOW TO SEE THE PARK

St. Lawrence Islands National Park is both easy and difficult to visit. You can reach Mallorytown Landing area by car from Highway 401, which

Wild calla, in the Arum family

runs from Toronto to Kingston and Montreal. The highway exits are well marked. But, to visit an island, you must take one of the privately run charter water taxis that operate out of local towns, or rent a boat from a regional marina. The staff at the park have up-to-date information on where boat rides are provided. For a longer stay, it is also possible to rent commercially owned houseboats.

Visiting the Islands

For people with their own boats—even canoes—the park really comes into its own. Sixteen of the island locations have docking facilities, and another, **Thwartway**, has mooring and a beach only. Many offer toilets and picnicking; some have weather shelters with cook stoves and fire-wood, small tent-camping areas, and drinking water. Most islands are four to 12 hectares (10 to 30 acres) in area. They all have easy walks, amid varied and interesting plants and animals, and water is close for swimming, fishing, or boating. You can canoe among the islands, near the protection of the mainland shore. Although the park provides its own maps for an overview of the islands and waterways, nautical charts are essential for safe boating. These charts are numbered 1436, 1437, 1438, and 1439 metric, for the whole park area.

Aubrey Island has tent-camping facilities for a few, scattered sites, as do a number of other islands. Since the island is small (no more than a 10-minute walk down its length), more sites would result in crowding. Cooking shelters are situated at each end of the island, pit toilets at either end, and each site has its own picnic table and small, raised cooking grill. In season, a supply of firewood is provided at the two boat landings. There's a pump for water, but be prepared to work hard for it.

Exploring the Mainland

The short **Mainland Nature Trail** runs behind the park headquarters, starting at the north side of the parkway. It covers a wide variety of habitat, for an easy, 30-minute walk. Eight hundred metres (2400 feet) of the trail have been made accessible for disabled visitors. I visited in early May, on several clear, warming days, and it proved to be an intense experience of concentrated springtime. Skeins of geese were fly-ing over, the rare rue anemone bloomed, along with the trillium, hepat-ica, and May-apples. Nearby, the first brown thrashers and yellow war-blers of the year also sang constantly. Chipmunks and black squirrels were active everywhere and, in contrast, a big porcupine sat immobile

Snapper laying eggs

on a fork of a tree above my head. At the end of the walk was the most cottony-tailed cottontail rabbit I've ever seen!

PARK FACILITIES AND SERVICES

Interpretive Program

At Mallorytown Landing, the Interpretive Centre is situated right at the shoreline, next to the swimming beach. A few metres away is the Browns Bay wreck display—a resurrected gunboat that sank in the last century. Since so many of the park's visitors are active boaters and do not remain in one place for long, roving interpreters travel the waterways of the park in boats. The interpretive staff have prepared a large selection of booklets on many aspects of the park—its sports fish, geology, climate, birds, mammals, plants, reptiles, amphibians, and history; a newsletter is also provided.

Primitive Camping

Eleven of the islands have primitive campsites, with drinking water, pit toilets, and flat areas for tents. There are cooking shelters and picnic tables, but no hook-ups. There is a docking area with a limit of three consecutive nights docking per island. **Grenadier Island** has individual campsites and group camping at the centre island location. A self-registration system is in place, to collect docking, camping, and firewood fees on the islands. Some interpretive presentations charge admission. Park maps, which are available at the Interpretive Centre, provide a helpful chart that outlines the facilities on each island.

Other Accommodation, Gas, Food, and Supplies

The Thousand Islands area has many motels, a few hotels, and a number of very attractive campgrounds, situated along the Thousand Islands Parkway and in larger cities, such as Gananoque and Kingston. The park and many of the business establishments provide informative brochures, supplied by the local travel and tourist associations. For more information, contact the Kingston Tourism Information Office, 209 Ontario Street, Kingston, Ontario K7L 2Z1, (613) 548-4415.

Gasoline, food, and supplies are easily obtained along the Thousand Islands Parkway or in Mallorytown. There are several marinas and marine-supply stores.

Recreational Services

Mallorytown Landing contains the main recreation complex, with its children's playground, swimming beach, changing rooms, washrooms, and boat ramp. The parking lot is large. The main season runs from June through Labour Day. These facilities are accessible for disabled visitors.

Fishing   About 20 species of fish are commonly caught in Thousand Island waters. Check in any fishing or sports store, for information on requirements for provincial fishing licences for certain fish.

Boat Trips   Brockville, Rockport, Ivy Lea, and Gananoque offer boat tours or boat-rental businesses during the summer.

Related Activities or Places of Natural or Historic Interest

Ontario Tourism can provide information for all kinds of visitation in the province and direct you to local Travel Information Centres. Call (416) 314-0944.

Activities and Places to Consider Visiting:

• Charleston Lake Provincial Park for hiking trails, canoeing, and camping on the Frontenac Axis.

Related Activities Cont'd

- For historic interest: Fort Henry in Kingston; Upper Canada Village in Morrisburg; Historic Thousand Islands Village in Gananoque; Brockville Museum in Brockville.

National Historic Sites:

- Ottawa to Kingston: The Rideau Canal

- Kingston: Bellevue House, Kingston Martello Towers

- Prescott: Fort Wellington, Battle of the Windmill

For More Information

St. Lawrence Islands National Park
R.R. 3
Mallorytown Landing, Ontario
KOE IRO
Phone: (613) 923-5261
Fax: (613) 923-2229

Thousand Islands Gananoque
Chamber of Commerce
2 King Street East
Gananoque, Ontario
K7G 1E6
Phone: 1-800-561-1595

LA MAURICIE

National Park

La Mauricie National Park is little known outside Quebec and yet, year-round, it is one of the most accessible and well-serviced parks in the Canadian system. Located just 200 kilometres (124 miles) northeast of Montréal, La Mauricie encompasses 544 square kilometres (212 square miles) of the Quebec Laurentians. The Laurentians here are knobbly, wooded mountains, incised by dozens of brooks and cascades and elongated lakes.

The Laurentians sit on the Canadian Shield, part of the Earth's first continental plate. About one billion years ago, tremendous mountain building activity on this section of the Shield caused uplifting, folding, and fracturing of several thousand metres of sedimentary rocks and formed a mountain range as high as the Rockies. During this process, rocks forming at great depths were transformed by tremendous temperature and pressure into metamorphic rock before rising to the surface. Hundreds of millions of years of erosion eventually eliminated the layer of sediments, and left a plateau of hard metamorphic rock. Beginning about one million years ago, and ending 10 000 years ago, four periods of glaciation filed and smoothed the rough edges of the Laurentians, deepened the valleys, deposited crushed rock, and created the numerous small lakes.

Except for its southern boundary and half of its western edge, the park is bounded by two very large rivers—the Matawin over half of the west and half of the north sides, and the St. Maurice on the northeast and east. More than 150 lakes and ponds are located in the park, many of which— Wapizagonke, du Caribou, Edouard and Lake à la Pêche—are accessible, not only to canoeists, but also to car-based visitors.

In its present protected state, La Mauricie is densely covered with a jigsaw puzzle of forests. Thirty tree species are found here. In rich, well-drained, and deep soil, sugar maple is the dominant species, both in number and in size, with yellow birch and some beech mixed in. On the

Marylee Stephenson

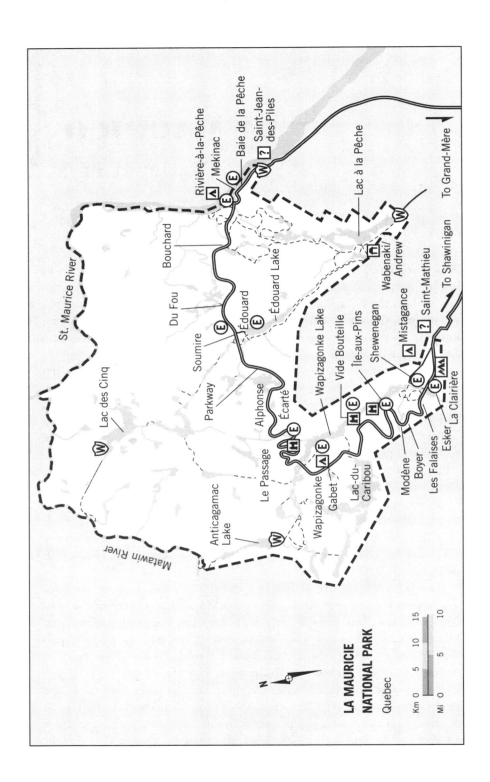

LA MAURICIE NATIONAL PARK

Quebec

N

Km 0   5   10   15

Mi 0   5   10

St. Maurice River

Matawin River

Anticagamac Lake

Lac des Cinq

Le Passage

Wapizagonke Gabet

Lac-du-Caribou

Écarté

Alphonse

Parkway

Soumire

Édouard

Du Fou

Bouchard

Édouard Lake

Wapizagonke Lake

Vide Bouteille

Île-aux-Pins

Shewenegan

Modène

Boyer

Les Falaises

Esker

La Clairière

Mistagance

Saint-Mathieu

Wabenaki/ Andrew

Lac à la Pêche

Rivière-à-la-Pêche

Mekinac

Baie de la Pêche

Saint-Jean- des-Piles

To Grand-Mère

To Shawinigan

Marylee Stephenson

Water runs from hillsides to other lakes, to form an intricate
web of streams and cascades

thin-soiled slopes and in the damper soil of the valleys, pine, fir, and
spruce dominate.

People have played a considerable role in the park's history. For more
than 8000 years, the forests were home to a sub-group of the native
Algonquin people, known as the Attikameks. These nomadic people
travelled the lakes and forests, as they hunted game or foraged for
berries, roots, and other plant materials.

The arrival of Euro-Canadians in the area significantly affected the
environment. Since 1970, much restoration has been undertaken,
including reforestation, the closure of logging roads, the restoration of
water bodies, and the gradual eradication of white spruce plantations.
Now one of the major threats is from acid rain.

HOW TO SEE THE PARK*

To appreciate the geological history, and the story of the lakes, forests, and human history of the park, it's best to combine participation in the interpretive program with hiking and driving on your own. From June through September, daily guided activities are offered, and a slide talk is provided in each of the three amphitheatres every night of the week.

From May until mid-October, slide shows are offered at the Visitor Reception Centre at Saint-Jean-des-Piles, and occasionally an interpretive event. The canoe tours are a great way to learn more about lakes.

All the talks are given in French, but since the interpretation is unique, and the walks, canoe paddles, and drives are through wonderful scenery, much of the language barrier is overcome.

To explore on your own, drive from one end of the park to the other, to get an excellent idea of the shapes created by the cracking and eroding of the land. The most spectacular viewpoint, **Le Passage**, is located near the northern end of **Wapizagonke Lake**.

To see how a forest grows and changes, there is the beautiful trail, **Les Cascades**, which starts from the major day-use area at the Shewenegan picnic area. After crossing the big wooden bridge, you travel through many types of forest. From this trail, you can take a side trip to the **Les Falaises Trail**.

To learn more about the maple-birch forest, try the excellent interpretation trail to **Lake Gabet**. It is an easy 1.5-kilometre (one-mile) walk that winds gradually uphill, through a forest that is 80 percent sugar maple, with yellow birch and American beech also present. As the trail approaches the lake, conifers take over and the forest becomes predominantly balsam fir and red spruce.

If it's winter, and you are cross-country skiing along the 80 kilometres (50 miles) of trails, look at the shelters for the interpretive panels that explain the winter fauna.

For a very special visit, explore the **Esker Bog** on the short interpretive **Tourbière Trail**. To get there, take the L'Esker turnoff from the main road at the south end of the park, just before the first bridge over Lake Wapizagonke, or follow the **Vallerand Trail** from the Shewenegan area. It is about 1.5 kilometres (one mile) to the bog trail. The trail is mostly a

---

*Julie Cartier visited this park for me in August, to round out my spring and fall visits. She participated in the French-language interpretive events, and experienced the park at its busiest season. I am indebted to her for much of this chapter's material.

boardwalk, which takes you out on the peat-moss mat located at the edge of the small lake, and then back through the black-spruce-and-tamarack forest that has taken hold where the ground has become more compacted. The peat is now up to seven metres (20 feet) thick.

For the human history of the park, you must rely on the interpretive programs and the exhibition room in the Saint-Jean-des-Piles Visitor Centre. Once you have heard the stories, the park takes on another dimension; lakes become canoe routes, moving masses of logs; forests become sources of food and shelter; history surrounds you.

PARK SERVICES AND FACILITIES

This is a year-round park, with very heavy use from late June through mid-August, extensive cross-country use in winter, and moderate camping, hiking, and day-visiting use in late spring and well into autumn.

Interpretive Program

The park has an invaluable interpretive program and a number of self-guided walks. There are schedules, posters, and bulletin-board notices at the entrances to campgrounds and picnic areas.

The Saint-Mathieu Centre provides maps, and a desk run by the local park cooperative association, Info-Nature Mauricie, sells books and souvenirs.

Parks Canada

Visitors learn about the park from the attractive graphic displays

At the Saint-Jean-des-Piles side, the Centre offers all this, and much more. It is a much larger building, with a theatre and extraordinarily attractive indoor and outdoor graphic displays of the natural and human history themes of the park.

For day visits, there are several picnic sites and a large kitchen shelter at the Lake Edouard picnic area, which includes an interpretation exhibit. The shelter can accommodate a group of 60 people.

Camping

Three large campgrounds, which are accessible by car, are open in summer: **Mistagance,** nearest the Saint-Mathieu entrance; **Wapizagonke,** about a 30-minute drive north, just off the park's main road; and **Rivière à la Pêche,** located a few minutes from the Saint-Jean-des-Piles entrance. All campgrounds are wooded. They all have hot showers, washrooms, flush toilets, picnic tables, fire grates, and (except Mistagance) kitchen shelters. Firewood is available for a fee. Mistagance, with 90 sites, is closest to the boat concession and swimming beaches at south Lake Wapizagonke. Wapizagonke is actually situated at a beach and is the largest site, with 219 sites. Rivière à la Pêche has sites with electricity and facilities for people in wheelchairs. It is also located at the trailhead of the entire system of hiking and cross-country-skiing trails that cover the southeast segment of the park. Each campground has an amphitheatre for the nightly slide talks. In the spring and fall, the Wapizagonke Campground is closed, but there is plenty of room at the others. There are no trailer hook-ups, but there are waste-disposal stations. Reservations can be made by phoning (819) 533-7272.

Primitive Camping

Since there is such an extensive network of canoe routes in the back country, many primitive campsites are situated along the way. You must register at the Visitor Centres and indicate which sites you intend to use, to avoid overcrowding. Some sites have firewood and fire grates, while others require portable campstoves. In times of high fire hazard, only campstoves may be used. Open fires are never allowed. All sites have tent pallets and pit toilets.

Group Camping

Group camping is available from mid-May to early October at La Clairière, near Lake Wapizagonke. There is a kitchen shelter with woodstoves, campfire facilities, picnic tables, and washrooms and showers. Only tents are allowed and the area is restricted to non-commercial parties of 10 or more. Reservations are required.

Other Accommodation, Gas, Food, and Supplies

A number of commercial campgrounds are located outside the park; a list is available from the park. In the park itself, in summer, there are snack bars at the Shewenegan and Lake Edouard day-use areas, and a small convenience store at the Wapizagonke day-use area. There is no gasoline in the park. In the villages just outside both entrances to the park, there are small grocery and supply stores and gasoline. Just before the entrance on the Saint-Mathieu side, there is a grocery store and snack bar, which are open only during the summer.

Recreational Services

Note for Senior Citizens Lakes Boyer, Modène, and Alphonse are reserved for use by senior citizens, for fishing only.

Facilities for the Disabled Organized groups of persons with disabilities are invited to inquire (c/o the Superintendent) about the availability of interpretive and other services that can be arranged for their group. Both Visitor Centres, the major day-use areas, the Interpretive Centre, and most viewpoints are wheelchair accessible. An interpretation trail at Lake Edouard has been designed for universal access.

Canoeing Most of the lakes are accessible for canoeing. A number of lakes touch upon, or are within a short walk of, the main highway. Canoe- and row-boat rentals are available every day from mid-June to Labour Day, at the Shewenegan day-use area, at Wapizagonke and at Lake Edouard, and on weekends only, from Labour Day to Thanksgiving, at Shewenegan. For canoeing for a few hours or so, the lakes most often used are Wapizagonke, Edouard, and du Caribou. The many kilometres of back-country canoe routes are connected by portage trails. Request the brochure on canoe routes in the park. You must register in and out for overnight trips, and must also pack out all garbage. There is self-registration during spring and fall, at the Visitor Reception Centre.

Hiking Trails vary in length from one to 15 kilometres (0.5 to nine miles). In general, they are easily accessible and some are interpreted.

Swimming Unsupervised swimming beaches are located at the day-use areas of Shewenegan, L'Esker, Wapizagonke, and Lake Edouard. In addition, many sandy lakeshores offer canoeists the possibility of a quick dip.

Fishing   Fishing is allowed in 39 lakes. You must purchase an inexpensive permit, available at Visitor Centres, at campground kiosks, or from convenience stores in Saint-Gérard-des-Laurentides, Saint-Mathieu, or Saint-Jean-des-Piles. At the same time, you can find out which lakes are open to fishing and what early limits are. Fishing season is from the last Saturday of May to Labour Day.

Winter Use   The park has an extremely well-developed winter-use program, centred on the Saint-Jean-des-Piles side at the eastern entrance. Ask for the brochure that has a map of the numerous trails, and describes the equipment and skills necessary for enjoyable and safe cross-country skiing, snowshoeing, and winter camping.

There are 80 kilometres (50 miles) of skiing trails of varying degrees of difficulty. Winter camping is possible at the Rivière à la Pêche Campground, which has pit toilets and a kitchen shelter with wood stove. Every five kilometres (three miles) along the trail system, there are warming huts, which have firewood, stoves, and pit toilets. It is possible to camp in primitive campsites if you are equipped with tents and other equipment, but there is no overnight use of the shelters. Near the south end of Lake à la Pêche, there are two lodges—Wabenaki and Andrew—which can accommodate 46 people. You must reserve at Info-Nature Mauricie, (819) 537-4555, from the third Monday of November, to assure a place. It is accessible only on skis, and a modest nightly fee is charged.

You can rent ski equipment in the small villages near the park entrances, or in Shawinigan and Grand-Mère.

Related Activities or Places of Natural or Historic Interest

Tourism Quebec is an excellent information service for all kinds of visitation in the province. Call 1-800-363-7777. La Mauricie Park is located in the "Mauricie-Bois-Francs" tourism region.

Activities and Places to Consider Visiting:

- Parc des Chutes between Shawinigan and Shawinigan-Sud.
- Boat cruises on the Saint Maurice River (from Grand-Mère and other towns).

Related Activities Cont'd

- For historic interest: Village du Bûcheron in Grande-Piles, which recreates a logging camp at the turn of the century.

National Historic Site

(Contact Canada Parks Service for the "Discover a living heritage" information booklet on the sites in Quebec):

- Trois-Rivières: Forges du Saint-Maurice

For More Information

Parks Canada
La Mauricie District
Place Cascade
794, 5th Street
C.P. 758
Shawinigan, Québec
G9N 6V9
Phone: (819) 536-2638
Fax: (819) 536-3661

Info-Nature Mauricie
776, 5th Street
C.P. 174
Shawinigan, Québec
G9N 6T9
Phone: (819) 537-4555

Economic Development Corporation of the Central Maurice Region
769, 5th Avenue
Shawinigan, Québec
G9N 1G1
Phone: (819) 537-7249

SAGUENAY-
ST. LAWRENCE
Marine Park

Visiting Saguenay-St. Lawrence Marine Park was like coming home to a French-Canadian side of the family I didn't know I had. It is a warm, friendly family, whose waterfront view includes whales passing by and whose backyard is actually one of the longest fjords in the world.

Each of Canada's national parks has its own distinctive character, which is one of the reasons they have been selected to be part of Canada's parks system. But Saguenay-St. Lawrence has its own special qualities—not simply because it is a marine park, or because of its fjord and whales, but because it has been established in the midst of 24 municipalities and a Quebec provincial park. As such, it is an example of a partnership between the federal government, the province of Quebec, the communities and tourism areas, hundreds of private businesses and non-profit organizations, and thousands of residents. In 1990, the federal government and the province of Quebec agreed to begin the process of establishing the park.

Strictly speaking, the federal government is responsible for two land sites and for the waterways of the park—up to the high tide line. This includes responsibility for traffic on the fjord and St. Lawrence estuary, since these are national waterways. The province of Quebec has responsibility for Parc du Saguenay, which extends along the forested shores of the fjord for over 80 kilometres (50 miles) and includes the bed of the Saguenay River and the seafloor of the St. Lawrence estuary. But local residents and businesses and organizations also have interests and responsibilities in the area, as they carry out their daily lives. As a visitor, you too are an important part of the life of the Saguenay-St. Lawrence environs.

When you visit the park, you will not be aware of who "owns" what, or who is responsible for what. Rather, you'll move easily between the land and the water, learning about the marine life or the geological forces that created the fjord. The diverse quality of the area led to the park's motto—"crossroads of life, source of exchange and richness."

Marylee Stephenson

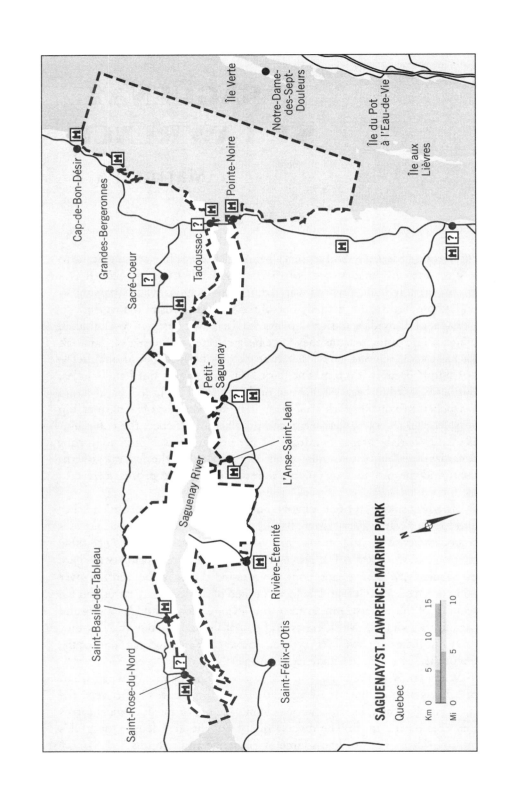

SAGUENAY/ST. LAWRENCE MARINE PARK

Quebec

Km 0   5   10   15

Mi 0   5   10

Cap-de-Bon-Désir

Grandes-Bergeronnes

Sacré-Coeur

Tadoussac

Pointe-Noire

Île Verte

Notre-Dame-
des-Sept-
Douleurs

Île du Pot
à l'Eau-de-Vie

Île aux
Lièvres

Petit-
Saguenay

L'Anse-Saint-Jean

Saguenay River

Rivière-Éternité

Saint-Félix-d'Otis

Saint-Basile-de-Tableau

Saint-Rose-du-Nord

Marylee Stephenson

The scenic coastline of the Saguenay fjord

HOW TO SEE THE PARK

Saguenay-St. Lawrence Marine Park is located at the mouth of the Saguenay River, where it flows into the St. Lawrence River. The park is shaped roughly like the letter T, if it were lying on its side, with the cross-bar at the east, covering parts of the lower and upper estuary of the St. Lawrence, along its north shore. This estuary cross-bar runs about 90 kilometres (56 miles) northeast and southwest of the mouth of the Saguenay River. The long line of the T is the Saguenay fjord. The fjord is an extension of the Saguenay River. Because of a fault in the underlying Cambrian Shield, the river bed plunges as deep as 275 metres (825 feet) in places. Because of this depth and the high cliffs and steep slopes that border it, the river becomes a fjord. The Saguenay fjord extends 100 kilometres (62 miles) to the east, as it meets the St. Lawrence estuary near the village of Tadoussac. It is one of the southernmost fjords in the world, and is unusual in that it opens on to a river estuary instead of the ocean.

The St. Lawrence itself is very deep along its shore here, plunging to over 300 metres (900 feet) in places. The river brings in very cold and salty water from the Atlantic. The St. Lawrence is tidal, and twice a day it pours its cold water into the Saguenay. This cold water sinks and forms a very slow-moving layer that is as cold and salty as water found in the Arctic Ocean. The warmer Saguenay water from the land run-off and its other river tributaries flows nearer the surface of the fjord and into the St.

This interpretive site is run by a non-profit community group

Lawrence. There, this layer of fresh water begins to be mixed vertically at the confluence of the two rivers. This layering and mixing of waters of the fjord and the St. Lawrence make for a rich and varied plant and animal life in the area.

It must be noted, however, that this marvellous, unique natural environment has suffered greatly from some of the worst pollution in North America, as industries along the Great Lakes and the St. Lawrence River, and at the source of the Saguenay River and its tributaries, have poured toxic wastes into the river system for more than 100 years. Efforts to end these practices have met with limited success, and clean-up of such severely damaged river beds is almost impossible. In fact, the features that draw us to this beautiful place—water, woods, whales, fish, and birds—continue to be threatened.

Marine Park Visitor Sites

The southern boundary of the park starts at Saint-Fidèle, located on Highway 138. As you drive north, notice several lookout sites along the shore. These include Port-au-Saumon, Saint-Siméon, and Baie-des-Rochers, all of which have observation sites.

As you go along the main road northeast, you will come to one of the main visitation centres of the Marine Park area—**Pointe Noire**. This is an interpretation and observation centre, located at the mouth of the fjord and just south of the dock for the ferry to Tadoussac, which is the largest community in the park area. Pointe Noire is a light station that is run by Transport Canada, but is now owned by Parks Canada. Because Pointe Noire is situated at the edge of a very steep cliff, where the water is very deep and up-welling, it is a favourite place for whales to feed. Often the minke whales come very close in and you can see them easily, and the belugas are also there.

Pointe Noire is also a great place to see the tidal movements and currents where the waters of the Saguenay and St. Lawrence meet. You can even hear the sounds of the tides changing!

Pointe Noire is one example of the partnership between Parks Canada and the local community. Transport Canada operates the automatic land-based navigational light system for ships entering the treacherous waters at the entrance of the Saguenay fjord. Parks Canada maintains the physical site, and a local non-profit research and education group provides the interpretation activities.

The other main visitor site is **Cap-de-Bon-Désir**, a 20-minute drive north of Tadoussac. Here again is a lighthouse and Interpretation Centre. This Centre is managed by Parks Canada and the Bergeronnes Tourism Corporation.

This is also a splendid place to watch whales. You walk through a narrow band of forest, follow a short network of boardwalks, and then settle down on gently sloping rocks by the water's edge.

The Saguenay Fjord and the St. Lawrence Estuary

Regardless of where you go in the park, the fjord and the estuary will be part of your visit. You will see them, walk beside them, boat on them, and maybe even dive into their chilly waters. There are approximately 25 boat-tour operators, and about 60 boats actually cruising the waters of the park. You will have many to choose from, ranging from kayaks to zodiacs to small and large cruise boats. Your choice of activity and location will depend on your interests. If you go into the fjord, you are likely to see belugas, which go as far up the fjord as Saint Fulgence.

If you want to see the sweep of the St. Lawrence and cruise through the choppy standing waves at the confluence of the two rivers of the park, then one of the larger cruise boats may be your best choice. When I was out we saw a gannet from the Gaspé, several belugas glowing ghostly white in the distance, and several other whales somewhat closer. We also circled the huge Haut-Fond Prince lighthouse, which juts out of the water at the Prince Shoal of the St. Lawrence.

The Communities of the Marine Park

The Saguenay-St. Lawrence area has a very long and interesting human history. Its location at the confluence of two major waterways made it an important corridor for travel. Because of the rich resources of marine and land-based plants and animals, the area was inhabited by aboriginal peoples as long ago as 8000 years. Archeological sites are located along the shore between Tadoussac and Les Escoumins, and a number of other sites are also situated in the area.

European contact began in the sixteenth century. Whalers, fishers, fur trappers, and traders took advantage of the natural resources in the area. In the 1800s and 1900s, forestry moved to the forefront of economic activity. The logging and transporting of logs had a direct and negative effect on the marine environment, however. Furthermore, the coming of industrialization in the form of pulp and paper plants, dams for hydroelectric power stations, and massive mining operations changed the environment yet again.

Tadoussac is the pivotal community of the Saguenay-St. Lawrence Marine Park. It houses the headquarters of Parks Canada and has the largest of the marine interpretation centres—the Centre d'Interprétation du Milieu Marin (CIMM). CIMM has very attractive displays and a number of talks and videos, and is located close to the wharf, which in turn marks the beginning of one of the essential trails for you to take—the **Pointe de l'Islet**. The trail takes you through a little bit of forest and then over the rocks that slope gently to the river, which seems like an ocean because of the width of the St. Lawrence here. Watch for minke whales, because they come in very close to the land here.

Tadoussac also has several important historical sites, including **La Chappelle des Indiens**, a church built in 1747 by the Jesuits. There is a replica of the first fur trading post, built in 1942 on what is believed to be the place where the original had stood. Guided tours are provided, with displays, films, and examples of furs. These two sites are part of the "Heritage Trail," which was established by the community in 1990.

On the way north from Tadoussac to Les Escoumins is another important place to visit—not a community but rather an interpretive site, **Maison des Dunes**. This refurbished two-storey house serves as an Interpretive Centre. The dunes are really a high, sandy cliff that leads to a point out into the St. Lawrence. You can walk down to the shore and along one of the relatively few sandy beaches in the area.

Les Escoumins is a 40-kilometre (25-mile) drive northeast of Tadoussac, if you continue along the shore of the St. Lawrence. It is located at the northern border of the park and is an excellent place for whale-watching from cruise boats as well as from the shore. A non-profit community group has created an Interpretive Centre ("Le Centre des Loisirs Marins des Escoumins") on the low cliffs overlooking the St. Lawrence. The Centre is distinguished for its emphasis on exploring the underwater world through diving. It offers guided dives and specialized services and facilities for divers. Land-locked visitors can walk down to the smooth rocks below the Centre to settle in to watch for whales.

Saguenay Provincial Park and Its Communities

You can think of the Saguenay Provincial Park and its communities as the land base of the Saguenay-St. Lawrence Marine Park. Tadoussac marks the beginnings of the Saguenay Park component of the Marine Park, but many villages are nestled along the shoreline of the Saguenay fjord. They are wonderful places to learn more about the history of the area and to experience the rich French-Canadian culture of the Saguenay of today. The surrounding forests, lakes, and streams also offer one of the best hiking trail systems in the East.

At least 10 villages are in, or on the border of, the Saguenay Park. One way to reach them in a leisurely day or two is by driving. Some of the particular attractions include an Interpretive Centre and wonderful bird-watching along the tidal marshes at **Saint-Fulgence**, the salmon ladders at **La Baie**, an Interpretive Centre at **Baie Éternité**, beluga-watching at **Baie Sainte-Marguerite**, and the covered bridge and traditional architecture of **L'Anse-Saint-Jean**. And don't forget the community of **Grandes-Bergeronnes**, where Cap-de-Bon-Desir is located, and **Baie-Sainte-Catherine**, the location of Pointe-Noire.

The trail systems and wilderness camping sites in the Saguenay Park are truly impressive. And keep in mind, they are available year-round, with cross-country skiers using them for day trips and overnight in winter. For both winter and summer there are short trails that follow the shore or loop inland, or that lead from campsite to campsite. The trails are concentrated on the south side of the fjord, but there is a 15-kilometre (nine-mile) trail that runs from the Maison des Dunes west to Cap de la Boule.

If you have time, round out your visit to the park by exploring its water and land from every possible angle. Drive, walk, ski, camp, sit, read, watch—even dive if you can.

PARK SERVICES AND FACILITIES

Because of the park's distinctive nature, the organization and availability of services and facilities differ from the other national parks. First, the national park supports other service providers rather than providing most of the direct services itself. Park staff are available to you by phone or fax, and you may want to drop by park headquarters in downtown Tadoussac to ask questions and get started on your visit. No campgrounds or other accommodations are provided by Parks Canada, because the land is not under the federal jurisdiction. However, there are many places to stay or camp in the communities and in the park itself. You will find that precisely because of the partnerships between the levels of government and the local community that there is one of the widest choices of services and facilities that you will find in any of the national parks.

Interpretation Program

A variety of sources offer many different programs and services. You can get information on these at park headquarters, but most of the Interpretive Centres and many of the local businesses and accommodations also carry a range of information. The hours and days of opening vary, depending on the nature of the service, time of year, and so on, so check first, especially before mid-June and after Labour Day.

Camping

There is a privately run campground at Grandes Bergeronnes (near Cap-de-Bon-Desir) and in Tadoussac. There are other private campgrounds in the area and the provincial park has many campsites—some "primitive" ones and some for car-based campers. For details, write or call either the Canadian Parks Service or provincial Ministry of the Environment and Wildlife numbers listed below.

Other Accommodation, Gas, Food, and Supplies

There are also dozens, if not hundreds, of other accommodations, ranging from the upscale Hotel Tadoussac to modest bed-and-breakfasts, and a great variation in between.

Of course, with all of the villages and towns in the area, you can find anything you want. If you are driving up the main highways from Montreal or Quebec, many superstore malls are located along the way to stock up on basics.

Recreational Services

Ice Fishing There is ice fishing on the fjord in winter and open-water fishing the rest of the year. You should become familiar with the regulations by contacting the provincial Ministry of the Environment listed below. Snowmobiling is an increasingly popular recreational activity in the area, with trails set aside for this use.

Kayaking   Kayaking is also increasingly popular, and local companies can provide supplies or guides for trips in the fjord. The intricate shoreline and many islets make for a fascinating experience.

Whale-watching   Of course, whale-watching is a central part of most visitors' expectations for their visit. You will have no shortage of choices, in terms of vessel, route, duration of the trip, degree of luxury on the boat, and cost. Collect brochures, talk with people, and make your decision. But don't forget the amazing opportunities to see these wonderful mammals right from the shore. There is no cost in some places and in others there will be a fee of a few dollars for entry where a non-profit organization manages the site.

Bird-watching   Wherever you go, but especially near or on the water, bring binoculars for bird-watching. The St. Lawrence is a highway for birds and some unusual ones are to be seen, from boats or the shore.

HOW TO GET THERE

Most people drive, and you can make your trip more interesting (and a bit more time-consuming) if you take a ferry at least one way across the St. Lawrence. The usual crossings are at Rivière-du-Loup to arrive at the south end of the park or Trois-Pistoles for the north end. The main route from Montreal is Highway 40 for the north shore of the St. Lawrence, or #20 for the south shore. Highway 40 becomes #138 from Quebec City, and this route takes you into Tadoussac. The east-west routes along the fjord are #172 on the north shore and #170 along the south shore.

The tourist guides from the province of Quebec (see below) provide detailed information on the places to visit along the way. The booklets have a number of "auto-tours" from various departure points in the area.

Ferry Information:
For departures from the South Shore of the St. Lawrence:
Riverière-du-Loup (418) 862-5094
Trois-Pistoles (418) 851-4676

For North Shore departures:
Baie-Sainte-Catherine/Tadoussac (418) 235-4395

Les Escoumins (418) 233-2202
Saint-Siméon (418) 638-2856

Related Places of Historic Interest

A number of national historic parks are located around Montreal and Quebec City (which is a historic site in itself). You can combine a historic site visit with a visit to a national park, by visiting the Forges de Saint-Maurice, on the north shore of the St. Lawrence, and then continue northwest on that road to La Mauricie National Park.

FURTHER READING

Le Fjord du Saguenay, Merveille du Quebec (text in French) by Yves Ouellet (Editions du Trecarre, 1993).

Les Iles du Saint-Laurent (text in French) by Andre Croteau (Editions du Trecarre, 1995).

For More Information

Parks Canada
Chief, Visitor Services
Saguenay-St. Lawrence Marine Park
182, de l'Eglise Street
Tadoussac, Quebec
G0T 2A0
Phone: (418) 235-4703
Fax: (418) 235-4686

Parc du Saguenay
Parc Marin du Saguenay
Ministere du Loisir, de la Chasse et de la Peche
3415, boul. Grande-Baie Sud
La Baie, Quebec
G7B 1G3
Phone: (418) 544-7388

Tourism Quebec
From Montreal: (418) 873-2015
From Quebec, rest of Canada and the United States: 1-800-363-7777
(year-round, 7 days a week, 9 a.m. to 5 p.m.)
Ask for the tourist guides to Saguenay-Lac-Saint-Jean and for the
North Shore (Cote Nord)
The Tourism Centre in Tadoussac can be reached year-round at (418)
235-4744/4977
Parks Canada Office in Quebec City: 1-800-463-6769

MINGAN
ARCHIPELAGO
National Park Reserve

Between the second and third editions of this book, I was able to visit Mingan Archipelago, and it was surely worth the trip! It is a long drive—a good two days from Montreal—but if you treat the trip like a major adventure to a truly wondrous land, then the length of the trip there is nothing. The archipelago has always been well known in Quebec for its exotic shorelines and wealth of wildlife, but it was added to the national park system only in 1984.

The reserve protects some 40 islands and many islets, which are part of the Eastern St. Lawrence Lowlands natural region. The archipelago is located along the north shore of the St. Lawrence River, with the islands parallelling the mainland shore at an average distance of about 3.5 kilometres (two miles). The whole reserve stretches some 150 kilometres, starting across from the town of Longue-Pointe. About halfway along the length of the park, on the mainland, is the town of Havre-Saint-Pierre. What makes the Mingan Archipelago so distinctive, aside from the fact that it is off the beaten track, and camping out on islands is pretty special in itself?

A major feature of the islands is their dramatic topography. The islands are limestone-based, unlike the exposed Canadian Shield of the mainland. The limestone bedrock has undergone repeated cycles of uplift and submersion, with the latest uplift occurring at the end of the last glaciation. This is the place to see raised beaches, now high and dry, to wander among sea stacks that punctuate island beaches, and to explore the largest concentration of shoreline arches and grottoes in Canada. You can trace the layers of sediment deposited on what was once the bottom of the sea. Fossil remains of over 200 marine organisms are evident in the rocks of the reserve. Hiking, camping, beachcombing, or kayaking, it's all very easy to get close to these characteristic features of the archipelago.

But the influence of the sea goes much beyond the impact of waves or chemical processes. The archipelago is at a meeting place of a relatively mild boreal maritime climate and much more harsh semi-Arctic conditions.

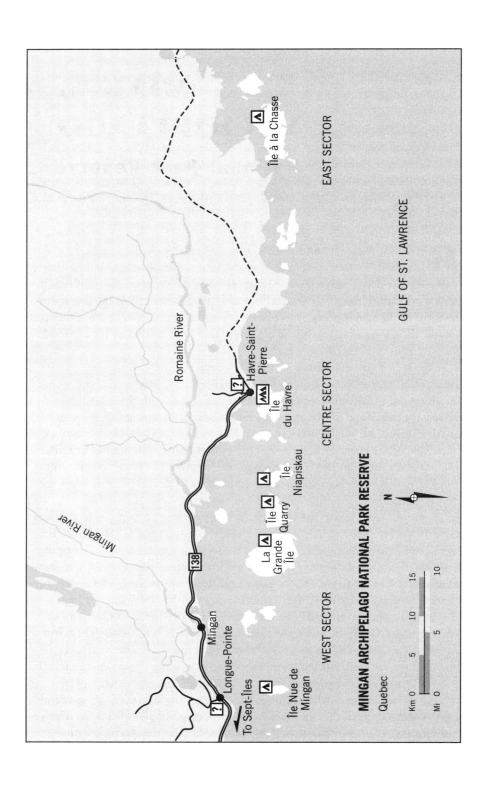

MINGAN ARCHIPELAGO NATIONAL PARK RESERVE

Quebec

Mingan River

Romaine River

Longue-Pointe

Mingan

To Sept-Îles

Île Nue de Mingan

La Grande Île

Île Quarry

Île Niapiskau

Havre-Saint-Pierre

Île du Havre

Île à la Chasse

WEST SECTOR

CENTRE SECTOR

EAST SECTOR

GULF OF ST. LAWRENCE

N

Km 0   5   10   15

Mi 0   5   10

On the one hand, most of the land mass of each island enjoys a boreal maritime climate, which means that, because of the moderating influence of the sea, the average yearly temperature is over one degree Celsius.

On the other hand, there are cold upwellings passing by islands. These currents contribute a real chill to the prevailing winds that strike the east-facing shorelines of the islands in particular. This in turn creates tundra-like conditions on these islands, a situation usually found much farther north.

The cliffs of the islands, and there are about 45 kilometres (28 miles) of them in all, rising to a maximum of 15 metres (45 feet), also have much more in common with the Arctic than with the boreal forest that makes up the gently sloping interior of most of the islands.

In all, there are more than 450 species of vascular plants in this small area. About 100 of these are of scientific interest because they are rare, or usually found much farther away, or are endangered.

The richness of the plant life is mirrored by the diversity and accessibility of the animal life. The waters of the area are visited by nine members of the whale family, some of which—like the minke whale—can be seen from the islands. On occasions, humpback whales be seen much further out to sea, and you will need to take one of the boat tours to reach them. Grey, harbour, and harp seals can generally be seen from as early as May.

At least 200 species of bird have been recorded in the islands. Many of the shorelines, moors, and cliffs are breeding grounds for gulls, terns, and kittiwakes. Double-crested cormorants, razorbills, the black guillemot, and that most attractive of seabirds, the Atlantic puffin, nest on some of the islands, as well.

The islands are an important resting and feeding area for migrating shorebirds, and considerable numbers gather there in spring and fall. The archipelago is also an important wintering area for ducks.

HOW TO SEE THE PARK

Once in the park area, there are tour boats operating out of the villages of the park. Once you are there, there are water taxis that will drop you off and pick you up from the islands.

Even though camping on the islands can be an important part of a visit to the area, it is possible to camp on the mainland, or to stay in local hotels, motels, bed and breakfasts, or a youth hostel (located west of Havre-Saint-Pierre, near the Romaine River). You can take day trips on cruise boats, water taxis, or bus boats to the islands. You can hike, picnic,

Parks Canada, M. Boulianne

The Atlantic puffin

and beachcomb for an afternoon or a day at a time. (Just remember to make your beachcombing "no-impact," because every rock and blade of grass is protected in a national park, and they may not be disturbed, much less removed.)

Many of the park's shorelines are breeding grounds for seabirds

Some islands are especially good for bird-watching, or for good views of the seals, or for exploring exotic plant life.

PARK SERVICES AND FACILITIES

The major mainland facilities are the visitor reception and interpretation centres at Longue-Pointe, at the western entrance to the park, along Highway 138, and at Havre-Saint-Pierre. There is also a park information kiosk at the marina of Havre-Saint-Pierre. They are both open daily, from mid-June through Labour Day.

Any overnight use of the park requires a permit, which you can purchase at the information kiosk or the reception centre at Longue-Pointe beforehand. So do register in and out, and be prepared for cold, wet, and surprises. One essential element of that preparation is including at least two days extra food if you are camping, because it is quite common to be held down, when the weather gets bad and kayaking or water-taxi transport becomes impossible.

Interpretive Program

The park has a varied interpretive program, and some of the most informative and attractive publications in the park system. They are additionally distinguished by being in three languages—French and English, of course, but also in Montagnais, the language of the local Native people. At the two Visitor Centres, you can see fixed displays about the natural and human history of the islands, and about how to plan your visit. There is also a movie on the archipelago. There is a regular schedule of evening slide-show talks at the centres, and interpreters visit several of the islands, on a rotating schedule, to give guided walks to visitors.

Camping

There are primitive campgrounds on six islands, and a group campground at one of them (Île du Havre). Primitive or wilderness sites have tent pads, pit toilets, picnic tables, wood-burning cookstoves, and sheltered firewood. The group campground has ten pads, two of the stoves, four tables, and two firewood shelters. A camping permit is required, and is available from the two Visitor Centres. It is important to return your permit to a centre when you leave the reserve. The islands and number of sites are Grande Île (four sites at Havre à Petit-Henri and four at Barachois à Montpetit), Île à la Chasse (six sites), Île du Havre (four sites), Île Niapiskau (six sites), Île Quarry (six sites), and Île Nue (two sites). It is possible to camp in the off-season, for those who can get there on their own, when water taxis are no longer operating. The permit is available from the park office in Havre-Saint-Pierre. You can reserve individual sites up to seven days in advance, and the group site can be reserved up to six months in advance.

There is a maximum stay of six nights in the park reserve, though you can extend your stay indefinitely by moving from site to site. There is a camping fee. The water transport services are commercially run, and their prices vary according to your destination and the size of the group. You must pack in and pack out everything, including cigarette butts. The park supplies garbage bags.

Other Accommodation, Gas, Food, and Supplies

The park has an excellent booklet that includes information on local private accommodation and services. Call or write ahead for it. It lists a municipal campground of 54 sites in Havre-Saint-Pierre, a bed-and-breakfast phone number, an 84 room hotel in Havre-Saint-Pierre, a hotel in Mingan and Longue-Pointe, a youth hostel near Romaine River, and you can camp there as well. There are two motels in Longue-Pointe, and a 30-site private campground. Bus, ferry, and water-taxi information are listed, as well as a central number for information on restaurants in the area.

Because Highway 138 is a primary provincial road, you will be able to find gas and other auto services along your route.

It is possible to top up your food and camping supplies in local stores, but it is probably best to bring your essentials along with you from home.

Recreational Facilities

Boating   Pleasure boating is a major activity in the area. However, it is important that you be very familiar with the nautical charts and weather and water conditions of the area, and that your boat and equipment meet all Canadian Coast Guard standards for safety. The charts you will need are 4432, Mingan Islands, and 4454 and 4456.

Ocean Kayaking   Kayaking is an ideal way to explore the area—if you are fully prepared to kayak in very cold conditions, with erratic weather and unpredictable seas. Of course, the standards for pleasure-boating apply to kayaking as well, but there are additional factors to take into account when kayaking in this wonderfully scenic area. One is that you are in an ocean, not a river, and the other is that you are in near-Arctic conditions. You must have a wet suit at the very least, but a dry suit is preferable. You should take at least two extra days of food with you. You will find that the early morning or late afternoon are the best times for travelling any distance in these waters.

Scuba Diving   This is an increasingly popular sport in the area, but it too, requires your being prepared to dive in semi-Arctic conditions. You don't need a diving permit, but it is a good idea to register at the park office for safety reasons. A dry suit is essential, and the usual safety precautions, such as never diving alone, using a dive flag, and having a lookout at the surface at all times, are particularly important here.

HOW TO GET THERE

Even if the drive to Mingan is a long one, actually getting to the park is quite easy. The main access route is Quebec Highway 138, which follows the north shore of the St. Lawrence to Havre-Saint-Pierre. There is also ferry access from Rimouski on the south shore and from the Gaspé peninsula. You can arrive by air from Quebec City and Montreal. Both ferry and air travel go to Havre-Saint-Pierre.

Related Activities or Places of Natural or Historic Interest

Because the trip to Mingan is likely to be a major one for you, I suggest that you take your time and visit two of the other national parks along the route — whether on your way to or from Mingan. If you drive you will be very near to La Mauricie National Park, north of Trois-Rivières, halfway between Montreal and Quebec City. Then north several hours driving from Quebec City is Saguenay-St. Lawrence Marine Park. You can't miss it. There are a number of national historic parks around Montreal and Quebec City (a historic site in itself), and the Forges du Saint-Maurice National Historic Site on shores of the St. Lawrence, near the turn-off for La Mauricie.

For More Information

The Chief, Visitor Services
Mingan Archipelago National Park Reserve
P.O. Box 1180
1303 Digue Street
Havre-Saint-Pierre, Quebec
G0G 1P0
Phone: (418) 538-3331
Fax: (418) 538-3595

AUYUITTUQ
National Park Reserve

Auyuittuq* means "the land that never melts." A great part of this arctic park is glacier, which melts at its edges in the summer, but is brought back into line in winter. However, much of the ground is in the zone of permafrost, where the earth's moisture, not far below the soil's surface, is forever in an icy form. For summer hikers, it may seem that the tussocks and gravel and mud below their boots are completely liquified. Knowing that there is frozen earth a few centimetres below provides no comfort, and no foothold, whatsoever. But raise your eyes to the glaciers pouring down between the high valley walls, or come close to the glacially carved peaks of Odin and Thor, and you are unlikely to regret the hardship of a true arctic wilderness experience.

This is Canada's second-most northern park. Its 18 644 square kilometres (7200 square miles) protect a pristine part of the eastern Arctic, on Baffin Island. The coasts of Baffin are extremely rugged. The glaciers formed the U-shaped valleys and multitude of fjords that radiate from the heights of the main island and the ridges of its peninsulas.

Glacial action is still having an impact on the park's topography. Approximately one-third of the park's surface is covered by the Penny Ice Cap—the central part of the mountainous Penny Highlands. A number of the mountains of the highlands are over 2000 metres (7000 feet) high, but the ice cap dominates them. Glaciers, some as long as 25 kilometres (15 miles), swoop down to the sea at Davis Strait, located on the northern boundary of the park, and emerge before visitors' eyes along the main travel route of the park, the Pangnirtung Pass, which crosses the peninsula from north to south.

However, it would be a mistake to envision Auyuittuq as a place of only ice and jagged mountains. In fact, unless visitors have come to the park specifically to climb mountains, most of their visit will be spent in

*Pronounced, approximately, Eye-you-eé-tuk.

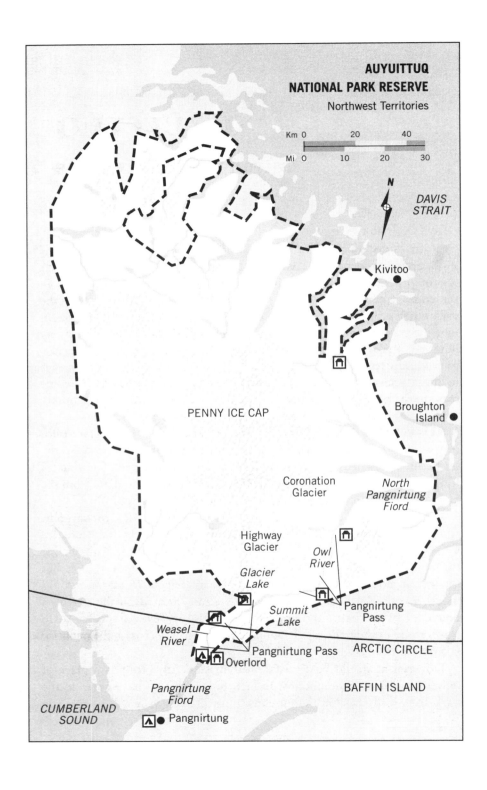

AUYUITTUQ
NATIONAL PARK RESERVE
Northwest Territories

Km 0   20   40
Mi 0   10   20   30

N

DAVIS
STRAIT

Kivitoo

PENNY ICE CAP

Broughton
Island

Coronation
Glacier

North
Pangnirtung
Fiord

Highway
Glacier

Owl
River

Glacier
Lake

Summit
Lake

Pangnirtung
Pass

Weasel
River

Pangnirtung Pass   ARCTIC CIRCLE

Overlord

Pangnirtung
Fiord

BAFFIN ISLAND

CUMBERLAND
SOUND

Pangnirtung

the ice-free valley of Pangnirtung Pass, which is only 400 metres (1400 feet) at its highest point.

The arctic ecosystem is shaped by the interrelation of soil conditions, climate, water supply, and length of days and seasons. In general, the soils in the park range from rock or gravel outwash from glaciers, which can support little vegetation aside from mosses or lichen, to tundra communities, based on deposits of wind-blown sand supporting dwarf shrubs or some grasses. These grasses often grow in large tussocks, almost a metre (three feet) tall, in a pillowy growth called a "thufor."

Tidal-flat plant communities have developed on the edges of fiords, where the walls are not too steep, and along the coastline of the Davis Strait. Finally, there are patches of snow (not ice) that persist throughout the year and, in summer, a few kinds of flowering plants can grow there.

Soil that is poor in nutrients and very thin, weather that is very cold, and summers that are very short—these factors severely limit the kinds of plants that can exist here. The one compensation is that Auyuittuq, which is located almost completely above the Arctic Circle, enjoys 24 hours of daylight in the summer.

The sparse vegetation growth, and its limited diversity, mean that the number of species of animals is small. You can expect to see only lemmings, the large arctic hare (up to five kilograms!), ermine, and arctic fox.

R. Marois, Parks Canada

Arctic plants crouch low to survive high winds

From June to August, the most apparent wildlife in the park for summer visitors is the bird life. Although there are just 32 species of birds, the population of each kind is fairly large.

A variety of marine mammals (seals and whales) can be seen in the coast water of Auyuittuq, and in the late summer polar bears can be observed.

HOW TO SEE THE PARK

Auyuittuq is a rugged wilderness park. Having a safe visit depends on being in good physical condition, having considerable outdoor experience, making detailed plans for the timing of the visit, choosing the proper equipment, and taking plenty of supplies. However, visitors should not take more than they can carry, since they must be totally self-sufficient and ready to meet any emergency. Once out on the trail, help may be several days away. Airborne rescue is available on occasion, weather permitting, and mountain rescue is limited.*

The Pangnirtung Pass Route

Although there is one main route through the park for hikers, there are several ways to go about it. Overall, the pass is 97 kilometres (60 miles) long. It follows the **Weasel River**, from the south at **Pangnirtung Fiord** to **Summit Lake**, situated about one-third of the way along the total route, and then along the **Owl River** to **North Pangnirtung Fiord**. Travelling the whole route thus takes the hiker right across the Cumberland Peninsula.

If your goal is to hike the entire route, remember that the southern segment of the trail is closer to the stations at **Overlord**, and that this segment has four shelters, and somewhat more visitation. The incline to the adjoining **Summit** and **Glacier Lakes** is steeper in this northern direction than from the lakes located on the northern end of the route. Consequently, if you want to do the more isolated section of the hike when you are fresh, avoid slogging the steeper segments of the trail while wearing a nearly full pack, and be closer to "civilization" on the last two to four days of the trip, then consider doing the whole route from **Broughton Island** south to Overlord. Allow nine to 12 days.

It is not essential to travel the entire route, however, to get a strong sense of the arctic environment. Many visitors start out at the 12-tent

---

* I did not visit this park. I am basing this chapter on printed material from Parks Canada, and especially from the book, *The Land that Never Melts*. For the visitor-use section, I am relying on interviews with staff and visitors to the park.

campground at Overlord, in the south, and then make a round-trip trek to Summit Lake, or on past it to Glacier Lake, and then back to Overlord through the other bank of the Weasel River. There is the full range of spectacular glacial scenery, of arctic plant life, of rushing glacial-melt streams to ford, and maddening thufor tussocks to circumnavigate. This round trip takes at least a week.

For any kind of hiking, always plan to travel much more slowly than you expected, and to eat much more than you believed possible. The Weasel Valley has designated trails, but in the Owl Valley this is not the case, and a lot of time is spent in localized route-finding. Getting lost is not a problem, because the pass walls define the limits of travel. However, north of Glacier Lake there are no designated trails, because frequent use of one route on permafrost-based soil is quickly destructive. Also, established routes would often be obscured by changing stream direction, spring avalanches, and so on. As a result, within the broad valley walls, hikers are on their own.

Also, hikers must be extremely cautious when crossing the numerous streams that flow into the pass. Try to cross very early in the day, before the midday heat increases the melting and, thus, the stream volume. Rope up, if there are three or more people. Use a stout pole if you're not roped and, above all, *unfasten your pack's hip belt*. People have drowned, even in shallow water, when they slipped and could not release their heavy packs.

The weather is very capricious on Baffin Island, and the Pangnirtung Pass may have snowfall any month of the year. On average, one day out

M. Beedell, Parks Canada

Emergency shelter and warming hut at Summit Lake

of three or four will have frost, throughout the summer. Rain is frequent, and wind is constant.

By spending a few days at either of the Inuit settlements of Pangnirtung or Broughton Island, and by hiking for a number of days in the pass, Auyuittuq should provide you with an unforgettable introduction to Canada's eastern Arctic, the life of its people, and its very special natural history.

PARK FACILITIES AND SERVICES

Interpretive Program

A wilderness park does not offer the interpretive programs and visitor services found in the southern parks. Wardens at Pangnirtung or Broughton Island patrol the trails and maintain the few emergency shelters, toilets, and garbage depots. The shelters are for emergency use only and, for most of the trail, human waste must be disposed of by shallow burial, and garbage must be packed out. Hikers are expected to register in and out with the wardens, who can advise about trail conditions, freight-canoe availability, reservations, and so forth. User fees for visits are in effect. Wardens can operate a limited rescue service, but climbers cannot expect rescue unless they have returned to the valley floor.

Camping

The park offers three primitive campsites at **Overlord, Windy Lake**, and **Summit Lake**. Overlord has 12 tent sites, pit toilets, fire grates, and water from streams. All other camping in the park is according to visitors' choice. Seven main shelters are located along the whole trail, which people may use in case of extreme weather or a physical emergency. Every shelter area has flat places for tents, and primitive toilets. Dryer, gravelly areas are recommended.

Other Camping

In Pangnirtung, there is an eight-site campground, which is run by the territorial government. It has toilets, kitchen shelters, and drinking water.

Other Accommodation, Food, and Supplies

A lodge in Pangnirtung provides accommodation for 33 people, in 17 rooms. In Broughton Island there is a hotel, which costs about $150 a night. There are Hudson's Bay stores in Broughton Island and Pangnirtung. They are small and expensive, and supplies are often limited. There are supply boats in August and September. Since most visitors come in July and August, supplies will be at their lowest. Plan to carry all supplies from home, but it is just possible that the store will have that one item you forgot.

Recreational Services

Mountain-Climbing This is a definite draw for visitors. There are a number of very rugged peaks about 2000 metres (6560 feet) high. The desire to make a first ascent of a remote mountain, or to scale clean, granite rock faces that no one else has touched, has brought increasing numbers of climbers to the park in summer, for more than a decade. Check back issues of the *Canadian Alpine Journal* (Numbers 37, 47, 49, 55, 56 and 57), for descriptions of some of these climbs. Write to the park, at least a year ahead, for information on routes, other climbers' experiences, equipment required, and so on. A favourite trip for climbers is skimobiling in from Pangnirtung in mid-June, climbing for days or weeks in cold, but possibly clear weather. This is the time with the minimum amount of snow, and the maximum 24 hours of daylight. By the end of August, there will be snowfalls regularly at 600 metres (2000 feet) and up.

Fishing Fishing for arctic char in the fiords of Davis Strait is very good, but is usually not the main goal of a visit to the park.

Other Services Various commercial outfitters, located near the park and from other areas of Canada, will take groups into the park. Also, outdoor clubs, such as Canadian Youth Hostels, sponsor an annual trip to the park. Write to the park for information, or to Travel Arctic, a service of the territorial government, for names and addresses. Several of the nature/conservation magazines carry advertisements for these services.

HOW TO GET THERE

There are regular jet flights from Montreal and Ottawa to Iqaluit (Frobisher Bay), on southern Baffin Island. From there, flights go to the village of Pangnirtung, on the southern edge of the Cumberland Peninsula, or to the Broughton Island settlement, on the Davis Strait. From either settlement, you must travel by boat to the trailheads, located at the north or south end of Pangnirtung Pass. The Inuit run this service after the sea ice breaks up, usually in late June or early July at Pangnirtung, and early August at Broughton Island. The ride from Pangnirtung to the southern trailhead at Overlord takes about 90 minutes. The ride from Broughton Island to the northern trailhead, at the mouth of the Owl River, takes between four and five hours.

Visitors must write ahead to the park to find out what kinds of service may be expected—times, cost, capacity, and so on. This is especially the case for the Broughton Island service, because it is much less used. Once you reach either settlement, check with the wardens and local tourism officers to ensure transportation at the end of the trip. It is also possible to be skimobiled from either end of the entry to the pass in June, before the ice breaks up. The pass will be snow-free, and the weather quite stable. The thin edge of ice along the rivers also makes hiking easier.

Related Activities or Places of Natural or Historic Interest

NWT Tourism Information is an excellent information service for all kinds of visitation in the territory. Call 1-800-661-0788.

Activities and Places to Consider Visiting:

- Kekerten Historic Park, in Pangnirtung Fiord south of Auyuittuq, is an historic whaling station.

- In Pangnirtung visitors can view a reconstruction of a whaling station, with replicas of whaleboats, artifacts, and displays of the period. There is also the Angmarlik Visitors Centre—a museum with displays on the life of the Thule and modern Inuit.

- The Pisuktinu-Tungavik Campground, located south of Auyuittuq.

- Visitors can take outfitted trips for arctic-char fishing or floe edge trips by dog team or boat to see wildlife.

FURTHER READING

The Land That Never Melts, Auyuittuq National Park, edited by Roger Wilson (Peter Martin Associates, 1976).

The Baffin Handbook, edited by W. Richard Hamilton (Nortext, 1993).

For More Information

The Superintendent
Auyuittuq National Park Reserve
Box 353
Pangnirtung, Northwest Territories
X0A 0R0
Phone: (819) 473-8828
Fax: (809) 473-8612

FORILLON

National Park

Forillon stretches its full length into the sea. The relationship between land, sea, and people gives the park a special character. Explore this park by driving, bicycling, or walking along its paths and shorelines.

Forillon lies at the tip of the northernmost continental reaches of the Appalachian Mountain chain, which extends southward as far as Alabama. The steep, grey-white cliffs, gleaming over the ocean, are formed from limestone. Over time, the elements have broken down this limestone in places into pebbles, creating the beautiful, crescent-shaped beaches that dot the perimeter of the Gaspé Peninsula.

Forillon has more than a spectacular coastline to offer visitors. The mountainous interior, with its wooded hills and valleys, stretches back into the inner peninsula and out to the steep edges of the sea. The woods are mixed boreal (fir and white spruce) and Acadian (maple and birch). On the periphery of the forest, in places such as the exposed cliff faces

Limestone cliffs, seen best from a boat

271

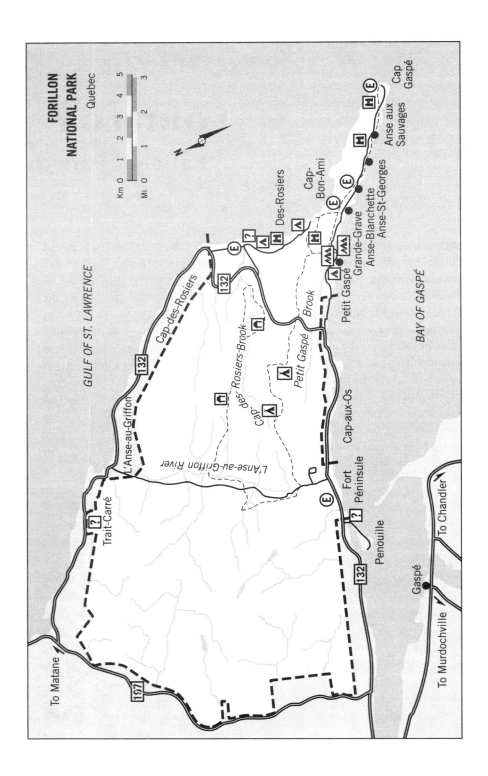

and talus slopes, where other plants cannot survive, about 30 species of rare arctic-alpine plants grow.

The Penouille beach area, located at the southwestern edge of the park, is a low peninsula about 1.5 kilometres (one mile) long. Long, smooth beaches and low dunes grace its open side, and a rich salt marsh lies on its inland edge. In the centre, vegetation that is usually located hundreds of kilometres farther north in taïga conditions thrives. Reindeer lichen carpets the sandy soil.

HOW TO SEE THE PARK

There are three good ways to explore the shape of the peninsula, and the plant and animal life on and around it. First, visitors can see it from the sea. The sea trip can be taken on a cruise boat, which is privately operated from the wharf located just north of the campground, at **Des Rosiers**. Up to six sightseeing cruises operate each day. From the boat, it is easy to see the geological structure of the soaring cliffs, the patches of orange lichen that colour them, and how they have become homes for sea birds, such as kittiwakes, black guillemots, common murres, double-crested cormorants, and razorbills. The narrow beaches, which are formed of sheared-off rocks, produce nesting places for eider ducks. The harbour seal gives birth in the water surrounding the peninsula, and the grey seal arrives with its young already born. A whale-watching cruise is also available, which leaves from **Grande-Grave** in the south sector of the park.

Visitors can see seals along the peninsula

The second way to see the peninsula is to view the underwater life. Check the interpretive-program timetable for the diving display, which is given twice a week at **Grande-Grave Beach**. Divers go down to progressively greater depths, bringing back characteristic plants and animals from each level. On shore, interpreters with aquaria receive the marine life, and explain what is brought up and how it survives at its level.

The third way to explore the shape of the peninsula is from its summit. Take the **Grande Montagne Trail**, which leaves from behind the **Grande-Grave Harbour** area and goes straight over the narrow neck of the peninsula, toward Des Rosiers Campground. In fact, you can walk from the **Cap-Bon-Ami** and Des Rosiers campgrounds all the way to the Grande-Grave Harbour, if you want a few hours' stroll. There is also an observation tower, which provides an unobstructed view of the park area and surroundings located on the highest point of Mont St-Alban.

At each major turning, carefully fenced lookouts give a thrilling sense of being poised between the flower-strewn woods behind and the vast ocean in front—about 200 metres (650 feet) below, in places.

People on the Land and Sea

Fishing, gardening, and lumbering have been an integral part of the Forillon area for hundreds of years. People no longer live on parkland itself, so there is no more gardening or lumbering, but they fish in the harbour of **Cap-des-Rosiers,** and from the quay at **Grande-Grave**. A wharf is located at Grande-Grave that is used mainly for local boats. Pebbly beaches line the peninsula, and the beach there is larger than most—about 400 metres (1200 feet) long. The park has preserved part of the little village that was once a centre of fishing and fish processing, including a store and a small homestead. You can go into the restored buildings.

Half a kilometre (0.25 mile) from the homestead is the Hyman & Sons store and warehouse. Both buildings are now open to the public, and are staffed by park interpreters. The store is stocked as it would have been in 1920 and the warehouse contains exhibits of the international cod trade at that time.

Close to the store, the three-kilometre (two-mile) trail—**Une tournée dans les parages** ("a walk around the area")—leads you through the fields where haying was done, and then into the woods, which were the source of heating and building materials. A fascinating scenic walk brings you much closer to at least some aspects of the former life of this area.

Another walk, located on the south side of the peninsula, dramatically displays the hardships that fishing entails, and the ingenuity that the people showed in meeting these obstacles. The road past Grande-Grave ends a few minutes' drive farther east, at **Anse aux Sauvages**. There is a wharf, still sturdy enough to walk on, an old cemetery, a picnic area with water and toilets, and an excellent pebble beach.

But to experience more of the Gaspé way of life, **Les Graves**, out to the lighthouse at the tip of the Gaspé peninsula, is the route to follow. The trail nears the cliff, overlooking the sea. Every few hundred metres, the ground seems to drop away beneath you, as the trail touches the border of a pebbled cove. You can look down in several places, and see the weathered remains of the stone-filled platforms and long ramps that were built to facilitate the transport of people, fish, and even boats over the vertical cliffs to the land above.

The trail that extends past these coves takes you out to the **Cap Gaspé Lighthouse**. The trail loops and, if you follow it all the way to the upper level (a 10-minute walk), you will be right in the middle of some of the park's boreal forest. It opens out suddenly on to the clearing, where the white-and-red lighthouse sits, booming out its warning on foggy days.

Penouille Beach

Penouille Beach creates a striking contrast to the wooded mountains, white cliffs, and wind-and-sea-sculpted pebble beaches of the rest of Forillon. It is low, sandy, and sparsely vegetated in some places, with rich mud flats in others. It is located at the southwestern entrance to the park, near an information centre, where staff can help plan a visit, provide maps and pamphlets, or sell posters and books on natural history. Visitors to Penouille park their cars at this centre, and travel the 1.5 kilometres (one mile) to the point by propane-powered tram. The point has a snack bar, changing rooms and showers for swimmers, toilets, and picnic tables.

PARK SERVICES AND FACILITIES

Interpretive Program

The park provide two Information Centres—one at Penouille near Cap-aux-Os and the other at Trait-Carré near L'Anse-au-Griffon, and an Interpretive Centre at the harbour of Cap-des-Rosiers. There are four aquaria, with live specimens of the park's underwater fauna, and video displays are shown on a regular basis. In general, the programs are provided in French, but some are in English. All of these facilities are wheelchair accessible.

Camping

The park offers three areas for single tents or trailers, and one group campground. There is a trailer-waste disposal facility in each, and all have water. **Petit Gaspé**, in the southwest, is the first campground to fill. It has 171 sites (35 with electrical hookups), in a beautiful, wooded area. Most of the sites are on split levels—one for the vehicle and one for the tent. Excellent kitchen shelters and washrooms with showers are provided, as well as a small playground and firewood. **Des Rosiers Campground**, located at the north side of the park, has about 200 sites, including 42 with hook-ups. This site is situated on a large, treed slope, with the ridge of the peninsula rising behind it and the ocean bordering its front. It is an easy walk to the beach, and to paths leading to the tip of the peninsula. This campsite boasts excellent showers, washrooms, and kitchen shelters. Firewood is available. The amphitheatre is located in the middle of this campground, and the Interpretive Centre is close by. The quay, for taking boat tours, is a short drive or easy walk from here.

Cap-Bon-Ami Campsite is a short drive farther along the peninsula, on the road past Des Rosiers. This is a small area, reserved for tent camping only. There are earthen platforms for tents, and cars can park between the sites. There are kitchen shelters, toilets and showers, picnic tables, and a broad field for playing games. The campground is situated very close to the mountains rising behind, and near the sea and the trails up to the peninsula tip. There is a picnic area and lookout near it, for day visitors. Nearby, a spectacular lookout overlooks bird-nesting cliffs and the picturesque Cap-Bon-Ami.

Group Camping

Reservations are necessary for this site, near **Petit Gaspé**; write to the Superintendent in advance.

Other Accommodation, Gas, Food, and Supplies

Small villages are located to both the north and south of the park, which offer motels and private campgrounds, small grocery and camping-supply stores, and gas stations. There is a youth hostel on the south shore at Cap-aux-Os. In front of the hostel, there is bicycle rental and diving gear rental and charter.

Recreational Services

Swimming Swimming is popular at the point of Penouille, but is unsupervised. People often wade at other pebble beaches. The water is cold, but not intolerable. Supervised swimming is only provided at the pool in the recreational centre.

Scuba Diving The park encourages scuba diving, because of its varied underwater habitat. This is one of the few places in the park system where visitors can see arctic-water plant and animal life. In summer, water temperatures in most areas vary from 8° to 19°C (46° to 60°F) at the surface, and 2° to 3°C (35° to 37°F) at 18 metres (60 feet).

Recreational Centre Located next to the campground in the Petit-Gaspé area south of the park is a recreational centre offering a swimming pool, tennis courts, playground, snack bar, and souvenir shop.

Winter Use There are plenty of opportunities for cross-country skiing and snowshoeing. Shelters equipped with wood stoves, picnic tables, and dry toilets are found on most trails.

Three of the five ski trails are rated easy and suitable for beginners. These are the fairly even La Vallée Trail, a seven-kilometre (four-mile) return trip starting at L'Anse-au-Griffon in the north; Le Portage, a 15-kilometre (nine-mile) return trip starting near Penouille in the south; and Le Castor, a loop trail starting near Cap-des-Rosiers in the east. There are two somewhat more strenuous trails in the interior of the park—La Cèdrière and Le Ruisseau. The five trails interconnect.

Winter camping is encouraged in the Petit-Gaspé group campground. The campground is located three kilometres (two miles) from the parking lot and can be reached on snowshoes or skis by way of an unmarked trail.

Fishing Fishing is free, and no licence is necessary to fish from the various oceanside wharves. No quotas are imposed. Mackerel is the usual catch.

Related Activities or Places of Natural or Historic Interest

Tourism Quebec is an excellent information service for all kinds of visitation in the province. Call 1-800-363-7777.

Activities and Places to Consider Visiting:

- The Parc de la Gaspésie, located in the heart of the Gaspésie peninsula.

- For historic interest, consider visiting the Musée de la Gaspésie and the Monument to Jacques Cartier in Gaspé. In Pointe-au-Père you will find the Musée de la Mer.

Related Activities Cont'd

National Historic Sites

(Contact Canada Parks Service for the "Discover a living heritage" information booklet on the sites in Quebec). Sites include

- Pointe-au-Père: Pointe-au-Père Lighthouse

- Pointe-à-la-Croix: Battle of the Restigouche

For More Information

The Superintendent
Forillon National Park
Box 1220
Gaspé, Quebec
G0C 1R0
Phone (418) 368-5505

KOUCHIBOUGUAC

National Park

Kouchibouguac* National Park offers a wonderful opportunity to appreciate a maritime plain. Its land slopes gently to the sea, and 25 kilometres (15 miles) of white, dune-edged beaches protect warm lagoons and rich salt marshes. At first, Kouchibouguac seems an unimposing place, remarkable only for its beautiful beaches. Perhaps because no part of the plain is higher than 30 metres (100 feet), visitors tend to think of the park as a place that is simply good for swimming, bicycling, or picnicking. It is not immediately apparent that this is a place of rich natural history and spectacular change. In fact, Kouchibouguac has one of the most dynamically changing ecosystems in the whole range of national parks: the chain of barrier islands lining its eastern border forms constantly shifting dunes, reefs, and lagoons.

The barrier islands are formed and changed largely through the power of the sea. The action of waves, particularly during storms, tears the sand from the land and from the sea bottom, and throws it up into ridges, which you can see on a stroll along the beach. The crests of the dunes are the result of further shaping by winds and longshore currents, which shift the fine sand exposed as the barriers are built up from underwater. Three major island dunes—North Kouchibouguac, South Kouchibouguac, and North Richibucto—have existed for about 2500 years.

This island system is not an isolated land form; it has important effects on the character of the area behind it, because the barrier calms and controls the effects of the sea on the land. Water that slips around the ends of the islands, through inlets, does not scour the sandy bottom, or disturb the many marine plants and animals. Rather, the sand is more stable and, near the edges of the tidal flow, mud can build up. Nutrients collect, seeds take, and molluscs and fish feed and shelter in the salt-tolerant plant life, in the fairly stable mud, and in the warm, sluggish water.

---

*Pronounced KOOSH-uh-BOOG-oo-WACK.

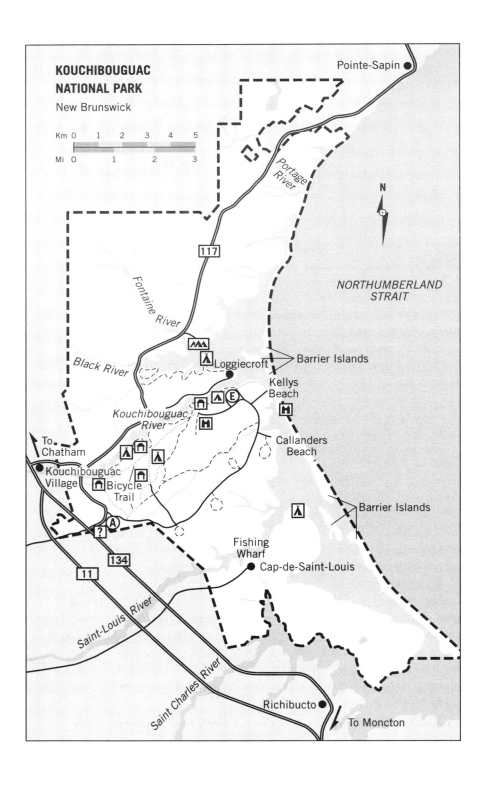

KOUCHIBOUGUAC
NATIONAL PARK

New Brunswick

Km 0   1   2   3   4   5

Mi 0   1   2   3

Pointe-Sapin

Portage River

117

Fontaine River

Black River

NORTHUMBERLAND
STRAIT

Loggiecroft

Barrier Islands

Kellys
Beach

Kouchibouguac
River

Callanders
Beach

To
Chatham

Kouchibouguac
Village

Bicycle
Trail

Barrier Islands

Fishing
Wharf

Cap-de-Saint-Louis

134

11

Saint-Louis River

Saint Charles River

Richibucto

To Moncton

N

The rivers and streams that cut through the plain, flowing to the sea, unite at this special place. The fresh water meets the tidal lagoon water, mixes with it, and is partially held in the lagoons by the barrier islands. As a result, the sea water is diluted in the slowly flushing lagoons, and thus plants and animals can survive in the estuaries at the river mouths, and in the nearer parts of the lagoons. There are also salt-water marshes in some places, with the grasses that waterfowl love to visit and breed among.

The forest and fields in the interior of the park have been moulded by people, as surely as the coastal area has been moulded by the sea. In the last 300 to 400 years, the forest was logged and burned repeatedly. The tall white pines were cut for ships' masts; other trees were taken for ship-building and construction. Occasionally a white pine was spared, because it was gnarled or distorted. Along the Claire Fontaine Trail or Ruisseau Major, it is possible to see several huge white pines, each with a quirk or kink in it. Fields were cleared for domestic animals to graze, or for crops to be grown. Both the forest and the cleared areas are being allowed to return to their natural state.

Bogs comprise 21 percent of the park's total area, though they are accessible only at Kellys Bog. High humidity and a low moisture-evaporation rate in this area produce the perfect conditions for bogs to form. There are raised bogs, whose sole source of water is rain and snow. They build up layer after layer of sphagnum moss and small shrubs, and become gently domed in shape. Kellys Bog is more than five metres (18 feet) deep in sphagnum moss, and the condensed layers that comprise it have become peat.

HOW TO SEE THE PARK

The Barrier Islands, Beaches, Lagoons, and Salt Marshes

The first destination for most visitors is Kellys Beach. A large parking lot, snack bar, changing rooms, showers, and toilets are part of a complex in the wooded area behind the beach. All facilities are accessible to persons with disabilities. Paths to the beach are all boardwalk, to protect the fragile plant life and shifting sands. The five-minute walk starts in a narrow band of woods, where visitors may see warblers, thrushes, and flycatchers, or hear owls at night. (A wheelchair could be taken here, with little difficulty.) Woods give way to the grasses of the salt marsh, where savannah sparrows abound. Then comes the first stretch of lagoon, which runs parallel to the beach. The boardwalk leads visitors to the start of their beach walk, situated on the sheltered side of the **South Kouchibouguac Dune**. The boardwalk ends at the ocean side of the dune. The dune ridge is covered

Parks Canada

Canoeing is a popular way to see the park

with marram grass—the primary colonizer of this sandy, shifting environment. In slightly more stable areas, the searocket and bayberry are taking hold. Down on the beach itself, there are kilometres of firm, clean sand to walk on. The ocean water is warm enough for swimming in summer.

The fall season (between September and November) provides an especially rich experience in that the brilliant autumn colours are complemented by the spectacular waterfowl migration. Thousands of terns and gulls nest at **Tern Island**, situated just at the south of the South Kouchibouguac Dune. A pair of binoculars helps, but isn't essential. You can also see grey seals basking on the quieter islands and beaches.

A number of tour-boat operators are available to take visitors into the Northumberland Strait—the waters bordering the park.

It is possible to canoe or kayak in the lagoons, though wind in the afternoons can pose a problem in some areas, and boaters should be well protected against insects, cold, and wet (in case of swamping).

The Forests

There are excellent walks in both the north and south of the park. (The Kouchibouguac River is the customary dividing line between north and south.) In the north, the three-kilometre (two-mile) **Claire Fontaine Trail** is well marked and easy. It rounds a wooded point, which juts out into Kouchibouguac Lagoon. Here, the forest is typical mixed Acadian birches, white pine, and several other kinds of conifer. The ground is fairly open, with trilliums, trout lilies, and bunchberry.

Several open areas, with benches, overlook either the stream side or the lagoon side. The loop trail begins and ends in a bog area, with kalmia, lots of fungus, and several very damp spots. Short stretches of boardwalk are provided.

Beaver Trail is located about halfway along the road between the Information Centre and the campground. This very short loop trail provides a fascinating example of change in the Acadian forest, as it is affected through altering water levels. Beavers have built a lengthy crescent of dams, and the pond formed has killed a number of big, old trees, but makes an excellent environment for water-tolerant bushes and trees such as alder. Canada warblers and American redstarts nest in the thickets at the border between dried and drowned forest, in the company of the common yellowthroat, magnolia, Tennessee, and yellow-rumped warblers. Dead trees in the middle of the pond provide havens for several kinds of woodpeckers. I saw five species of butterfly, and four types of dragonfly. The Beaver Trail and other nature trails in the park are enhanced by interpretive exhibits in the form of large, colourful fairy-tale-style books with cartoon-like characters created by well-known Canadian artist, Michael Fog.

The Fields

Most of the fields lie east of the main road to the campground. The best way to see them is by bicycle. You can rent bikes at Ryan's Landing, though many people bring their own. The Major Kollock nature trail has been converted to a one-way mountain bike trail. Pedestrians may use this trail to explore the park's interior but should be extremely careful to avoid the mountain bikes that blast down the trails. Trails start at the **Major Kollock Creek Bridge**, located at the eastern edge of the campground, or at several places marked from the main road.

The Bogs

Kouchibouguac is such a dynamic environment that even its slow-moving features change quickly. This is true of **Kellys Bog**. Bear in mind that most bogs in eastern Canada have existed for approximately 8000 years. But at only 4500 years of age, the sphagnum and peat in this bog is deeper than much older bogs. Visiting the bog is easy—just drive or walk two kilometres (one mile) past the campground toward **La Source**. Then walk to one of the gems of the park's interpretive program—the boardwalk

Parks Canada

Kellys bog: arethusa orchid and pitcher plants

into the middle of the bog. It is self-guiding, with colourful, informative signs along the way.

The first part of the trail is through the narrow band of woods surrounding the bog. This moist, densely treed area is excellent for warblers. Just as the woods open on to the vast bog, there is a three-storey viewing tower with a wide, spiral staircase and several flat areas to rest and look out from.

The boardwalk leads you past small ponds, where common bladderwort nod. These are carnivorous plants, similar to the more common pitcher plants and sundew.

Located at the far end of the boardwalk is a partially enclosed area with benches on three sides. It's a good place to stay for a while, and enjoy the atmosphere of the bog.

PARK SERVICES AND FACILITIES

Interpretive Program

The park's interpretive service attempts to bring the program to the visitor, rather than trying to assemble visitors at fixed locations. Schedules are posted in French and English at the campgrounds, the Information Centre,

Kellys Beach, and at other key visitor gathering points. These programs are presented in the language posted, but since most of the staff is bilingual, if you miss a program in one language, it will likely be offered again.

Camping

During busy July and August weekends, there is often a queue for camping sites. On these days, names are taken when visitors arrive, and places are given out in the early afternoon.

The park offers two main campgrounds. The largest one is **South Kouchibouguac**, which is undergoing a major upgrade and expansion to 311 sites, 46 of which will have electrical hook-ups. There is also a trailer-waste disposal area. The sites are beautifully designed for space and privacy—set well back from the road, with shrubs and some trees screening each site. The tent area is smooth lawn—not an extremely natural environment, but a very comfortable one. There are tables, and fire rings with cooking grates. Firewood can be purchased near the entrance. The large and handsome kitchen shelter is equipped with large wood stoves, sinks, and washrooms. Clean, hot showers are available in one area, and large washrooms with sinks and hot water in four places. The campground has an accessible shower located in loop three of the campground. All washrooms are accessible. This campground has a marvellous adventure playground, set in a huge field. **Côte-à-Fabien Campground** is the other main camping area, with 21 drive-in sites and nine walk-ins. This campground is located between the Black and Kouchibouguac Rivers, and is quite removed from the park's main activity areas. If you really want to get away from it all and have a very "natural" park experience, this may be the place for you.

Primitive Camping

Three sites in the park have room for four tents each—**Sîpo***, **Petit-Large**, and **Pointe à Maxime**. These sites are accessible by canoe, except for Petit-Large, which can be reached by bicycle or hiking. They have dry toilets, firewood, and water. Register at the Visitor Reception Centre. There is a minimal fee.

Group Camping

There is a group area, with kitchen shelter, firewood, toilets, and pump water. Write to the Superintendent for reservations.

---

*Pronounced Seeboo

Other Accommodation, Gas, Food, and Supplies

Several small towns are situated at either end of the park, and halfway along its length. Richibucto is the largest town in the area. There are motels and a good selection of private campgrounds, which are very close to the park and all its activities.

The surrounding communities of Kouchibouguac, Pointe-Sapin, Saint-Louis-de-Kent, Richibucto, and Rexton have grocery, hardware, and department stores, gas stations, credit unions, and banks.

Recreational Services

Swimming   There is supervised swimming, from mid-June through Labour Day, at Kellys Beach. Swimming is unsupervised at Callander's Beach, which has big fields for picnicking, and a kitchen shelter.

Boating and Canoeing   There are many kilometres of lagoon and river waterways. A publication by a local group and the park's own air-photo mosaic outline these routes. Visitors can rent rowboats, canoes, and recreational kayaks at Ryan's Landing, located near South Kouchibouguac Campground. Motor boats are permitted on the major rivers. Kayakers with ocean-going kayaks can make a trip to the isolated barrier islands.

Bicycling   The park is unique for its extensive development of bicycle trails and, given the distances, much of the park is best seen from a bicycle. A six-kilometre (four-mile) mountain-bike trail is now available. Bikes can be rented at Ryan's Landing.

Winter Use   The park emphasizes cross-country skiing and snowshoeing. Maps are available that show trails and warm-up shelters. An annual marathon and other community events are held during the winter. The terrain is not rugged, and there are many places to go. Winter camping can be arranged for groups; contact the Superintendent.

Fishing   Fishing is not a popular activity in the park. To do it, however, you must purchase a National Park fishing licence. Cod, mackerel, and flounder are the catch. Although a licence is not required for shellfish, there are limits in place and certain species may not be harvested. Check with a park warden before you head out to harvest shellfish.

Bird-Watching   The park is very good for shorebirds and pelagic species (seen from a distance). The fall waterfowl migration is spectacular. The park is one of the few breeding places of the endangered piping plover. The park is protecting the nesting area, but speak with the interpreters about other areas where you might catch a glimpse of this tiny bird.

Related Activities or Places of Natural or Historic Interest

The New Brunswick Department of Economic Development and Tourism is an excellent information service for all kinds of visitation in the province. Call 1-800-561-0123.

Activities and Places to Consider Visiting:

• Pays de la Sagouine, a 30-minute drive from Kouchibouguac, provides an excellent immersion in the Acadian lifestyle.

• Bonar Law Historic Park, located in the village of Rexton, a 20-minute drive from the park.

For More Information

The Superintendent
Kouchibouguac National Park
Kouchibouguac, New Brunswick
E0A 2A0
Phone: (506) 876-2443/876-2446

FUNDY
National Park

S ince I first visited Fundy National Park, it has undergone some of the most significant changes of any of the parks in our national system. One of the main changes is that its rich forests, dramatic shoreline, and lakes, rivers and bogs, are now much more accessible to visitors. A new network of trails is provided in the back country, which links up many of the familiar, shorter trails. Along with bringing nature closer for visitors, the park has endeavoured to reintroduce several species of wildlife not seen in the park for many years. The park has been successful in this respect with the peregrine falcon.

HOW TO SEE THE PARK

Visitors can become familiar with Fundy Park in a variety of ways—by camping, driving the car trails, exploring the walking trails, referring to the many brochures and signs, or speaking with the interpreters.

The Tides of the Bay of Fundy

The park is famous for the extreme tides of the Bay of Fundy. Pushed by the Atlantic ocean tides, the water in the Bay of Fundy rises to meet the land twice a day. The water rises higher here in the Bay of Fundy than anywhere else in the world, due to the fact that the length of a bay determines the timing of water rocking up and down its basin. Here, the timing happens to coincide with the Atlantic ocean tides (caused, of course, by the gravitational pull of the moon). So, like a child on a swing, the Bay is getting a push by the ocean tide at just the right time to generate the giant tides.

You can witness this phenomenon in several places. The **Headquarters Campground** is beautifully situated on a cliff, located at the eastern edge of the park. A short walk or a two-minute drive to the village of Alma will place you on the beach of the bay itself. You can walk out on the flats, at

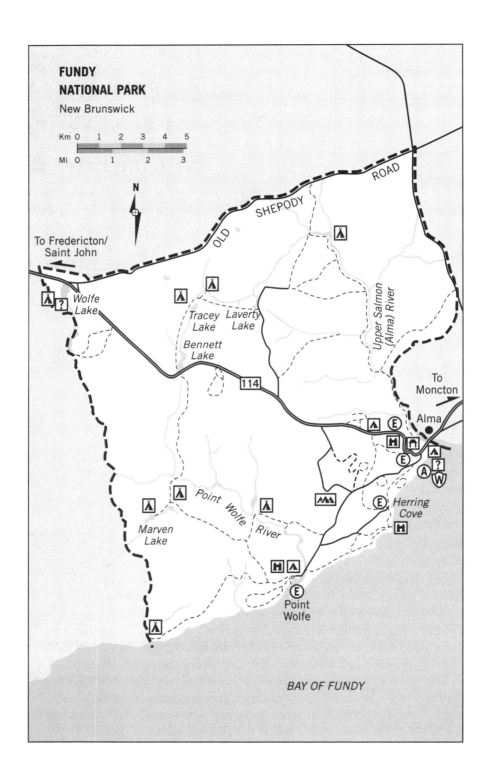

FUNDY
NATIONAL PARK

New Brunswick

Km 0 1 2 3 4 5
Mi 0 1 2 3

N

To Fredericton/
Saint John

Wolfe
Lake

OLD SHEPODY ROAD

Tracey
Lake

Laverty
Lake

Bennett
Lake

Upper Salmon
(Alma) River

114

To
Moncton

Alma

Point Wolfe River

Marven
Lake

Herring
Cove

Point
Wolfe

BAY OF FUNDY

Bay of Fundy

low tide, as far as a kilometre (0.5 mile), but remember that the tide advances across this area at a rate of 1.5 metres (almost five feet) per minute, so don't leave your shoes too far away.

Herring Cove is another good place to learn about intertidal life. An interpretive display helps, or you can join a guided group. **Point Wolfe** provides another opportunity to be close to the ocean's changes. Look for signs to the **Shiphaven Trail**, which is a wonderful walk.

Of course, you need not be on the beach itself to appreciate the beauty and fascination of the tides and the bay. Trails such as **Coastal, Dickson Falls, Devil's Half Acre,** and **Coppermine** all offer dazzling vistas of the bay, or spine-tingling views down to the rocks and shore far below.

The Forests

Of the eight types of forest region in Canada, the Acadian occurs over most of the Maritime provinces. An Acadian forest has both evergreens such as red spruce and balsam fir, and hardwoods such as red maple or white birch. It also features bogs, where glacier movements have scoured out depressions in which water from rain or snow now collects.

Some areas of the Maritimes will have only the coniferous forests, or may be largely boggy, or predominantly hardwood. What makes the narrow coastal area that borders the Bay of Fundy so distinct is that it encompasses all three types of habitat.

Dickson Falls Trail is self-guiding; interpretive signs help you understand the distinctive features of this coastal forest. It is quite easy to walk along the boardwalk that takes you to the foot of the low, but beautiful two-tiered falls.

Devil's Half Acre is part of a foggy, red-spruce forest. Here, you see the coastal forest precariously clinging to its foothold on the rugged, steep hillsides sloping to the sea. Years of freezing and thawing of ground moisture, with its attendant forces of expansion and contraction, have helped to create this startling landscape.

The park has made this area accessible by constructing a very convoluted railed stair and bridge system, without which visitors would be unable to reach this intriguing place. When the mists from the sea below begin to rise, the trees and mossy wooden walkways assume the mood of a Japanese scenic painting.

Hardwoods and broad-leaved forests are found mainly in one zone of the park, the middle uplands, located about three kilometres (two miles) from the headquarters. The beautiful **Maple Grove Trail** is accessible by car, along the **Hastings Auto Trail**. The trail is mostly among the trees but, since the predominant ground cover is ferns, you can easily see into the many light-filled clearings, where deer graze in the early morning or at dusk.

Raised Bog Habitat

A peat bog is a beautiful place, but walking in it can pose problems. What looks like solid ground is really a huge mat of sphagnum moss. At Fundy, on the **Caribou Plain Trail**, the problem is solved. After a brief walk from the parking lot, through beautiful and increasingly moist woods (watch for many pink lady slipper orchids in June), help is thoughtfully provided. A solid, winding boardwalk is situated just centimetres off the sphagnum moss mat. The boardwalk passes a pond created by the largest beaver dam in the park. This is a good place to watch beaver at dusk or early morning.

Once at the bog, it is worthwhile to closely examine the pink-and-green carpet of sphagnum moss, which forms the basis of bog plant life. Along the lakeshore, you may see that most fascinating plant—the sundew. It looks like a collection of tiny, reddish tennis racquets with pink bristles radiating off the rim.

Taller than the sundew is the Labrador tea bush, which appears either in small clumps or as an extensive carpet. It grows about half a metre (two feet) high and, in June, has beautiful, white flower clusters.

A striking red globe—two to six centimetres (one to two inches) across—hanging from a stem 10 to 20 centimetres (three to eight inches)

Parks Canada

Toad and three-leaved false Solomon's seal

high, signals another well-known bog resident—the pitcher plant. The flower of the pitcher plant towers above its rosette of curved red-and-green leaves, or "pitchers," which collect water.

On the bog, the tallest plants are the trees, but even these are miniatures—often no more than a metre tall. You can begin to understand the slow process of change in nature, and the limited growth potential in a peat bog, when you learn that a tamarack or black spruce, which stands less than a metre (three feet) tall, may have taken 100 years or more to reach that height. The same plant, grown in deep, rich soil in another location, could be 30 metres (90 feet) high.

In the bog, insects abound. In terms of amphibians, only the mink frog and perhaps pickerel frog can successfully breed in the naturally acidic bog pond. Birds hunt insects over the bog and its lake; swallows swoop ceaselessly.

The Caribou Plain Trail is 3.4 kilometres (2.5 miles) long, leading you through coniferous forest, across the bog and back to the parking lot over a dry hardwood ridge with maples and birches.

Human History

The original inhabitants of the Maritime provinces were the Maritime Archaic Indians, and then the Mi'kmaq and Malecites, who hunted and fished, settling briefly here and there, as they followed their food supply.

Settlement in the park area came with the growing demand for timber—for buildings, for ships, and eventually for pulp. Initially, the forests surrounding the major river systems were harvested, and later, portable sawmills allowed harvesting of interior forests. Sawmills polluted the fishing in the nearby rivers and inshore. Today, with the park's protection, the salmon are recovering and the trees have a chance for a natural life span.

The best evidence of farming in the area is provided at **Matthews Head**. A trail there criss-crosses the now-deserted fields.

For other traces of earlier human settlement, follow the self-guiding **East Branch Trail**, or hiking trails such as **Coppermine** and **Goose River**.

PARK SERVICES AND FACILITIES

Interpretive Program

The park offers a modest Visitor Centre, which houses temporary displays and provides a focal point for the visiting public. Visitors can view a 12-minute video presentation on the park in either French or English, obtain an interpretation schedule, permits, information, maps, and a visitor guide.

A central attraction of the interpretive program is the evening slide shows and animations presented in the outdoor theatre in the headquarters area.

A number of guide books and informative brochures on the park's natural and human history are available, and on trails and other interesting places to visit. The main bookstore is located in the Visitor Centre and the other is open from May to October at the Wolfe Lake Information Centre.

Camping

The park offers 600 campsites in three main campgrounds, plus a number of primitive campsites for those hiking in the back country. Primitive campsites must be reserved in advance (by calling the park or on-site). In winter, part of the Headquarters Campground is kept open for tent camping. The roads there are plowed and the public washroom (no showers) behind the nearby Visitor Centre remains open.

All campgrounds have toilets, showers, and enclosed kitchen areas where you can cook on woodstoves and eat at picnic tables. **Headquarters Campground** is lawned and treed, with one edge overlooking Alma Harbour and the tidal marsh at the mouth of the Upper Alma River. **Chignecto North Campground** has wooded sites, and is located on the plateau portion of the park, near several trails. A major recapitalization project at Chignecto North has resulted in newly renovated washroom/ shower facilities and kitchen shelters. A bike path now circles the campground and an adventure playground has been developed (great fun!). Each site now has a fire pit. Firewood can be purchased on site. A number of sites are now wheelchair accessible and are equipped with specially designed picnic tables. The renovated washroom facilities are also wheelchair accessible. **Point Wolfe Campground** is lawned and treed, and is located close to the Point Wolfe River. A children's playground is also provided. The campground is a short walk to the beach and to the start of a number of interesting trails. **Wolfe Lake Campground** (self-registration) is suitable mainly for tenting. There is no electricity and water is from a common tap. **Micmac Group Campground** is located in what was once farm fields. It has a lot of rolling open space, with occasional fruit trees and some treed field edges. Reservations are required for groups.

Other Camping

Several private camping grounds are located in the village of Alma, just a short drive from the eastern park entrance.

Other Accommodation, Gas, Food, and Supplies

Thirty-two chalets are located near the park headquarters (in the park), and a similar number are situated two kilometres (one mile) west on Highway 114. The facilities are park-owned, but privately operated. To reserve chalets, call (506) 887-2808 or 887-2930. Several modest, well-kept motels with and without housekeeping facilities are located in and near Alma and toward Albert. There are more than 10 bed-and-breakfasts.

There is a concession-run restaurant, in the same building as the pro shop. It serves standard Canadian fare. The town of Alma, located just down the hill from Headquarters, on Highway 114 east, has two small grocery stores, a bakery, and several small restaurants. A gift shop, which sells park mementos and regional crafts, is situated near the Fundy Park Chalets and golf course, as well as a few craft shops with locally made collectibles.

There are no gas stations in the park, but one in Alma and two in nearby Albert.

Recreational Services

An extensive sports area is located within a few minutes' walk from the Visitor Centre.

Hiking   Fundy has improved its hiking trail system considerably, and you would be well advised to contact the park staff, even before you visit, to find out about the back-country opportunities in particular. The most interesting back-country experience is hiking the 50-kilometre (30-mile) **Fundy Circuit**. It takes about four days to complete the entire trail, though you can join it from a number of places and do day hikes, or camp in one of the primitive campsites by a lake or along a river. The Fundy Guild sells an excellent trail guide for the Circuit and the many other, shorter trails. Some of the shorter trails have their own interpretive booklets, which tell you about the natural and human history of the area in which you are walking.

Golf   The park offers a beautiful nine-hole course, with a pro shop for last-minute golf equipment needs. Fees are modest.

Tennis   Three paved courts are located adjacent to the Clubhouse Restaurant. Equipment can be rented in the golf pro shop.

Lawn Bowling   A lawn bowling green is located beside the tennis courts. Fees are modest.

Swimming   Aside from the beaches, most of which are perhaps better for wading, a heated salt-water pool is open throughout the summer. It is a 10-minute walk downhill from the assembly hall. Bennett Lake and Wolfe Lake have swimming beaches (unsupervised), and the water is comfortably warm by mid-June.

Boating   Canoeing is possible at Bennett Lake where rowboats and small sailboats can be rented. No motor-driven boats are allowed in the park, though they are used in the bay waters. Canoeing clinics are sometimes given in summer months.

Fishing   Fishing is allowed in the park. You buy a National Parks licence at the entry (good for all national parks in Canada). Information on seasons and limits is available there.

Winter Use   There is increasing emphasis on cross-country skiing in the park. Fifty kilometres (30 miles) of groomed trails loop through the back country, over old horse trails, roads, and paths. Some of the more gently rolling interpretive trails can also be used. Snowshoeing can be done nearly anywhere, but the opportunity to follow the interpretive trails in the winter is very appealing. At the headquarters area, a toboggan run provides for hours of fun. Winter camping is becoming more popular, especially at the cabin at the Laverty Trail (for reservations, call 506-887-6000).

Related Activities or Places of Natural or Historic Interest

The New Brunswick Department of Economic Development and Tourism is an excellent information service for all kinds of visitation in the province. Call 1-800-561-0123.

Activities and Places to Consider Visiting:

- The 32-kilometre (20-mile) scenic drive from Alma to Riverside-Albert (Hwy 915) provides beautiful beaches and superb viewpoints, particularly at Cape Enrage.

- The Shepody Bay Western Hemisphere Shorebird Reserve at Marys Point is an excellent birding area, especially during the July and August migrations.

- Rock Provincial Park at Hopewell Cape where the tides have carved out giant flowerpot-shaped rock formations. The best time to explore is at low tide.

- The Museum-in-a-Gaol and old Albert County Courthouse at Hopewell Cape, operated by the Albert County Historical Society.

For More Information

The Superintendent
Fundy National Park
Alma, New Brunswick
EOA IBO
Phone: (506) 887-6000
Fax: (506) 887-6008
TDD: (506) 887-6015

PRINCE EDWARD ISLAND

National Park

O ne early summer morning at Prince Edward Island National Park, I went to the beach near my campground and walked alone there, seeing no one for hours. Later in the day and farther up the beach, I wandered through crowds of people swimming, picnicking, and playing on these same warm, pink sands. The contrast was great, but both experiences highlighted the main joy of Prince Edward Island National Park—it offers something for almost anyone.

This park is a narrow, broken strip of land, 40 kilometres (25 miles) long, that runs along the northern shore of Prince Edward Island. A drive along the Gulf Shore Parkway or a bicycle ride along its pathway border showcases the park's central feature—its dune system. On the north side of the road is the Gulf of St. Lawrence. As far as 20 kilometres (12 miles) out, the water is no more than 15 metres (50 feet) deep, which makes for warm water and gentle waves. Sand bars parallel the coast, which play a role in bringing in sand for the beaches and dunes that build up.

As dunes become established, marram grass gradually takes hold on the sand of the gently sloping southern, or bay, side. This grass sends down roots more than a metre (three feet) deep, which hold the sand in place against the buffeting of the wind and water. The longer the grass grows on a dune, the more fresh water and organic matter can collect there and, eventually, seedlings from other plants, such as the fragrant bayberry or the wild rose, take root. Trees, such as the white spruce, begin to do the same, though they never reach more than a metre or two (three to six feet) in height.

Farther inland, to the south, are older dunes, which are now completely covered with mature spruce forest, rather than the earlier mixture of small bushes and scrubby trees. But the wind and salt water leave evidence of their power at the first row of tall trees rimming the forest to the north; they are shorter and their branches twist to the south, like a flag blowing steadily in the wind. This is an example of *krummholz*, or

301

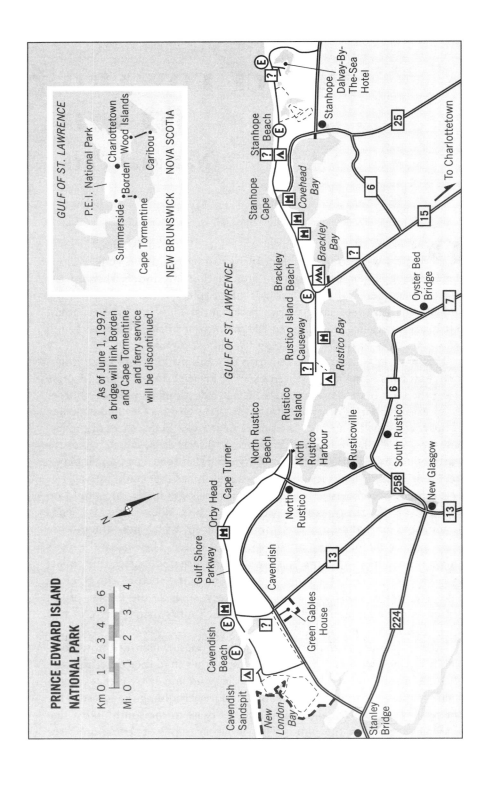

PRINCE EDWARD ISLAND
NATIONAL PARK

Km 0 1 2 3 4 5 6
Mi 0   1   2   3   4

GULF OF ST. LAWRENCE

P.E.I. National Park

Summerside Charlottetown
    Borden Wood Islands
Cape Tormentine Caribou

NEW BRUNSWICK   NOVA SCOTIA

As of June 1, 1997,
a bridge will link Borden
and Cape Tormentine
and ferry service
will be discontinued.

N

Cavendish
Beach

Cavendish
Sandspit

Cavendish

New
London
Bay

Green Gables
House

Stanley
Bridge

Gulf Shore
Parkway

Orby Head

Cape Turner

North Rustico
Beach

North
Rustico
Harbour

North
Rustico

Rusticoville

GULF OF ST. LAWRENCE

Rustico
Island

Rustico Island
Causeway

Rustico Bay

Brackley
Beach

Brackley
Bay

Covehead
Bay

Stanhope
Cape

Stanhope
Beach

Stanhope

Dalvay-By-
The-Sea
Hotel

South Rustico

New Glasgow

Oyster Bed
Bridge

To Charlottetown

258

13

224

13

6

7

15

6

25

An earth-star fungus and grasses on the inner dunes

"twisted wood." At a certain point in their development, the trees can no longer withstand the constant, searing salt wind, but their skeletons provide a protective wall, enabling succeeding spruce to grow.

HOW TO SEE THE PARK

Dunes and Beaches

The dune and beach system in Prince Edward Island National Park is varied in character. Most of the beaches are backed by dunes. The few that are not are bordered by the steep, red sandstone cliffs that provide the basic material for the dunes formed elsewhere. It is wonderful to walk along the clifftops, to overlook the edge of the sea at places such as Orby Head or Cape Turner, both of which are located in the park's western section. Take care not to venture too close to the edge due to the danger caused by rapid erosion and undercutting of the cliffs.

During the summer, frequently held beach walks with interpreters will enhance your awareness of the dune-beach environment. Some guided walks are held specifically for bird-watching. Several of the evening talks in the campgrounds focus on the changing nature of the dune-beach environment. We watched a slide show on dune formation, and learned that it takes a 20-km/h (12-mph) wind to blow grains of sand down the beach. We also learned how easy it is for dunes to be damaged by random walkers, and how important it is to walk alongside the dunes on the beaches, rather than on the dunes themselves. To reach the beaches, boardwalks or carpeted paths through the dunes have been established, which minimize dune destruction.

Woods and Fresh Waters

The beauty of Prince Edward Island National Park isn't confined to sand and sea. South of the beaches, on the landward side of the Gulf Shore Parkway, are long, narrow stretches of forests, broken occasionally by meadows and fresh-water ponds. Walks along the **Bubbling Spring Trail** or the **Farmlands Trail** are short, easy ways to see how the forests have overtaken old dune lands or more recent farm fields. Bubbling Spring Trail leads you past a pond overlook, and then dips back into the woods. A beautiful spring flows at the top of the trail, and the pink sand bubbles up like a cool cauldron.

The wind sweeping down from the north is responsible for the dune beach development, and for the subsequent freshwater-pond creation. All along the south side of the park are small barachois ponds. "Barachois" is a uniquely Acadian word, which means "barricade." Where there is a salt-water inlet in the shoreline, or where a fresh-water stream has formed an inlet, sand may slowly build up until the open end is choked off (except, sometimes, for a narrow outlet going to the sea). No more saltwater comes in, the fresh water from rain and the existent streams or springs slowly fills

Parks Canada

The transition from dunes to grass to forest

in the land-locked bay, and a rich new environment for fish, plants, insects, and birds evolves. A great place to see this phenomenon is on the **Reeds and Rushes Trail**, which has a floating boardwalk that allows you to walk on Dalvay Pond.

Located just west of the entrance of the Cavendish Campground is the start of the Homestead Trail. This is an excellent trail for either hiking or cycling. The full trail runs for eight kilometres (five miles) and a shorter loop takes you 5.5 kilometres (3.5 miles).

Human History

Bases of old earthen fences can be seen on the **Farmlands Trails**. The remains of small pits are also evident, which some enterprising residents made for stashing illicit rum barrels during Prohibition days.

But the sight that means the most to a literature buff is **Green Gables House**, located at Cavendish in the western area of the park. This house inspired the setting for Lucy Maud Montgomery's novel, *Anne of Green Gables*. A tour of the house and a walk along **Lover's Lane** and the **Balsam Hollow Trail** or through the **Haunted Wood** will bring Anne's world very close to visitors of today. Preserved within the park since 1937, Green Gables House is open daily from May to October.

At the eastern end of the park is the elegant Victorian home **Dalvay-by-the-Sea**. Built in 1895 as a summer home, it was declared a national historic site in 1993. It is now operated as a hotel through a lease agreement.

PARK SERVICES AND FACILITIES

Activities

A busy and innovative summer activity program is offered at the national park and historic sites. The schedule is available at entry kiosks, and on bulletin boards throughout the park. Exploring the park is quite easy. There are several self-guiding trails, with easy access to the woods and beaches. The roads through and around the park are wide and gently rolling—great for leisurely drives. Bicycling is a favourite activity in the park and the surrounding countryside.

Camping

Prince Edward Island National Park offers four campgrounds, with over 500 sites in all. Situated on the western side of the park is **Cavendish**, a lightly wooded site that is very popular with campers.

Stanhope and **Rustico Island Campgrounds** are located in the eastern section of the park. Stanhope is a bustling, wooded site, situated across the road from a supervised beach. Rustico Island, which faces Rustico Bay, offers wooded and meadow sites. It is the quietest campground, and the last one to fill up at busy times.

There are a variety of individual site facilities; Cavendish and Stanhope offer three-way trailer hookups, Rustico Island does not.

The **Brackley Group Tenting Area** is available for organized groups. Reservations are required and can be made by calling (902) 672-6350.

The main season is early June to late September.

Other Camping

An estimated 1500 campsites are available in the area surrounding the park, so you should be able to find accommodation within a few minutes' drive of the park, even during the busiest season.

Other Accommodation, Gas, Food, and Supplies

Numerous hotels and motels are located near the park, and even a couple of concessions within the park. For further information, contact the Prince Edward Island Visitor Services at 1-800-463-4734 or write to them at PO Box 940, Charlottetown, PEI C1A 7M5.

Fast-food stands are located at the Brackley, Stanhope and Cavendish supervised beach centres. A souvenir gift shop is open beside Green Gables House. Parks and People Association operates a gift shop in the Cavendish Visitor Centre.

There are stores near the park, and a full range of food, gasoline, camping supplies, and so on is available in the surrounding villages.

Recreational Services

Swimming The park offers several supervised beaches. Guard season is from July 1 to the end of August.

Bicycling Bicycling is especially good in the park, because one-metre-wide strips are reserved for cyclists on either side of the Gulf Shore Parkway, which runs the length of the park. The Homestead Trail located near Cavendish Campground provides 8.5 kilometres (5.5 miles) of cycling through woodlands and fields with views of New London Bay. The land outside the park is rolling farm country with narrower roads, but is heavily used for bicycling.

Boating Rowing and canoeing are allowed in the fresh-water lakes and ponds. Power boats are not permitted. You can charter ocean-going sightseeing or fishing trips at Tracadie Harbour, North Rustico Harbour, and Covehead Harbour.

Tennis Three double courts are available in the park.

Golf Green Gables golf course, located in Cavendish, is an extremely beautiful and popular 18-hole course.

Winter Use During the winter, the park offers cross-country skiing, snowshoeing, and skating.

Related Activities or Places of Natural or Historic Interest

Visitor Services provides an excellent information service for all kinds of visitation in the province. Call 1-800-463-4734.

Activities and Places to Consider Visiting:

• PEI has a wealth of historic sites to visit. Among those nearest the park are Great George Street, Confederation Landing Park, Confederation Centre of the Arts Art Gallery and Museum (all in Charlottetown), and the Acadian Museum in Miscouche. Contact the Community Museums Association of PEI for more information (902-892-8837),

• For devotees of Lucy Maud Montgomery, other sites to visit include the Lucy Maud Montgomery Birthplace in New London, the Anne of Green Gables Museum in Park Corner, the Site of Lucy Maud Montgomery's Cavendish home in Cavendish, and the Confederation Centre of the Arts Art Gallery and Museum in Charlottetown.

• There are several provincial parks on the Island and a number of hiking trails. The Island Nature Trust publishes a Nature and Trail Map of PEI (contact them at 902-892-7513).

National Historic Sites

(Contact Canada Parks Service for the "Vacation Planner" information booklet on the sites in Prince Edward Island). Sites include

• In Charlottetown and area: Fort Amherst/Port-la-Joye, Ardgowan, Province House

For More Information

Department of Canadian Heritage
Parks Canada
Prince Edward Island National Park
2 Palmers Lane
Charlottetown, Prince Edward Island
C1A 5V6
Phone: (902) 672-6350
Fax: (902) 672-6370

KEJIMKUJIK

National Park

F resh water, forests, and people have always been the key elements of Kejimkujik National Park. Recently, however, the scope of the park has been extended to include a Seaside Adjunct—a 22-square-kilometre (nine-square-mile) segment of rugged coast on the south shore of Nova Scotia, near the community of Liverpool. Access to the Adjunct is limited but, over time, it may play a larger role in the visitor's experience of the park.

The typical fresh-water pattern of this part of Nova Scotia is one of many irregularly shaped lakes, dotted with islands. Rivers and lakes comprise about 15 percent of the park's 381 square kilometres (147 square miles), and the largest lake is the park's namesake, Kejimkujik. This island-studded lake, and the meandering Mersey River, dominate the visitor's experience of the park.

Rainfall in Kedge* is high: it averages 150 centimetres (60 inches) a year, giving the park a very warm, moist climate. The rain is essential to maintain the levels of lakes and streams, for few are spring-fed. The richness of the plant life in bogs and meadows, and in coniferous and hardwood forests, depends on the high level of rainfall, because the shallow, nutrient-poor soil of the area could never support such abundance with a lesser supply of water. Acid rain is a concern and has been affecting the park area for many years.

The slow-moving streams, which flood regularly in the spring, and the numerous shallow lakes, are often edged with bog areas. These provide special habitats for animal and plant life.

The forest of Kejimkujik is the Atlantic uplands variety of the Acadian type. In the lowest and least well-drained parts of the park, the trees are typically black spruce, tamarack (larch), and perhaps some balsam fir. In somewhat dryer and higher areas, there are the red spruce, balsam fir, and occasional white pine of the softwood forest. Where the soil is deeper and better drained, hardwoods, such as maple, birch, and oak, thrive.

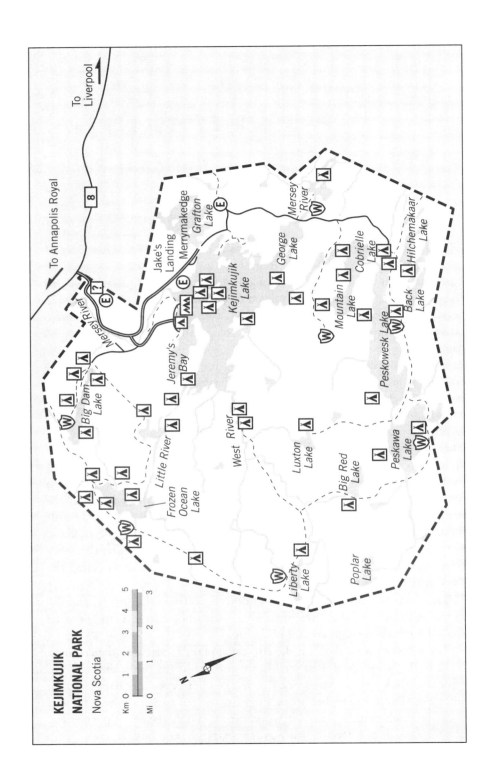

Parks Canada

Cancer root along a woodland trail

The woods and rivers provide excellent homes for deer, rodents (including beaver, muskrats, and voles), and many amphibians. The forests are home to a great variety of birds, particularly woodland warblers. Bird-watchers may see the huge pileated woodpecker and, if they are extremely lucky, the black-backed woodpecker.

In the mixed-wood areas, which cover three-quarters of the park, an abundant variety of plants can be found.

For thousands of years people have played an important role in the area that is now Kejimkujik Park. The Mi'kmaq (pronounced "mik maw") people lived here, at one with the life-giving waters and forests. They fished and hunted, using the waterways as canoe highways, portaging where necessary, camping where they wished.

The Mi'kmaq almost disappeared during the nineteenth century, when Europeans moved into the area. Over the past 200 years, the entire area has been heavily logged and, with a few exceptions, all of the woodland has been seriously disturbed by protracted logging and burning. A few old, but small, stands of hemlocks and hardwoods have survived unscathed. In the late 1800s, a minor gold rush occurred, and remains of shafts and waste material can be seen in places.

By the turn of this century, Kedge was a sport-hunting and fishing centre, but this use, too, slowly dwindled.

Today, people seek not to exploit Kedge, but to preserve it.

HOW TO SEE THE PARK

There are two main ways to see the park. The first is through the independent wilderness experience, by hiking or canoeing in the undeveloped areas of the park (which is most of it). The second way is by camping in the developed sites, and being guided by interpreters in an appreciation of the park.

Independent Wilderness Experience

There are 140 kilometres (84 miles) of hiking trails. Most of that distance is taken up in trails that circle the perimeter of the park, with spurs leading from them into the interior. Primitive campsites are situated along the way, with tent pads, fireplaces, and toilets.

For the experienced canoeist, there are many kilometres of wilderness routes, including 23 portages, ranging from a few metres to over two kilometres (1.5 miles) in length. Because many of the lakes are large and shallow, especially Kedge, they can become very rough when the weather is windy; experience and caution are expected of the canoeist. Primitive campsites are also provided for canoeists.

For the back-country explorer, the park's *Backcountry Guide* is available for purchase. Check with staff for additional details.

There are several embarkation points, with parking lots, for both the wilderness hiking trails and canoeing routes. Some primitive campsites, such as those at Big Dam trailhead, are located within walking distance from parking, and it is possible to experience something of the wilderness life, without a lengthy hike or canoe trip.

Guided Appreciation of the Park

To experience the park, most visitors rely on the varied programs offered by the interpreters. The developed campsites and interpretive programs are family affairs. Special attention is paid to children's interests, and there are specific displays for them, although adults are not ignored.

Begin your exploration of Kejimkujik at the Visitor Reception Centre. There is a very attractive, 60-seat theatre in the Centre. Several excellent, multi-projector slide shows are offered.

Once you've left the Visitor Centre, you can choose to participate in the interpretive program in various ways: through interpreter-guided walks; interpreted walks or "paddles" near the shores of the lakes or streams (canoes may be rented); illustrated talks in the evening; interpretive displays at the Visitor Centre; and numerous free pamphlets. The interpretive walks and paddles link the key elements of Kejimkujik. For the waters of the park, any interpretive event that goes along the Mersey River or to any lake is relevant.

Four self-guiding trails are also available, and they are well worth your time. One is the very short (0.3-kilometre) **Mersey Meadow Trail**, which leads along the edge of the Mersey River. The trail is a combination of boardwalk, paved trail, and high-quality gravel, and is wheelchair accessible.

The **Mill Falls Trail** is also very short, and attractively signed. It, too, follows the Mersey River, and is accessible from three places along the road to Jeremy's Bay. A distinctive feature of this walk is the fern life along the trail. A viewing platform overlooks the falls and is accessible to visitors with special physical needs.

Beech Grove Trail is located just across the river from the Visitor Centre. It is two kilometres (one mile) long, with nine interpreted points along the way. The park provides visitors with a small, portable cassette player that is keyed to the nine stops. Because of the richness of this environment and the fun of using the cassettes, you can easily spend 90 minutes on the trail.

A trail that shows some of the human history of the area is the three-kilometre (two-mile) **Gold Mines Trail**, located along the Peskowesk Road. It has a series of interpretive signs, which tell about the gold-mining efforts that went on in the park area between 1880 and 1940.

After taking guided tours of the river, try a walk on your own to a similar habitat, such as **Rogers Brook Trail**. It's quite a revelation; now you *understand* what comprises the habitat around you!

With the restoration of Grafton Lake to its pre-dam (1938) configuration, the **Grafton Lake Walk** offers an opportunity to observe an ecosystem as it reverts to a natural state.

For an appreciation of the special areas of the forest, the **Hemlocks and Hardwoods Hike**, beyond the Big Dam parking lot, is ideal. The park usually has a guided event along this trail, which takes a leisurely three hours, with stops to explore the rich environment in more detail.

For a better understanding of human involvement in the Kejimkujik area, the **Mi'kmaq Memories Walk**, or a guided tour of the small farmlands area, will show you some remains of the Indian and early settler experience. If you want to be alone, try paddling from Jake's Landing, just a little way up the Mersey, in the quiet of the evening.

The Seaside Adjunct

This coastal section of the park is located about 25 kilometres (16 miles) southwest of Liverpool, off Highway 103. It takes in the tip of the Port

Parks Canada

When the river floods, it clears the shoreline of trees and large bushes

Mouton peninsula, and is officially known as the Seaside Adjunct of Kejimkujik National Park. There are two spectacular white-sand beaches, tidal flats, salt lagoons, and salt marsh areas. The inland terrain is rugged, with a mixture of forest types. Bogs and ponds are common in some areas. It is a particularly good area for bird-watching, especially for fall migrations of shorebirds.

Access is limited, in that motorized vehicles and motorboats are not allowed in the area. There are two access points for walking into the area. One is a gravel road, five kilometres (three miles) long, from Southwest Port Mouton to the shore on Black Point. The other is an old cart track from the community of St. Catherines River, which has been upgraded with boardwalks in the wet sections. This track is two kilometres (one mile) long. There are no visitor facilities here, so pack in and haul out your picnic, hot drinks, and rain gear, and be ready for some wonderful views of the coast and the plant and animal life of the ocean, shore, and forest.

PARK SERVICES AND FACILITIES

Interpretive Program

The park offers a number of information newsletters, guides to trails, an excellent bird-watching pamphlet and checklist, and brochures about the main park and winter activities. There are bulletin boards at the campsites,

Visitor Centre, snack bar, and so on, with current information on schedules and descriptions of the guided walks and talks, evening programs and
other events. It is wheelchair accessible.

Camping

There are 329 developed campsites at Jeremy's Bay, which is open year-
round. It is subdivided into three sections. Each section has washrooms
with flush toilets and hot- and cold-water sinks, faucets for water between
every few campsites, well-equipped playgrounds for children, and an
unsupervised beach. Trails lead from section to section and these, in turn,
link up with some of the shorter hiking trails. Clean, tiled showers are
available in one building, and serve all campsites. It is a short walk or drive
from the campsites themselves. You can purchase firewood there, which
may only be used in the grates provided. This rule applies to both wilderness and developed campsites. There are no electrical hook-ups. A trailer-
waste disposal depot is situated across the road from the showers. Several
sites, and the washrooms, are wheelchair accessible.

Primitive Camping

You can reach 42 wilderness campsites by hiking or canoeing. Reservations
are accepted up to 60 days in advance. Due to the increased interest in
back-country camping, visitors are urged to use the reservation system to
avoid disappointment. There is a fee in the summer, and you must register
at the Visitor Centre.

Winter Camping

A winter campground is located in one loop of Jeremy's Bay campground.
Facilities include hot and cold running water and toilets, fireplaces, and
free firewood. You can trailer- or tent-camp here.

Group Camping

Write to the Superintendent for information about reservations.

Other Accommodation, Gas, Food, and Supplies

Located close to the park, from Maitland Bridge to Caledonia, are several
canteens, restaurants, food stores, and camping-supply outlets. An inn is
situated just three kilometres (two miles) from the park, and is open year-
round. Several local families offer bed-and-breakfast services, and many

craft outlets are also located near the park. Within an hour's drive are the towns of Lunenburg, Bridgewater, Liverpool, Annapolis Royal, and Bear River, all of which offer motels, lodging houses, supplies, and so forth.

Within the park, a snack bar, which carries a few basic groceries, is located at Merrymakedge Beach. Gas is not available in the park, but several stations are situated within a 10- to 15-minutes drive along Highway 8.

Recreational Services

Swimming   There are a number of clean beaches, with unsupervised swimming, at each campground. A supervised beach is located at Merrymakedge, which visitors are encouraged to use. This beach area, and the trail beside it, are wheelchair accessible.

Boating   Power boats are allowed on Kejimkujik Lake, with a 15 km/h (9 mph) speed limit. You can rent canoes and rowboats at Jake's Landing or bring your own. The Jake's Landing area is wheelchair accessible. The park encourages canoe use by people with physical disabilities, because it is an excellent way for visitors, who otherwise might not be able to do so, to get right out on the waters of the park and see the wildlife in the most natural setting. This part of the lake is sheltered, and all the equipment is available right there.

Fishing   There is good trout fishing in spring, with the season ending August 31, to conserve fish stocks. The park encourages catch-and-release. Otherwise, perch is the most usual catch. A National Park licence is required, which you can purchase at the Visitor Centre. You can also pick up the summary of anglers' regulations for the Atlantic Canada National Parks here.

Winter Use   The amount of snow for cross-country skiing varies a great deal, from year to year. In good years, there is excellent cross-country skiing and snowshoeing along the wider trails. Some trails are groomed, depending on snow conditions. Wood-heated shelters are provided at Merrymakedge Beach, Jim Charles Point, and Mill Falls.

Related Activities or Places of Natural or Historic Interest

Tourism Nova Scotia is an excellent information service for all kinds of visitation in the province. From the Halifax/Dartmouth area call 425-5781. From anywhere else in North America, call 1-800-565-0000.

Related Activities Cont'd

Activities and Places to Consider Visiting:

- Take the Kejimkujik Scenic Drive, which crosses from the Bay of Fundy to the Atlantic. It passes by the entrance to Keji National Park. (Phone 902-354-5741)

- North Queens Heritage House Museum, in Caledonia, just east of the park. (Phone 902-682-2989)

National Historic Sites

(Contact Canada Parks Service for the "Vacation Planner" information booklet on the following):

- In Halifax and area: The Citadel, Prince of Wales Tower, Fort McNab, York Redoubt

- Between Halifax and Wolfville: Fort Edward, Grande Pré, The New England Planters Exhibit

- Annapolis Royal area: Fort Anne, Port Royal

- Lunenberg: Bank Fishery/Age of Sail Exhibit

For More Information

The Superintendent
Kejimkujik National Park
Box 236
Maitland Bridge, Nova Scotia
B0T 1B0
Phone: (902) 682-2772
Fax: (902) 682-3367

CAPE BRETON HIGHLANDS

National Park

Most people associate northern Cape Breton with the Cabot Trail, which wends its way in a loop, encompassing much of this scenic area. However, few people realize that almost half of the Trail—106 kilometres (66 miles) of its northern arc—is an integral part of Cape Breton Highlands National Park. This park offers wonderful opportunities to view rugged coastal vistas, ramble through forests and barrens, walk along magnificent beaches, and visit the charming small communities that are interspersed along the Trail, on private land adjacent to the park.

The park has six well-equipped campgrounds: some quiet, some crowded; some protected by woods, others exposed on windy ocean beaches. Short, self-guiding walks are accessible directly from the Cabot Trail. Longer walks lead up plunging river valleys, over windswept highlands, and along wave-battered shorelines.

The diversity and grandeur of the Cape Breton Highlands is due to its distinctive geological history and its geographical location, the northernmost point of Cape Breton Island, jutting out into two very different seas—the Gulf of St. Lawrence on the western shore and the Atlantic Ocean on the east. The Highlands are the most spectacular part of the Maritime Acadian Highlands, one of the 48 Natural Regions in Canada. The Highlands are a huge plain that, long ago, was lifted to 532 metres (1600 feet) at its highest point, though the average elevation at the margins of this plain is 350 metres (1050 feet). It is tilted higher on the western side. The stress of this upward movement created long cracks in the earth's crust, which became straight, steep-sided valleys, carrying rivers to the sea.

Soil on the high central plateau is very thin, and supports taiga and heath plants and animals. On the lower eastern side of the park, and all along the valley sides and floors, forests can grow—boreal forests in the higher, more exposed areas, mixed hardwood and softwood forests in the more protected areas.

Marylee Stephenson

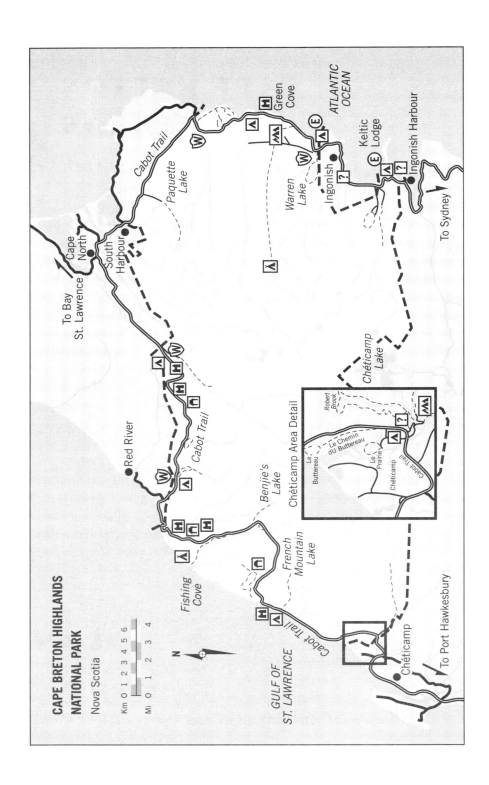

CAPE BRETON HIGHLANDS
NATIONAL PARK

Nova Scotia

Km 0 1 2 3 4 5 6
Mi 0 1 2 3 4

N

GULF OF
ST. LAWRENCE

Cabot Trail

To Port Hawkesbury

Chéticamp

Fishing
Cove

French
Mountain
Lake

Benjie's
Lake

Cabot Trail

Red River

To Bay
St. Lawrence

Cape
North

South
Harbour

Cabot Trail

Paquette
Lake

Warren
Lake

Green
Cove

ATLANTIC
OCEAN

Keltic
Lodge

Ingonish

Ingonish Harbour

To Sydney

Chéticamp
Lake

Chéticamp Area Detail

Robert
Brook

Le Chemin
dU Buttereau

Le
Buttereau

Le
Prairie

Chéticamp

Cabot Trail

The coastline itself is very imposing, with many of the huge wooded headlands dropping precipitously to the sea.

HOW TO SEE THE PARKS

Bogs and Barrens

To the early European settlers of the Cape Breton Highlands, who were interested in the land for farming or grazing, the plateau may have seemed barren. But, if you like kilometres of misty vistas, Labrador tea plants waist high as you walk among them, pink granite outcroppings covered with pearly-grey reindeer lichen or soft, green lichen, then the barrens are a rich source of life and beauty.

I drove the short, rocky road to **Paquette Lake**, and then began walking along the wide **Glasgow Lakes Trail** into the barrens. Reindeer lichen, heath plants, and tamarack trees clung to the thin soil and occasional granite outcroppings.

As I continued the gradual descent, there was a narrow, deep stream, and after fording it on some old logs someone else had left as a makeshift bridge, I came out on to a very wet open meadow. Surely one of the special areas in the park, it was sewn with dozens of orchids!

Several trails can take you on to the barrens, and one self-guided boardwalk, the Bog Trail, which is right by the Cabot Trail at **French Mountain**.

Marylee Stephenson

Flowers survive even on rocky terrain

The Forests, Rivers, and Mountains

From the Cabot Trail in July, it seems as if everything in the park that isn't ocean is lush forest. It's hard to tell that there's more than one type of tree growing there; variations in the shades of green, or the occasional white gleam of a birch trunk, are the only clues.

Any of the walks or drives up the valley sides and on to the plateau will reveal the progression from deciduous forests, near the valley floors, to the evergreen forests, located higher up. The **Acadian Trail**, from behind Chéticamp Campground, is an excellent way to cross through this whole sequence and return, in three to four hours. There are spectacular views of the interior of the park, of the Chéticamp River Valley and Chéticamp village, and also of the flatlands and barachois ponds that border the ocean, before it stretches out off to the horizon. Barachois ponds are formed when sand dunes or reefs build up at the mouths of freshwater streams.

Franey Trail, near Ingonish, provides sweeping views of the ocean and shoreline, and this is one of its main attractions. However, it is also a good opportunity for another magnificent experience of the forest, rivers, and highlands of the eastern part of the park.

For a gentle walk that leads to a woodland lake, try **Jigging Cove Trail**, located just off the Cabot Trail, a short drive from the Black Brook day-use area. You can walk around the lake in less than an hour, enjoying the mixed forest, the dark lake, and its beautiful vegetation. Bird-watching here is really rewarding.

At **Benjie's Lake**, a short trail in a higher, more boreal woodland will bring you to carpets of spring flowers. The highlight of the walk turned out to be a mother moose and two calves, which startled me as I came around the bend in the narrow, tree-lined trail.

For woodland rivers and streams, try the **Corney Brook** or **MacIntosh Brook** trails. Both end at waterfalls. The valleys of both brooks are rich and well drained, and support mature deciduous forests, with maples and other hardwoods. Spring flowers are a treat, and these are the areas to visit to see the changing colours of autumn.

Another favourite visitor site, nestled in a mature deciduous forest, is **Lone Shieling**, a short drive east of the MacIntosh Brook trailhead and campground. The shieling is a reproduction of Scottish sheep crofters' huts. This lone shieling was erected in 1942, to commemorate the Scottish heritage of so many Cape Bretoners. But, for the nature buff, the setting of the shieling is striking, indeed, for the deciduous forest here has never been cut, and some of the trees (sugar maple, yellow birch, and beech) are more than 300 years old.

The Shoreline

Cape Breton Highlands National Park offers a number of places to walk, at one with the sea and the shore. The northwestern **Chéticamp** area has more precipitous shore edges, with the giant, high headlands plunging to the sea, so walking is often along ridges and crests overlooking the ocean. The **Skyline Trail**, which begins at the top of **French Mountain**, is not along the shore itself, but runs along the top of a 300-metre (900-foot) coastal headland. The trail offers one of the best "overviews" of the rugged western coast of Cape Breton. At sea level, near the Chéticamp area, there are two very good places to experience the shoreline environment up close. One is **La Bloque** beach and picnic area, which has interpretive signs telling about the life of the small Acadian fishing community that existed there at the turn of the century. The other is **Le Buttereau** Trail, near the Grande Falaise picnic area. There are views of the Chéticamp River, the Gulf of St. Lawrence, Chéticamp Island, and pillar rocks offshore.

On the Ingonish side of the park, the elevations are lower and the land slopes more gently to the sea. Here, you can walk at your leisure in areas like **Green Cove**, where trails right by the ocean take you through mushroom-studded forests, over low headlands that seem more like Scottish moors, and on to spurs of pink rock, washed by ocean waves.

Marylee Stephenson

Glacial erratic in the foggy barrens

Another gentle but spectacular walk is the one at **Middle Head**, which starts at the Keltic Lodge. There are great views of the coast here, and the bird life is rich. The **Coastal Trail** is another good opportunity for a shoreline and forest experience.

PARK SERVICES AND FACILITIES

Interpretive Program

The park has a rich, and quite complex, interpretive program, because overnight visitors are concentrated at the opposite sides of the park, and many people visit for a few hours only, as they drive along the Cabot Trail. Also, the strong Acadian and Scottish traditions of the area call for programs that interpret the park in both French and English.

The core of the summer interpreter-led programs is the nightly slide shows, which are given in the Chéticamp and Broad Cove outdoor amphitheatres.

There is also increasing involvement of local people in interpretive and recreational programming. The Park Cooperating Association (Les Amis du Plein Air—friends of the outdoors) sponsors Scottish Acadian concerts, which feature Cape Breton music and dance.

There are eight roadside exhibits along the Cabot Trail, and six self-guiding trails. These trails tend to be short and easily accessible.

The greatest single source of information on all aspects of a visit to the park is the Chéticamp Visitor Centre, which is also wheelchair accessible. The Centre focuses on what can be seen along the Cabot Trail, including its natural and human history. The main park map also provides hiking-trail information. There is a large topographic relief map of the park here, which cyclists find particularly useful.

The Ingonish Information Centre is the place to start your visit at the eastern entry to the park. It is not as large as the Chéticamp Visitor Centre, but there are staff to answer your questions, a smaller nature bookstore, a copy of the hiking trail photo album, and information on non-park visitor facilities nearby.

Camping

Because the two sides of the park are quite distinct in natural setting, it is wise to camp first on one side, and then move to the other.

The campsites of this park are among the most luxurious in the national system. Of the six developed campsites, **Broadcove** (256 sites) and

Chéticamp (162 sites) have many sites with three-way trailer hook-ups, showers in the washrooms, separate dishwashing areas, and kitchen shelters with woodstoves. Both Chéticamp and Broadcove offer wheelchair-accessible campsites and washrooms.

Chéticamp is the least crowded, the most wooded, and the quieter of the two campgrounds.

There are four campgrounds without any trailer hook-ups, but they do have water, washrooms, fireplaces, and kitchen shelters with woodstoves. Ingonish has 90 unserviced sites. It is the first campground to fill up, especially as the weekends approach, so arrive mid-week and/or early in the day. The others are **MacIntosh Brook** (10 sites), which is in cleared woodlands; **Corney Brook** (20 sites), which is near the beach on the west side; and **Big Intervale** (10 sites), which is cleared woodland and about halfway along the Cabot Trail. These three campsites are prized as rest-stops by cyclists.

Primitive Camping

There are two wilderness campsites, with fireplaces and pit privies. Most are located in the interior of the park, and have been set up particularly for people who are fishing. **Fishing Cove Campground** is along the coast, and **Lake of Islands** is on the plateau, quite far into the interior of the park. Both require a permit.

Group Camping

A group campground is located near Ingonish, called **Marrach**, and another by **Robert Brook** in Chéticamp. Write to the Superintendent for information about your group's camping there. Both of these campgrounds are situated near hiking trails and water.

Other Camping

Private campgrounds are situated south of the park, along the roads that lead into either side of the park.

Other Accommodation, Gas, Food, and Supplies

Keltic Lodge is a provincially run resort located in the park. There are motels in the small towns bordering the park, at either edge, and in the small villages scattered along the Cabot Trail.

The park itself does not provide gasoline, food, or supplies, but you will find them at the towns at Chéticamp and Ingonish, and in several villages along the Cabot Trail. You are never more than 30 minutes by car from a small, but sufficient, supply of gas, food, and so on.

There is a restaurant at Keltic Lodge in Ingonish. You'll find snack stands, small cafes, and restaurants in most communities along the Cabot Trail.

Recreational Services

Swimming   Ocean swimming is supervised at beaches at Ingonish Beach and Freshwater Lake. Unsupervised ocean beaches are at North Bay, Broad Cove, Black Brook, the Aspy Bay, La Bloque Beach, and sandy beaches near Chéticamp. You can swim in fresh water, north of Ingonish at Warren Lake.

Fishing   Two main species of fish are caught in the park: Atlantic salmon in the Chéticamp River, and Eastern Brook trout in the lakes and rivers that go to the sea. Also, most streams have a good run of sea trout. Ask staff at the entrance, or any warden, for a national park fishing permit and information on seasons and limits.

Golf   Ingonish offers an 18-hole highlands course, run by the Canadian Parks Service. There are daily, seasonal, and twilight fees, and special junior rates.

Tennis   There are three free hard-surface courts at Ingonish Beach day-use area. Players rotate every 45 minutes, on the honour system.

Winter Use   Like most of the national parks, Cape Breton Highlands is rapidly expanding its winter access. A winter activities bulletin is available from the park, which lists a wide variety of activities—snowshoeing, winter camping, tobogganing, and cross-country skiing. From January to March, the park offers a number of groomed and ungroomed trails. The bulletin lists their length and degree of difficulty. There are also good cross-country opportunities outside the park.

Bird-Watching   A wide variety of habitats and bird life can be viewed within the park, but visitors who wish to see offshore birds, such as puffins and razorbills, should follow signs outside the park, for boat charters to the Bird Islands near Bras d'Or, located about an hour south of the Ingonish entrance. Park information centres offer a supply of the relevant leaflets, if you have missed the signs.

Whale-Watching   Many whale-watching tours are offered in the park vicinity, leaving from Chéticamp, Pleasant Bay, Bay St. Lawrence, Dingwall, and Ingonish. There are good chances of seeing whales and, in any case, the chance to see the park area from offshore is well worthwhile. Contact the

Nova Scotia Department of Tourism, inquire at the park information centres when you arrive, or check at the various shops or other tourist facilities along the Trail for brochures.

Related Activities or Places of Natural or Historic Interest

Tourism Nova Scotia is an excellent information service for all kinds of visitation in the province. From the Halifax/Dartmouth area, call 425-5781. From anywhere else in North America, call 1-800-565-0000.

Activities and Places to Consider Visiting:

- Nature touring: Whale- and seal-watching tours operate out of several villages in Cape Breton, and there are a number of bird-watching tours, by boat or land. Refer to the Tourism Nova Scotia information books that they will send you.

National Historic Sites

(Contact Canada Parks Service for the *Vacation Planner for Cape Breton Island* information booklet on the sites in Nova Scotia). Sites include

- Baddeck: Alexander Graham Bell National Historic Site
- Glace Bay: Marconi National Historic Site
- Louisbourg: Fortress of Louisbourg
- St. Peters: St. Peters Canal
- Canso: Grassy Island National Historic Site

For More Information

The Superintendent
Cape Breton Highlands National Park
Ingonish Beach
Cape Breton, Nova Scotia
B0C 1L0
Phone: (902) 285-2270, or
       (902) 285-2691 (Ingonish)
       (902) 224-3403 (Chéticamp)
Fax: (902) 285-2866

GROS MORNE

National Park

Rugged, glowering mountains and long, pearly beaches are quite unexpected in this part of Canada, but Gros Morne National Park* has these and more; steep-sided fjords, trout and salmon streams, bog-engulfed lakes. Nestled in the grandeur of this setting are several small fishing enclaves. Walking along lobster-trap-laden wharves or dodging the occasional sheep on the roads, you get a sense of how, for the past 5000 years, people have made their living on this land at the edge of the sea; fishing the sea and the fjords, and gardening or hunting in the forested slopes.

The geological history of this particular combination of fresh- and salt-water fjords, coastal plain, and mountains makes Gros Morne an essential link in the preservation plan of the Canadian parks system. Since some of the rock formations exist in only a few other places in the world, Gros Morne is now a World Heritage Site—a location considered to be of exceptional interest and value, not just within Canada, but around the world. Gros Morne contains evidence of important stages in the geological evolution of the Earth—the opening (rifting) and closing of the Iapetus Ocean. In places, rock from the depths of the earth's mantle is exposed right beside rock of the earth's crust. At other sites you can clearly see the filigreed graptolites from the Ordovician period.

The park's variety of terrain and rock composition is largely the result of two processes. One is plate tectonics, where the forces of continental collision have caused land to be pushed upward, forming what is now known as the Tablelands. The other process is repeated glaciation, where the tremendous weight of the debris-filled ice rivers cut out fjords. The last glacial retreat began about 15 000 years ago, but the Gros Morne lowlands were not ice-free for another 5000 years or so.

Marylee Stephenson

---

*Gros is pronounced locally as "gross."

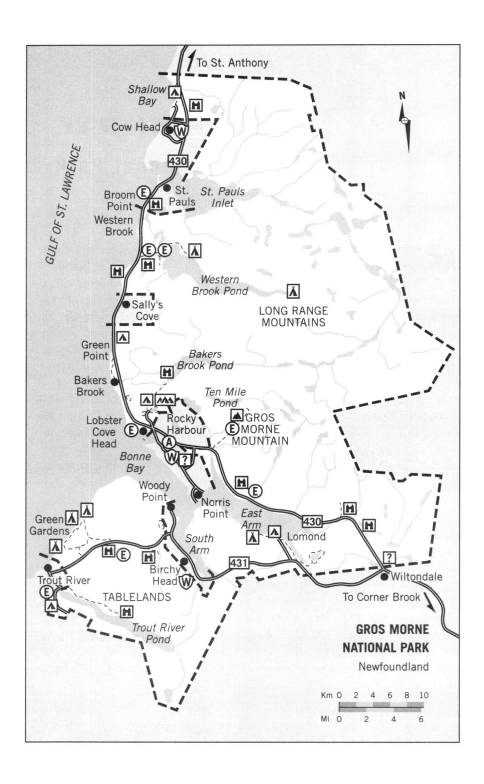

GROS MORNE
NATIONAL PARK

Newfoundland

HOW TO SEE THE PARK

To see as much of this park as possible in a visit of a few days, it's helpful to envision it as three levels, stairstepping upward to the east. First, there is the sea and its meeting with the land; second, the long, low coastal plain, with its forest, fjords, and bogs; and third, the rugged uplands of Gros Morne itself and other mountains, in the northern part of the park and the Tablelands in the south.

The Coastline

Within 15 minutes of entering the park from its southeast gate (the one nearest the Trans-Canada Highway), the role of glaciation, in forming parts of the coastline, becomes evident. For about 16 kilometres (10 miles) the road skims past a deep fjord, **Bonne Bay**. The views are spectacular. If you can take one of the private boat tours that are run out of **Norris Point**, at the mouth of the bay, you will get an even better impression of its expanse.

A 15-minute ride from the Woody Point landing is **Green Gardens Trail**. It has two trailheads, along Highway 431. The park recommends taking the Long Pond trailhead route, which starts 11 kilometres (seven miles) from Woody Point. There is a 4.5-kilometre (three-mile) hike to the coast, so you can come back the same way, in one day. It is also possible to continue on the route and loop back to the other trailhead at Wallace Brook. This is a more rigorous 18-kilometre (11-mile) trip that involves two stream crossings. The Green Gardens Trail takes you from the barren, plant-poor environment near the road, down into an increasingly lush, wooded valley and, finally, out to the clifftop meadows of Green Gardens, located at the edge of the rugged coast. There are sea stacks, and a giant sea cave accessible at low tide, and small coves and waterfalls scattered along the shore.

Heading straight north from Norris Point through the park, a few minutes past the turn-off to the park information building, is Rocky Harbour. As with the many other fishing villages on Newfoundland's coast that depended on the cod fishery, life is changing here. Fishing is now limited to lobster in the spring and early summer, herring and mackerel in late summer and fall, and a new experimental crab fishery.

A rocky coast wouldn't be complete without a lighthouse. Gros Morne provides one at **Lobster Cove Head**, located just north of Rocky Harbour. The light is now automated, but the keeper's house is open to the public every day from mid-June to late September. One room is a reproduction of how the lightkeeper's den might have been at the beginning of this century.

About halfway up the park's length is **Green Point,** situated just beyond the Green Point Campground. As you come around the head-land, walk along the level, tide-pooled slabs of rock; the low cliffs to the right are composed of sedimentary layers, thrown up vertically by the slow but huge earth movements that shifted rocks 450 million years old. At one point near a sharp indentation on the cliff line is a place where the rock spans the boundary between the Cambrian and Ordovician periods, with rock from the Cambrian era to the south and Ordovician to the north. Rock textures range from pockmarked to rippled, dimpled, smooth, or jagged.

The drive farther north passes the first real dune area of the coastline, at **Western Brook** picnic ground. Several picnic tables, a cook shelter, and washrooms are provided here.

North from Green Point is **Broom Point,** the site of the Mudge family cabin and fish store. The Mudge family fished from the site from 1941 until 1975, when they sold the property to the park. The buildings have been restored and are now run as an interpretive exhibit between mid-June and early September.

Near the north end of the park you come to **St. Paul's Bay,** which lies just outside the park boundary. This bay is glacially carved, but its sides are not as steep as the other fjords. Much of it is edged with salt-marsh flats. Basking seals, best seen from a tour boat, are not an uncommon sight on the sand bars, and the bird life is rich—migrating shorebirds, especially, abound.

Park near the bridge or in the tiny hamlet of St. Paul's, and walk along the crooked point of land that forms the inlet's lower edge. The sheltered beach is long and flat, with barnacles and beached shells, wood and sea-weed; this is a favourite place for blue mussels and razor clams. The nar-row channel out to sea is called a "tickle"—a deceptively mild term, for the sea rushes in and out with the change of tide, at alarming speed. Caution forbids walking too close to the edge at those times, but safe slopes, which turn into pastureland, are located nearby.

At the end of the point, the land is no longer the park territory, and you see again the local use of the coastline, where scattered sheep or horses graze. You may find, as we did, an old jaw of a whale that stretched about 2.5 metres (8 feet) long, with flowers growing in its shadow of protection from the wind. Boat tours of St. Paul's Inlet are offered by tour operators in St. Paul's.

As you continue your drive along Highway 430, rocky beaches and salt flats give way to long stretches of white sandy beach, edged by dunes or flower-dotted grassy fields. This landscape stretches for many kilometres at **Shallow Bay,** located at the northernmost part of the park.

To view a remarkable aspect of the Gros Morne area, though it is not actually located within the park boundaries, just walk south from Shallow Bay, along the water towards Cow Head, a peninsula jutting into the ocean. The point contains the renowned **Cow Head Breccias.** Close examination shows a light-coloured sedimentary rock, engulfing rough-edged chunks of another rock. Fossils are also embedded here and there. Breccias do occur elsewhere in the park, for example at Green Point, but this is where geologists first came to understand what appeared to be a paradox: in this cold northern climate, how could rocks laden with fossils of animals that could live only in shallow warm seas be found with fossils of species that lived only in deep water? The answer is that, long ago, these rocks were part of the shallow shelf of the continent, which stretched far into what was then the sea. Occasionally, underwater avalanches would occur at the edge, and the shelf, with all its living and sand-entrapped dead animals, would plunge suddenly down the slope, to the depths of the sea. These fragments would then be layered, over the millennia, with other debris, and compacted into a conglomerate. The ongoing movement of the huge plates that comprise our earth's crust slowly raised these areas, and moved them to where they are now.

The Coastal Plain

The coastal plain was once a shallow shelf, submerged by the sea, but the rebound after glacial retreat lifted it to its present level—the second level of the park. Now it slopes up slightly inland, and then changes dramatically into the highlands. This narrow band of plain contains a world of its own. Around the sheltered head of Bonne Bay, in the southern part of the park, the woods contain hardwood (temperate) species such as red maple, black ash (rare), and yellow birch as well as eastern white pine. Robins, jays, chickadees, and warblers of many sorts abound. Elsewhere, the boreal forest dominates, with its balsam fir, black and white spruce, and white birch. Moose, lynx, snowshoe hare, red fox, beaver, and otter all live in this habitat.

There are three good places to visit, if you want to enjoy the fjords, woodlands, and bogs of the lowlands. The first is the **Lomond** area, located at the south end of the park. Here, you can see the remains of a steam engine from the sawmill that once operated here and the garden escapes of the previous inhabitants.

The second location worth visiting is **Berry Head Pond**. A short walk, on the road north of the Berry Hill Campground, leads to a typical freshwater pond of the area. Irises, marsh marigolds, and bog orchids grow tall by the pond. A large, raised bog spreads out from one side of the pond. Bogs are rarely as accessible as this one. The wetter part is traversed by a narrow boardwalk.

The third place to visit lies farther north, and offers one of the most exciting experiences of the park—the hike to **Western Brook Pond**, and a boat ride on it. "Pond" is the rather modest local term used for the massive, land-locked fjords that slash through the park. The lower talus slopes support some trees and shrubs, but higher up the cliffs are nearly perpendicular, and only the gulls can cling to tiny cracks and shelves. Waterfalls sheet down, sometimes turning to mist curtains in the wind, at their upper heights.

To see all this you must take a boat ride—a service offered by a licensed concession in the summer. The Visitor Centre will have the telephone number for reservations.

The enjoyment of Western Brook Pond begins with the walk in. The three-kilometre (two-mile) trail through boreal forest takes you over various wetland types, including sphagum bogs, larch scrub, and alder

Parks Canada

The sweeping shoreline of Gros Morne park

swamp. There are also four slightly better drained areas on bedrock ridges that support a balsam fir forest. The damp areas have a wide boardwalk. You may spot beaver, caribou, or moose.

Even if the boat trip isn't possible, the hike is worthwhile. At the boat dock area, there is space to picnic and walk along the lakeshore or skip rocks across the water. There is also a large waiting area with shelter, interpretive exhibits, and benches and picnic sites nestled in the woods.

Mountainous Areas

These regions of the park contain vegetation with an arctic-alpine element. There are essentially three areas in the park where this environment occurs: the **Long Range Mountains**, the **Tablelands**, and **Gros Morne Mountain** itself. Much of Gros Morne National Park is composed of the Long Range Mountains, an alpine plateau that runs from the north to the south of the park's eastern boundary. This area is not easily accessible to visitors.

The Tablelands plateau comprises much of the southwest segment of the park. Access to this area is by Highway 431, which turns to the left at Wiltondale, the hamlet at the edge of the park. It is also easy to reach from Woody Point, if the ferry from Norris Point is operating.

The looming Tablelands are made of peridotite, a rock that is found in the earth's mantle—the dense, but active, layer located just below the earth's crust.

Peridotite is also interesting because, when it is exposed to water under very high pressure, or to heat, serpentine can be formed from this rock. Along the Winterhouse Brook at the base of the Tablelands, and at a few other locations, rocks show exposed sheets of serpentine, gleaming green in the light. This area can be further explored via **Trout River Pond Trail** or the Tablelands boat tour, both of which depart from the Trout River day-use area.

Gros Morne, the park's namesake mountain, is located less than halfway up the main park road. The experience of hiking into its base, and then struggling up its face to the stark, rock-littered top will stay with you for a lifetime. The trail reaches more than 805 metres (2600 feet) up to a flat expanse, where quartzite, shattered by water freezing and thawing on the chilly, windy surface, has created nine square kilometres (three square miles) of *felsenmeer*, a "sea of rocks." This felsenmeer is probably very old, and formed over millions of years of exposure to the elements.

The views from Gros Morne are fantastic. Glacial valleys, surrounding the mountain, cut sharply into the land around; other mountains rise as sharply in the distance. The coastal plain, with its mixed bogs, forests,

The trail to Gros Morne's top is easy to follow, but requires hard
work on the scree slope

lakes, and streams, spreads out below, and the blue of the coast with Bonne
Bay and the distant gulf accentuate the grey and green world all around.

It's an extremely rugged hike to the top, and it can take more than
three to four hours each way.

If you choose to go to the top, you first have to scramble up a large
and very steep scree slope. On top, a trail is clearly marked with rock
cairns. This is a strenuous climb, but the view is marvellous.

PARK SERVICES AND FACILITIES

Gros Morne was established in 1973. It has excellent visitor facilities, a
wide range of trails for a variety of hiking experiences, and informative,
extensive interpretation programs. These programs take place all over the
park, but are coordinated at the Visitor Centre at Rocky Harbour. This
centre is a beautiful building, with excellent displays and a good indoor
theatre for evening presentations.

Camping

The park offers 287 campsites in all. None have electrical hook-ups, but
the Berry Hill and Shallow Bay Campgrounds have trailer-waste disposal

facilities, and a water supply for filling storage tanks. All campsites are on a first-come, first-served basis. Cooking grates are provided and firewood is available for a fee, but bring your own hatchet and small saw. Most sites have picnic tables. At **Berry Hill**, 153 sites are situated in a densely wooded area, located four kilometres (2.5 miles) inland. The trees provide a lot of privacy. The campground is equipped with hot showers, washrooms and toilets, excellent kitchen shelters with running water, sinks, and sophisticated wood stoves. There are three sandbox and play areas for small children; one is very large, with a well-designed adventure playground. There is a trail to a good lookout point, leading from the back of the campground, a trail leading around a small pond behind, and a five-kilometre (three-mile) trail to Bakers Brook Falls. There are three bulletin boards, with information on the interpretive programs.

Six "walk-in" campsites are situated on a small lake. Parking is located nearby. These sites are more secluded, but the walk to the facilities is longer.

Green Point campground offers 18 sites, nestled into the low, coastal tuckamore—the coastal border of windswept, gnarled trees. There is a kitchen shelter with a wood stove, and flush toilets. A central water supply is provided. The campground is self-registering, with the staff collecting the slips each day. There's a low cliff here, but a stairway descends to the beach. The sea is too rough for swimming, but the beach is great for walking and enjoying the marvellous sunsets. Being so close to the Green Point fishing settlement, and the fascinating geology of the cove, is the real advantage of this quiet, modest campground. There is a bulletin board, with a park map and announcements of the interpretive program. At **Shallow Bay**, 50 sites are located on an open field. This campground is located closest to the dunes and the wide, shallow beach that stretches for kilometres along the northern part of the park. It has an adventure playground for children. There are flush toilets and showers. Adjoining the kitchen shelter is a minitheatre, for weekend evening interpretive programs. There is a kiosk for registration and information. The **Lomond** area (28 sites) is situated at the southern edge of the park, on the western segment near the Tablelands. It is located four kilometres (2.5 miles) east of Highway 431, on the road to Woody Point. The grassy field for camping leads down the east arm of Bonne Bay. Three of the sites are "walk-ins," overlooking Bonne Bay. The brief walk is through meadows that are thick with flowers. With a licence, you can fish along the nearby Lomond River. There is a kiosk for registration and information. There is also an adventure playground for children.

Trout River campground has 33 sites overlooking Trout River Pond. There is an adventure playground, kitchen shelters, pumped water, and flush toilets. There is a kiosk for registration and information. Boat tours operate on Trout River Pond during the summer season, depending on weather conditions. Check with the Visitor Centre for rates, schedules, and reservations.

Group Camping

Group camping is now offered at Berry Hill campground. Write to the Superintendent for information and reservations.

Other Accommodation, Gas, Food, and Supplies

The villages of Rocky Harbour, Cow Head, and Woody Point have motels. There are private campgrounds near Rocky Harbour, on private land. Most communities provide gas, food, and supplies. There are guest homes now in Woody Point, Rocky Harbour, Cow Head, Norris Point, and Trout River and guest cabins in Rocky Harbour, Trout River, Cow Head, and Wiltondale (located near the southeastern edge of the park). The Superintendent should have listings, or contact the Newfoundland Tourism Department (toll free — 1-800-563-6353).

Recreational Services

Playgrounds   Adventure playgrounds are located at Berry Hill, Lomond, Shallow Bay, and Trout River campgrounds, as well as at selected day-use areas.

Swimming   There is no supervised swimming in the park, but many areas of shore and stream are good for wading or swimming. The community of Rocky Harbour offers an unsupervised beach on Rocky Harbour Pond, as well as a fitness park. Shallow Bay and Lomond day-use areas have unsupervised salt-water swimming. Both have changing rooms, and Lomond has outdoor showers for rinsing off. Trout River has fresh-water swimming, with changing rooms. Two kilometres (one mile) south of Berry Hill campground, on Highway 430, an indoor, 25-metre swimming pool overlooks Rocky Harbour. The shallow bay and a whirlpool complete the picture. This facility is open from mid-June through Labour Day.

Fishing   This is a very good area for Atlantic salmon or speckled trout. National Parks fishing regulations are in force. Park staff can give information, as can the local businesses servicing visitors, motels, grocery stores, camping suppliers, and so on.

Winter Use   Gros Morne maintains a system of groomed ski trails, managed by the co-operating association (709-458-2417). Winter camping is available at Green Point, and the major motels and cabins are open year-round.

Related Activities or Places of Natural or Historic Interest

The Newfoundland and Labrador Department of Tourism, Culture and Recreation is an excellent information service for all kinds of visitation in the province. Call 1-800-563-6353.

Activities and Places to consider visiting:

- Western Newfoundland provides a wealth of scenery. Nearby provincial parks include Pasadena Beach and The Arches.

- For nearby historic sites, visit the Pioneer Village in nearby Wiltondale or the museums in Corner Brook and Cow Head.

National Historic Sites:

- 42 kilometres from St. Anthony: L'Anse aux Meadows (also a UNESCO World Heritage Site)

- Port au Choix: Port au Choix National Historic Site

- Red Bay Labrador: Red Bay National Historic Site

FURTHER READING

Rocks Adrift: The Geology of Gros Morne National Park by Michael Burzynski and Anne Marceau (Gros Morne Co-operating Association, second printing, 1995).

For More Information

The Superintendent
Gros Morne National Park
Box 130
Rocky Harbour, Newfoundland
A0K 4N0
Phone: (709) 458-2066
Fax: (709) 458-2059
TDD: (709) 458-2996

TERRA NOVA
National Park

T erra Nova occupies over 400 square kilometres (155 square miles) along the eastern coast of Newfoundland, and is a great place to see the heritage of the Ice Ages. It is a park to see, literally, from the ground up; from the deep fjords, to the sweep of bog and fen, upward to the boulder-strewn slopes, to the boreal forest clinging to the shallow soil, and finally up to the bald, windswept hilltops.

HOW TO SEE THE PARK

Although much of the park is rugged, exposed, island-studded coastline, with hectares of mushy bog, the park is very accessible. The Trans-Canada Highway runs through 43 kilometres (27 miles) of the park. It provides many easily reached areas along its route, including car access to the hilltops by side roads, to the campground, hiking trails, day-use areas, and coastline.

During the last Ice Age there was a massive ice cap in southwest Newfoundland, which sent out rivers of ice that gouged valleys, deepened rivers, and ground bedrock to a high polish. As the ice cap began to melt and retreat, it left a trail of sand, gravel, rocks, and boulders, which had been bound up in its ice. The gouging and scouring action of these deposits resulted in the varied topography of Terra Nova.

The Coastline

There are almost 200 kilometres (125 miles) of coastline in Terra Nova, with fjords, coves, and tidal flats lining the southern, eastern, and part of the northern edges of the park. In places, the land's edge is highly sculpt-ed with caves, cliffs, and rocky stacks; elsewhere, there are sand and pebble-strewn beaches. To appreciate the beauty and variety of the coast-line, take the coastal trail that runs along much of inner **Newman Sound**,

Parks Canada

343

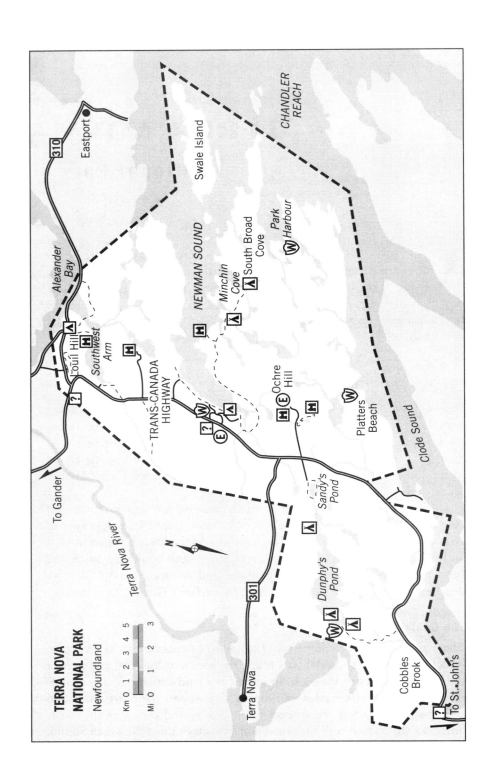

from **Buckley's Cove** to **South Broad Cove**. You can reach the trail from several roads off the Trans-Canada Highway, which runs the entire north/south length of the park, or you can meet the trail near the Newman Sound Campground. This is a good trail for viewing the coastline, for wandering onto the beach at low tide, or for watching for boreal birds or flowers in the forest through which it weaves.

The shore area is rich in plant and bird life. Look for shore birds, ducks, and geese in spring and fall. Bald eagles and ospreys nest in the park, and can regularly be seen from this trail. You can stop near the wharf area to view **Pissing Mare Falls**, which is far more elegant than its name. You can fish at the wharf or simply watch others fishing.

The Fresh Water

Fresh water flows in many narrow swift streams, slows down in numerous ponds, and remains still in the bogs and fens. The Ice Age has also left its mark in this area. Some of the streams were cut out long ago by the melting water from the retreating ice. Some of the lakes and bogs were scraped out by glacial action, or built up when coarse soil was compacted by glaciers, so that the torrents of rain could not drain off rapidly.

For a good look at some of these wetlands, take the **Ochre Hill Ponds Loop Trail** or proceed past the Ochre Hill Ponds up to the Ochre Hill Lookout. Here you will walk on a gravel-and-boardwalk trail, through sphagnum-based bogs or sedgy fens dotted with little islands of tiny, twisted tamarack trees or spruce. The bogs give way to a stream littered with jagged boulders, which have most intriguing lichen patterns.

The trail also weaves in and out of the boreal forest that edges the bog and pond system. Eventually, you will reach a lake, with water that is clean but coloured brown by the tannic and humic acids that seep in from the surrounding bogs. You can follow this trail all the way to the overlooking Ochre Hills. The view from there reveals bogs spreading in almost every direction. The bogs at Bread Cove Meadow, located to the south, are the most fascinating. They look like half of a drowned coliseum, with the concentric half-circles of water forming the remaining tiers of seats.

Sandy Pond Trail takes you on a delightful walk around this freshwater lake. The scenic mix of water, shoreline, forest flowers, and other vegetation makes for a splendid walk.

The Sandy Pond Trail has self-guided signage describing boreal life in the park. Three large habitat signs and other smaller interpretive signs explain the animal and plant life found in the forest, bog, and fresh-water habitats.

Parks Canada

Bread Cove Hills, a glacially scoured area

The Forests

The boreal forests of Terra Nova support only the type of trees that can grow on thin soil, at low temperatures, with a very short summer. The predominant trees are black spruce and balsam fir. The coastal walk along **Newman Sound** and the Malady Head and Newman Sound Campgrounds offers opportunities to enjoy the boreal forest, with its bird sounds in the early mornings and evenings.

My favourite place, however, was on a short hike to **Malady Head.** A word of warning: this trail is hard to find. It begins near campsite 62, in the Malady Head Campground. Ask the kiosk operator for instructions on how to get there and where to park. When you reach the trail, you will be treated to the quiet, intense experience of a true boreal forest.

The forest floor is the familiar tumble of moss or laurel-covered rock-jumble, depending on the slope and dryness of each little area. Many varieties of moss thrive here in the humid environment—sphagnum being one of the most common.

The Barrens

Coasts, bogs, and forests of the park give way to barrens. At transitional levels, there is pearly-grey caribou lichen in puffs and rolls, interspersed

The scenic mix of forest flowers and other vegetation
makes for a splendid walk

with the occasional hearty tamarack or low-growing spruce. Some of
these black spruce trees send out their lowest branches in a wide circle,
and keep their tops less than a metre (three feet) tall. You can see this kind
of plant life on the slopes leading to the Ochre Hill Fire Tower Lookout
and Ochre Hills Lookout. But, at the top of both lookouts, the altitude
and winds have conspired to prevent even this much vegetation from taking hold. The Louil Hills are mostly exposed rock, remoulded through the
ages, with the occasional glacial erratic breaking its profile. The lichens
on the rocks are marvellous, and tenacious berry shrubs stretch out low
from rock cracks, and hold on tight.

PARK SERVICES AND FACILITIES

Interpretive Program

During the summer, the park offers an active interpretive program of
guided walks, evening presentations, children's programs, and special
events. Outdoor theatres are located at each campground, and a campfire
circle is situated at Newman Sound Campground only. Times and places
of park programs are posted on the campground bulletin boards, and listed in various park publications available at the kiosks and Visitor
Centres. Ski events and school and special group tours are available on
request in the fall, winter, and spring.

A new Marine Interpretive Centre at Salton's provides the focus for marine activity and marine interpretation, and also serves as the park's main Visitor Information Centre.

Camping

Two large campgrounds are provided in the park. Newman Sound is the larger of the two, with spacious, clean flush-toilet facilities, hot showers, kitchen shelters, laundromat, playgrounds, and grocery store. The setting is sparsely forested, with gravel pull-ins and a picnic table at each of its 387 sites. Malady Head is smaller and quieter, with only 165 sites. It is more densely treed than Newman Sound, and also has clean flush-toilet and shower facilities. No electrical hook-ups are provided at either site, but both have a trailer-waste disposal facility. At Malady Head, campfire pits are available at each site.

Back-Country Camping

The park offers six back-country camping areas, with pit toilets and picnic tables, for the use of hikers and canoeists. You must register for these sites. Park staff can provide more information on these.

Other Accommodation, Gas, Food, and Supplies

Gas stations are located at each end of the park, and a concession-run grocery, with a wide variety of food and other small camping supplies, is situated near the Newman Sound campground. The villages in the area have grocery and hardware stores and gas stations. Charlottetown is located near the central area of the park; Terra Nova and Eastport are about 16 kilometres (10 miles) outside its boundaries. Traytown is the closest village to the park—about two kilometres (one mile) beyond Burnt Point.

Recreational Services

Swimming   Supervised swimming is provided at Sandy Pond, 10:00 a.m. to 6:00 p.m., seven days a week, from June until Labour Day. Changing rooms and a snack bar are provided.

Canoeing   During the summer you can rent canoes and kayaks hourly, daily, or weekly at Sandy Pond. Waterproofed aerial-photo maps of the park, for canoe routes, are sold at a moderate price.

Fishing   There is fishing in a number of ponds and streams. A park permit is required. Salmon fishing is only permitted at the Northwest River and a special salmon licence is required in additional to the regular fishing permit. Ask any warden, or at the information kiosk, for further details.

Skiing   Cross-country skiing is a popular winter activity in the park. Groomed trails are open throughout the park for your skiing enjoyment.

Golfing   The scenic Twin Rivers Golf Course (18-hole) is located at the southern end of the park. Reservations can be made at the Terra Nova Lodge. Club-rental and dining facilities are available at the clubhouse.

Boat Tours   Regularly scheduled trips/boat tours leave several times daily from Headquarters Wharf, from mid-June to Labour Day. Special adventure and education programs are provided throughout the summer. Group rates are available. Call (709) 533-6024 for information.

Related Activities or Places of Natural or Historic Interest

The Newfoundland and Labrador Department of Tourism, Culture and Recreation is an excellent information service for all kinds of visitation in the province. Call 1-800-563-6353.

Activities and Places to Consider Visiting:

- The community of Eastport, located 15 minutes west of the park, is well known for its beautiful sandy beaches. Opportunities for whale-watching are available.

- Eastern Newfoundland has a network of provincial parks. Contact the local Visitor Information Centre for details.

- Several historic sites are situated near the park, particularly on the Bonavista peninsula. Try not to miss Trinity.

National Historic Site:

- Bonavista: Ryan Premises

For More Information

The Superintendent, Terra Nova National Park
Glovertown, Newfoundland
A0G 2L0
Phone: (709) 533-2801
Fax: (709) 533-2706

ELLESMERE ISLAND
National Park Reserve

Ellesmere Island National Park Reserve is located at the northernmost tip of the western hemisphere. (Reserve status means that, although the area is governed by the National Parks Act, the land claims of aboriginal people must be resolved in order for it to achieve full park status.) Ellesmere is surely the ultimate northern experience in the Canadian parks system, and quite likely there are few comparable experiences anywhere in the northern hemisphere. The park reserve was established in 1988, and the land set aside is 38 000 square kilometres (14 755 square miles) of the northern part of Ellesmere Island. The reserve protects a representative part of the Eastern High Arctic Glacier natural region.

Ellesmere Island is home to Arctic wolves

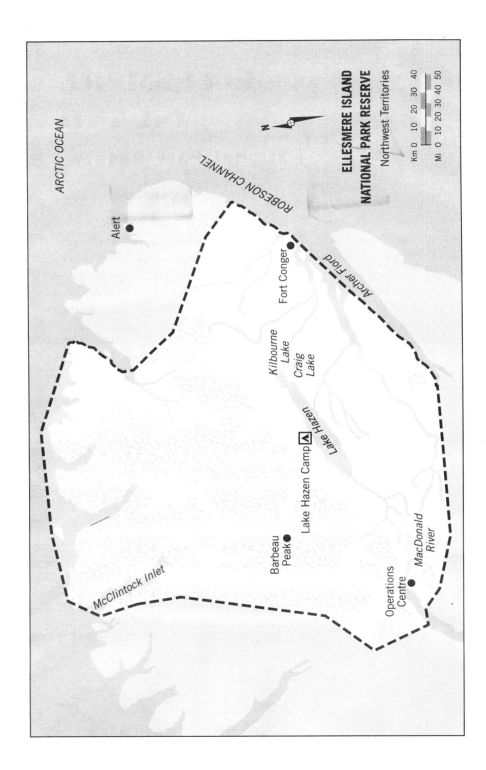

ELLESMERE ISLAND
NATIONAL PARK RESERVE
Northwest Territories

Km 0 10 20 30 40
Mi 0 10 20 30 40 50

ARCTIC OCEAN

Alert

ROBESON CHANNEL

Fort Conger

Archer Fiord

Kilbourne Lake

Craig Lake

Lake Hazen Camp

Lake Hazen

Barbeau Peak

McClintock Inlet

Operations Centre

MacDonald River

Ellesmere abounds with glaciers. These icefields, as much as 900 metres (2700 feet) thick, cover the Grantland Mountains located at the northern part of the park. Several of the peaks in the Grantland Range are over 2500 metres (7500 feet) high. Along the coast are many valleys, cut by glaciers, sweeping to the sea. Within the park is the 70-kilometre (44-mile)-long Lake Hazen. This area is especially rich in wildlife, because there is more moisture there. Moisture is a major issue for this rugged place, because it is actually a polar desert, with annual precipitation of only six centimetres (two inches)!

Plant and animal life is rich, with the landscape carpeted for the few weeks of summer, with dwarf willow, bright Arctic wildflowers, and colourful lichens and mosses. Musk ox, Arctic wolf and fox, bears, caribou, and many nesting birds are easy to see, and easy to approach and photograph.

Evidence of human use of the area is apparent as long ago as 4000 years—a use that has continued sporadically to this day. Along with the artifacts of aboriginal people, a number of sites show remains from Arctic explorers, who used the tip of Ellesmere as their jumping-off place en route to the North Pole.

Visiting Ellesmere Island Park Reserve is expensive, and requires that visitors either be very knowledgeable about travel in the High Arctic, or use

Auyuittuq National Park Reserve

The park's landscape is carpeted with bright arctic wildflowers

the services of tour companies that are licensed to operate in the reserve. The park offers a useful information handout about visitation, including lists of licensed outfitters, what conditions to expect, what to bring, associated costs, and so on. Because the season for visiting is very short—mostly July and August—and there is a great demand for transportation and guiding services, you must plan well in advance for your trip. And, once on your way, the conditions of northern travel may thwart your carefully planned schedule. However, for the truly adventurous traveller, I am confident that the trip will be worth the inconvenience.

Related Activities or Places of Natural or Historic Interest

Northwest Territories Tourism Information is an excellent source of information for visitation in the territory. Call 1-800-661-0788.

Activities and Places to Consider Visiting:

- Numerous private or outfitted trips are available out of Grise Fjord and Resolute Bay.

For More Information

Ellesmere Island National Park Reserve
P.O. Box 353
Pangnirtung, Northwest Territories
X0A 0R0
Phone: (819) 473-8828
Fax: (819) 473-8612

VUNTUT
National Park

V untut National Park is located in the northern Yukon Territory near the village of Old Crow. The initial agreement to establish the park was signed in May 1993, and the park officially came into existence in February 1995 with the effective date of the Vuntut Gwich'in First Nations Land Claim.

The park is 4345 square kilometres (1670 square miles) in size and is located between Ivvavik National Park to the north and the Arctic National Wildlife Refuge to the west. Vuntut lies within the northern portion of Old Crow Flats, an extensive plain with more than 2000 lakes and ponds. These wetlands are the Yukon's most critical waterfowl habitat and have been recognized by the Ramsar Convention as being of international importance. Each year, 500 000 birds use the flats as a breeding, staging, and moulting area.

In the Gwich'in language, "Vuntut" means "Crow Flats," and the entire flats, including the park, are part of a special management area established to protect the wildlife. The flats are only about 300 metres (900 feet) high while the surrounding mountains rise as high as 1500 metres (4500 feet).

The Old Crow Flats and surrounding area provide an important fall, winter, and spring habitat for the Porcupine caribou herd, whose range extends throughout northern Yukon and into Alaska. Other mammals found here include the grizzly bear, moose, and muskrat.

The park is dedicated to wilderness preservation and the maintenance of aboriginal lifestyles. The Vuntut Gwich'in people maintain harvesting rights within the park and throughout the flats. There are currently no Parks Canada staff or infrastructure in Vuntut National Park or the community of Old Crow. Parks Canada is working with the Vuntut Gwich'in First Nation and the community of Old Crow to develop a basic plan for the park operation that the land-claims agreement calls for. Staff estimate that it will probably be the summer of 1997 before Parks Canada has a presence in Old Crow.

Visitors to Old Crow are advised to be prepared to be self-sufficient and to make transportation and accommodation arrangements in advance. Most visitors come to travel the Old Crow and Porcupine Rivers or to hike on Old Crow mountain. Two businesses in town offer accommodation, and camping is permitted in a designated site near the centre of the town.

For More Information

Vuntut National Park
P.O. Box 390
Dawson City, Yukon Territory
Y0B 1G0
Phone: (403) 993-5462
Fax: (403) 993-5693

AULAVIK

National Park

A ulavik National Park is located on north-central Banks Island in the Northwest Territories. Established in August 1992, through an agreement between the Inuvialuit, the government of the Northwest Territories, and the federal government, the park consists of 12 275 square kilometres (4740 square miles) of arctic tundra and represents the Western Arctic Lowlands natural region. The nearest community is Sachs Harbour, located 250 kilometres (156 miles) southwest of the park.

The park is bisected by Thomsen River—Canada's most northerly navigable river—and its tributary, Muskox River, both of which flow north into M'Clure Strait. In the Inuvialuktun language, "Aulavik" means "a place where people travel"; the river has been a route for Inuit hunters for thousands of years. Mercy River is located on the east side of the park.

The park area is home to polar bears, 60 000 muskoxen, Arctic wolves, lemmings, and the Peary caribou (an endangered subspecies). Visitors are reminded to be cautious and keep their distance from the wildlife. Polar bears have been known to wander far inland and will, on rare occasions, stalk humans. The muskox, although appearing slow, can easily outrun a human and can be aggressive during the annual rut.

Birdlife is plentiful. In fact, the park encompasses the Banks Island Migratory Bird Sanctuary located in the northern portion of the Thomsen River valley. This area protects brant- and snow-geese habitat. Peregrine falcons, rough-legged hawks, and sandhill cranes are some of the many species nesting in the park.

Archeological sites within the park date back more than 3400 years. The first record of European visitation was during the search for the Northwest Passage when, in 1851, the English ship, the "Investigator" became trapped in the ice and was abandoned. In following years, the ship became a source of iron and copper for the Copper Inuit in the area.

HOW TO SEE THE PARK

Access to the park is by means of charter aircraft from Inuvik. Aircraft landing is carefully regulated. All visitors are required to register in and out of the park and to obtain a back-country use permit. If you intend to fish, you will need a Parks Canada fishing licence, which are available from the park office in Sachs Harbour or the district office in Inuvik.

July and August are the best months for visiting. It is generally fairly dry during this period, although often quite cool. The park does not offer any visitor facilities or services, and visitors must be totally self-sufficient. Canoeing, hiking, and camping are the main activities. Campers must practise no-trace camping, and must pack out all garbage. Arctic foxes on Banks Island have a high incidence of rabies, so visitors must be particularly careful to control garbage around their camps, to reduce its appeal for these beautiful animals.

The Thomsen River is the primary destination for canoeists. Because of its slow rate of flow, it is generally more suitable for canoes than for rafting. Visitors who intend to travel along the Thomsen between the Muskox River and Castell Bay, through the bird sanctuary, require an additional permit, which they can obtain from the Canadian Wildlife Service in Yellowknife.

For More Information

Aulavik National Park
General Delivery
Sachs Harbour, Northwest Territories
X0E 0T0
Phone: (403) 690-3904
Fax: (403) 690-4808

TUKTUT NOGAIT

National Park

uktut Nogait, Canada's newest national park, was established in June 1996. This remote park is located east of Inuvik in the Melville Hills, and represents the Tundra Hills natural region. The park covers an area of 16 340 square kilometres (6300 square miles) of the rolling tundra landscape of the Western Arctic, and includes the Brock and Hornaday Rivers, known for their spectacular canyons.

Tuktut Nogait means "caribou calves" in Inuvialuktun, which is the language of the Inuvialuit people of the Western Arctic. The park protects the calving grounds of more than 100 000 Bluenose barren-ground caribou. The park also protects the highest concentration of birds of prey in North America, including the peregrine falcon.

The creation of the park was initiated by the people of Paulatuk, who recognized the ecological and cultural importance of the region. Following Ivvavik and Aulavik, it is the third national park to be created within the Inuvialuit Settlement Region.

The park will be managed by representatives from Canada, the Northwest Territories, and the Inuvialuit. Park planning and management is currently in its early stages. Contact the park directly for further information.

For More Information

Tuktut Nogait National Park
Box 1840
Inuvik, Northwest Territories
X0E 0T0
Phone: (403) 979-3248
Fax: (403) 979-4491

WAPUSK

National Park

Established in April 1996, Wapusk is Canada's thirty-seventh National Park. The park is located in northern Manitoba, south and east of Churchill, between the Churchill and Nelson rivers. It represents the Hudson-James Lowlands natural region.

The park protects 11 457 square kilometres (4430 square miles) of critical wildlife habitat. "Wapusk" is the Cree word for "white bear." The area is one of the world's largest polar-bear denning sites. Other mammals found here include caribou, moose, wolves, and wolverines. The park also protects habitat for waterfowl and shorebirds that nest along the Hudson Bay coast in the summer and gather in the area to feed during spring and fall migrations.

The park was established as a result of negotiations between Parks Canada, the Manitoba government, the First Nations of Fax Lake and York Factory, and the District of Churchill. Existing aboriginal and treaty rights relating to hunting, trapping, and fishing will be respected within the park, and local residents can continue with traditional land use.

Park planning and management are in very early stages. Contact the park directly for information on visitor use.

For More Information

Wapusk National Park
c/o Churchill Office
P.O. Box 127
Churchill, Manitoba
R0B 0E0
Phone: (204) 848-7275
Fax: (204) 848-2596